Ace the IT Résumé!

Ace the IT Résumé!

Paula Moreira
Robyn Thorpe

Osborne/**McGraw-Hill**

New York   Chicago   San Francisco   Lisbon
London   Madrid   Mexico City   Milan   New Delhi
San Juan   Seoul   Singapore   Sydney   Toronto

Osborne/**McGraw-Hill**
2600 Tenth Street
Berkeley, California 94710
U.S.A.

To arrange bulk purchase discounts for sales promotions, premiums, or fund-raisers, please contact Osborne/**McGraw-Hill** at the above address. For information on translations or book distributors outside the U.S.A., please see the International Contact Information page immediately following the index of this book.

Ace the IT Résumé!

234567890 QPD QPD 0198765432

ISBN 0-07-219403-0

Publisher
Brandon A. Nordin

Vice President & Associate Publisher
Scott Rogers

Editorial Director
Gareth Hancock

Project Manager
Deidre Dolce

Freelance Project Manager
Laurie Stewart

Acquisitions Coordinator
Jessica Wilson

Technical Editor
Tim Sosbe

Copy Editor
Lunaea Weatherstone

Proofreader
Kelly Marshall

Indexer
Jack Lewis

Computer Designer
Maureen Forys, Happenstance Type-O-Rama

Series Design
Maureen Forys, Happenstance Type-O-Rama

This book was composed with QuarkXPress 4.11 on a Macintosh G4.

Contents

Part II   Résumé Encyclopedia

Chapter 12   Résumé Encyclopedia   179

Acknowledgments

It began as an idea—thank you, Gareth.
It became a project—thank you Mom, Dad, Andrea, and Rose for the encouragement.
It required a little sweat and elbow grease—thank you, Abbi.
It became reality by sheer persistence—thank you, Robyn.
And it was completed with love—thank you, Pano.

—Paula Moreira

We would like to thank our publishing and editorial team at McGraw-Hill and everyone at New Horizons Computer Learning Centers for their excellent advice and support. Plus, this book would not have been a reality without all of the résumé samples we have seen throughout the years—the good, the bad, and the ugly. Hopefully, our message will reach those IT professionals who are so talented in what they do, but need a little help to put their experience and knowledge onto paper. :)

Special thanks to Efi Rufael for his endless love, encouragement, and technical expertise, to my family—Larry, Jeanne, Ryan, Robert, Ross, Sharon, and Harvey—for helping me be a dreamer, and to Paula for bringing me along for the ride.

—Robyn Thorpe

Introduction

Top 10 Reasons Why You Should Buy this Book

1. Your résumé consists of your name, address, and phone number AND your MCSE certification.

2. You've sent out 100 résumés and haven't received a single call back.

3. Your résumé is four pages long.

4. Your résumé still includes your high school GPA.

5. You have no experience but you are trying to get a 60k+ job.

6. You are a career changer and realize that getting an IT job is not as easy as all those advertisements say.

7. You have been at the same job for so long that you *have* no résumé.

8. Your résumé begins with the line "I want to get a job in IT..."

9. You have been to all of the career sites on the Web and they haven't helped you improve your résumé at all.

10. You want to get your dream job and make the big bucks.

Why We Wrote this Book

When we were first approached about the idea of writing a résumé book just for IT professionals, we thought to ourselves, "Does Barnes & Noble really need another résumé writing book?" So, we visited our local B&N bookstore, found the careers section, sat down with a Starbucks decaf skinny double latte (we live in California now), and went through the book stacks. And were there plenty! There were books for dummies and idiots. There were bibles and just about every other collection that you could think of.

Then we looked through these books in search of samples of IT résumés. In most cases, we only found one or two samples out of hundreds! We couldn't believe it. For an industry that employs 7% of the U.S. workforce, how could there possibly be more sample résumés for secretaries than for the IT professionals that keep this country running?

We were convinced that there was a market for the tips, tricks, and advice we had to share. Between the two of us, we've been writing IT résumés, giving advice, and counseling IT professionals for over 15 years. We LIVE IT—literally. Not only do we work for a computer training company, but both our better halves are software engineers! We can't escape it.

What we wanted to do was the following:

- ▶ Make sure that we covered topics that were specifically relevant to IT professionals—things like paper certification, lack of hands-on experience, how to present technical skills and qualifications—all the things that other books didn't even come close to.

- ▶ Provide relevant examples for today's jobs, including web programming, security specialists, and helpdesk technicians. Each job has different requirements. We offer firsthand insight on what's important from a hiring manager's perspective.

- ▶ Share what we've learned ourselves as IT professionals.

As for who we were writing for, we thought our primary audience would be recent college graduates seeking their first jobs, but as we sifted through the hundreds and hundreds of résumés contributed by friends, colleagues, and friends of colleagues, we quickly realized our little project wasn't just for recent college graduates. This book is for any IT professional who is looking at a career in IT as an opportunity to be successful in a career that would be around for a long time—a way to provide for their families, and to afford a comfortable lifestyle.

To the thousands of job seekers out there—good luck and we hope that we can be a small part of your success.

—Paula Moreira and Robyn Thorpe, October 2001

Part I

Creating a Winning IT Résumé

In This Part

Chapter 1

Standing Out from the Crowd

Want to dramatically increase your earning potential, improve your lifestyle, and multiply your over-all net worth—all without diet and exercise? Get a job in Information Technology (IT).

The fast-paced, constantly changing IT world is an exciting place. The continuous introduction of new technologies and processes means endless opportunities to focus on what you really like and the chance to make a great living doing it. But to keep on top of the seemingly boundless prospects out there, you've got to keep on top of your most important tool: your résumé. It's your passport to all these adventures, within and outside your company. Whether the changes around you are the result of "going E" (e-business, e-learning, e-everything), a new CIO being hired, downsizing, or just looking for a new challenge, a résumé that will make you stand out from the crowd is a critical part of achieving your career goals.

Résumé writing is not the fun part of looking for a new job. Unless you are a professional writer, you will probably dedicate more time to writing your résumé than any other writing project in your career. An IT résumé has to have the right blend of technical skills and business acumen (the buzzword for business sense these days) whether you're applying for a tech support position or for the role of CIO.

Your résumé is your letter of introduction to the job you seek—your ticket to high-tech success. Keep it up to date even when you're not actively looking for a job, and you'll make the entire process easier when the right opportunity comes along. When a high-paying job opens up at a company you've always dreamed of working for, you'll get your résumé into the hiring manager's hands while your competition is still sharpening their pencils. Your dream job is out there. But hundreds of other professionals may think it's *their* dream job. This book is your secret weapon. It offers proven steps for writing a winning IT résumé, explanations even your mother can understand, and plenty of examples you can refer to for inspiration.

This chapter offers a high-level perspective on what it takes to get noticed. We'll go into much more detail later on. For now, these are skills to keep in mind throughout the résumé writing and interviewing processes.

In this chapter, we'll cover:

▶ The basics of getting noticed

▶ Getting past the HR recruiter and to the hiring manager

▶ Reading the hiring manager's mind

▶ Marketing the ten hottest skills

 FACT *IT employment currently accounts for approximately 7 percent of the U.S. total workforce (Information Technology Association of America [ITAA]).*

The Basics of Getting Noticed

At the core of getting noticed is a firm belief in yourself and your abilities. Yes, Mom always taught you not to brag, but unless she wants to keep doing your laundry and providing you with rent-free housing, she'll adjust to your new, confident manner.

IT fuels a competitive spirit in a way that just doesn't seem to be there with accountants. Who cares if there are hundreds of candidates applying for a single position? You deserve it, because you can solve the company's problem in your sleep. They're darn lucky you happened upon their ad and had a spare copy of your résumé.

But there's the rub: where does this self-assuredness and competitiveness go when you start to put your accomplishments down on paper? All too often, it gets lost in translation. It's one thing to tell your friends how terrific you are. But setting words to paper makes them seem more *real*, and that can be terrifying.

Confidence plays the most important role in getting noticed. You *must* genuinely believe two things (read them aloud if you need to):

▶ The right opportunity with the right company and the right team is out there for me.

▶ I have skills that employers need.

Your job is to keep believing in yourself while you work through this book. Once you acknowledge your accomplishments, we'll show you how to make employers notice them.

By the time we get through with your résumé, you won't believe the masterpiece you've created. That's right—you will create a high-impact, attention-grabbing résumé. Our job is to act as coaches in providing you with trade secrets on how to shine. Once you have compiled your new résumé, you may not believe that it actually describes you. You may even think that you are being dishonest about your capabilities. No one could possibly be this good, you may think to yourself. Before you hit the delete key in panic, let your new image grow on you. Try it out for size by sending it out. See the response. And as you start getting responses back and you go on interviews, your confidence will increase. Presenting a strong image on paper will get you in the door.

Let's take a look at how to make yourself stand out as the perfect candidate for the job of your dreams.

Controlling Your Image

Presenting a strong image of yourself through your résumé is important regardless of the position you seek. Most IT professionals, especially recent graduates or career changers, are not comfortable walking in and demanding high-paying, influential positions. They know that they can troubleshoot PC hardware and write VB code, but they don't quite know how to express in words how these skills can benefit an organization, much less promote themselves above other job candidates with similar skills.

To get noticed, you need to convey a strong image. In interview situations, this means how you physically present yourself. On a résumé, it's the words you use, the examples you provide, and the impression you create in the recruiter's mind. To convey a strong image you must begin with a positive attitude.

In many situations, modesty is appropriate and becoming. Regardless of how many years you have been in the IT industry, it's difficult to brag about experience and accomplishments. Face it, IT professionals are rarely salesmen or marketers, and with good reason. While marketers like to embellish and sell the features and benefits of a product (including themselves), most IT professionals stick to facts and analytical data (hence the binary nature of computers and computer languages). Marketers are comfortable making larger-than-life claims about their products. Techies tell you everything that works and doesn't about their products. This is not a good idea when the product is you and *you want that job*. So follow our crash course in self-marketing.

Our goal is to help you get your dream job, the one that will best fit your talents, knowledge, and lifestyle. We'll show you how to turn your skills and accomplishments into highly desirable competencies that will enable you to command top dollar. We'll provide detailed examples of exactly what you need to say and how to say it. Your job is to adapt these examples to your own set of skills and watch the magic of a powerful résumé go to work for you.

The Importance of Your Job Title

How can you possibly keep up with all the different IT job titles out there? Does anyone really know the difference between a network administrator and a network support specialist level I? How about a PC technician and a PC specialist? If you're confused, pity the employers wading through stacks of inaccurately titled résumés.

The reality is that titles are assigned by HR (Human Resources or personnel) professionals who may be a little out of touch with what really happens in the IT department. Don't get hung up on what your HR records say. We will help you master the art of the job title. The job titles you use on your résumé are important because they are used in three different ways by recruiters and employers:

▶ Job titles project your image

▶ Job titles are scanned for fit with the available positions

▶ Job titles show promote-ability

Image Projection

Of these two job titles, which sounds stronger: *programmer* or *software engineer*? The software engineer title instills greater confidence by projecting more experience, knowledge, and quality of work. In reality, the titles are interchangeable and can be used to describe the same person with one to two years of software development experience in VB. In actuality, employers will pay more for the software engineer applicant than they would for the programmer. The same with *helpdesk technician* versus *helpdesk analyst*. The lesson is that there are many similar job titles out there that project a stronger image. Whenever possible, use the recommended titles in Table 1-1 to project a stronger image.

TABLE 1-1 Powerful IT Job Titles

These titles ...	Are synonymous with ...
Systems engineer	Network engineer
	Network administrator
	Systems administrator
	LAN manager
	MCSE
Software engineer	Programmer
	Developer
	Software developer
Information architect	Content specialist
	Webmaster
	Copy editor
	Copy writer
Data architect	Database administrator
	Data warehouse manager
	Database analyst
Documentation specialist	Technical writer
User interface designer	Web designer
	Graphic artist
Helpdesk analyst	Helpdesk technician
	Helpdesk specialist
	Helpdesk support
	Helpdesk level I/II
Mail server administrator	Email administrator
PC maintenance technician	Desktop technician
	Helpdesk

TABLE 1-1   Powerful IT Job Titles *(continued)*

These titles ...	Are synonymous with ...
Quality assurance specialist	QA tester
Technical trainer	Instructor
Telecommunications analyst	Phone technician
Security administrator	Network engineer
IT project manager	Development manager
	Program manager
	Product manager
Network architect	Network planner
	Network designer
Development manager	Team leader
	Supervisor
	IT manager

Hit Rates

Employers receive hundreds of résumés for every available position. Somewhere in the pile is your résumé. Research shows that recruiters typically spend about five seconds glancing at each résumé. Talk about a short amount of time to make a first impression!

FACT *The most in-demand positions in IT these days are network and Web related (ITAA).*

A no-brainer, yet effective, way to make sure you get at least your five seconds of fame is to use the job title being recruited for as the title of your résumé. Remember, many job titles are interchangeable. So if you're a network engineer, don't hesitate to answer ads for system engineers, network administrators, systems administrators, LAN managers, or MCSE, and use the title the company uses. Simple and effective—and it gives the impression that you understand the company's way of thinking.

If you can't fit the job title into your work experience, find a way to work it into your career objective statement or your cover letter. It's crucial that the hiring manager see the exact phrase he's looking for if your résumé is going to make the cut.

TIP *We do not recommend listing certifications like CNE or MCSE as job titles. Most job ads include these as qualifications rather than as job titles. There are fewer hits on these as job titles versus more generic titles like network engineer.*

Unless you're applying for a position with a company-specific title, it is also important to select the most common job title for the type of work that you do. For example, if you are a Microsoft Certified Systems Engineer posting your résumé on the Web, think like an employer.

On job boards, the title "network engineer" returns more job postings than "network manager," "network administrator," or "LAN administrator." In other words, employers use the title "network engineer" more often than all the others, so that's how you should title your résumé.

Not sure which title to use? Go to an IT job search engine like Dice.com to find out which titles have the most number of positions posted. Table 1-2 provides some of the more common job titles and the number of job posting hits they returned on Techies.com in a recent search. We will cover Web job boards in more detail in Chapter 3.

TABLE 1-2 Most Popular IT Job Titles

Job Function: Network Administration	Job Function: Programmer
Systems engineer (20,000)	Developer (46,000)
Network engineer (10,000)	Software engineer (18,000)
Systems administrator (6,500)	Programmer (7,600)
Network administrator (3,000)	
LAN manager (1,500)	
MCSE (700)	
Job Function: Database Administrator	**Job Function: Helpdesk**
Database administrator (3,000)	Helpdesk support (673)
Database analyst (2,100)	Helpdesk analyst (200)
Data architect (1,200)	Helpdesk specialist (127)
Data warehouse manager (900)	Helpdesk technician (111)

TIP *A quick search on a job board will reveal the most popular titles to use based on your experience.*

Skill and Career Progression

Unless you're new to planet Earth, you know that companies don't like risk. Companies consider new hires a big risk—a risk that hiring managers try to minimize. Are you going to require a lot of ramp-up time? Do you have experience in similar positions using similar skills? List your skills in easy-to-read bullet points, and title each job appropriately. At least one of your previous positions should have the same title as the position you want. That way, you match the hiring requirements at a glance.

All that "rose by any other name" stuff is good if your experience is fairly close to what you want to be doing, but what if you're reaching? Focus on the part of your job that's closest to what you want to be doing. If your official title is Tech Level 1, you might be responsible for database administration, PC support, and webmaster duties. If you're hoping to move into DBA, list "database administrator" as the job title and as the first bullet describe your responsibilities in this function. Other bullets would describe additional responsibilities. For a final bullet you might consider "Additional duties associated with Tech Level 1 position."

Does this mean that you should lie about your job title? Not unless you really like the feel of egg on your face. Changes in job titles should be made after a careful self-assessment. Certainly you should be qualified for the position you're seeking. Otherwise, you will be wasting everyone's time (including your own) and sullying your reputation. By all means, use the resources in this book to find a stronger title, but be sure you are qualified for the position. Your goal is to *increase the likely match between what the employer is looking for and the skills you possess.*

If what the employer is looking for was only a part of your overall responsibilities, it is acceptable to put down the stronger job title as the primary descriptor of your role, but you will also want to include your other job responsibilities as part of the job description. The key is to find a job title that is interchangeable with your actual job title. The title should represent at least 50 percent of your job duties and should match or be a stepping stone to the position that you most seek. Demonstrate a growth in responsibilities, product knowledge, and skills.

If you are like most job seekers, the idea of replacing your actual job titles with more impressive job titles may scare you. Some job seekers fear that they will be discovered when employers check their references. No need to worry.

Before you list anyone as a reference, give them a recent copy of your résumé and tell them that you are currently exploring employment opportunities. Never offer a person as a reference who hasn't agreed beforehand.

Keep in mind that HR recruiters contact previous employers for employment verification, not to gather details on previous job responsibilities. It is highly unlikely that either the HR manager performing the reference checks or the HR manager at your previous employer will have any detailed understanding of your job responsibilities.

 FACT *The greatest demand increase for IT positions is for network administrators and enterprise systems professionals (ITAA).*

Selling the Benefits of Your Skills

Most people experience writer's block when they first sit down to write their résumé. They get caught up in the mechanics of how the résumé should be laid out, what font to use, what type of paper to print it on, and so on. In Chapter 2, we'll cover the particulars of formatting a professional-looking résumé. But beauty is only skin deep—if your résumé lacks substance, it'll be out of fashion faster than a failed dot-com.

In Chapter 4, we will help you identify and articulate your hidden traits and skills. We'll teach you how to present your skill set as benefits for employers by asking yourself, "Why would an employer care?"

Bad hires cost employers tens of thousands of dollars in time invested, recruitment costs, training cost and effort, and lost productivity. You need to demonstrate minimal risk. Grab employers' attention by focusing on the benefits that your skill set can provide their company. Bear in mind that the biggest benefit for employers of IT professionals is reducing technical ramp-up time and quick assimilation into the corporate culture.

Most people have a hard time identifying their skills, let alone understanding how those skills actually benefit employers. Your résumé, cover letter, and thank you letter should all explain and market the benefit of your skills. It is your job to make the employer feel good about your present skills and future potential.

Some of the things that employers are looking for (without even knowing it) when hiring IT professionals are:

Experience   Because it implies faster time to productivity

Trainability   Because it saves them time and money

Problem-solving abilities   Because such employees are extremely efficient

Same industry experience   Because it translates to faster time to productivity

Growth and promotional potential   Because it minimizes employer risk

Table 1-3 provides examples of how your skills and experience can translate into benefits for a new employer.

TABLE 1-3   Selling the Benefits of Your Skills

Benefit to Employer	Example for Résumé
Same industry expertise means increased productivity	More than ten years back office software development experience for medical services industry.
	Five years experience managing a centralized helpdesk supporting 20,000 weekly incoming calls.
Easiest to train	Certifications include MCSE Windows 2000, Novell CNE 5, and Cisco CCNA.
Problem solving	Decreased customer hold time by 20 percent by evaluating, selecting, and implementing a call tracking system.
	Saved $1 million in annual procurement costs by centralizing computer systems purchasing and implementing an online ordering system.
Growth and promotion potential	Recognized by management for increasing profitability by 12 percent within a one-year period of being hired.
	Managed departmental operations and staff of 25 with an annual operating budget of $1 million.

Marketing the Ten Hottest Skills

You might expect that the ten hottest skills for an IT professional would include technical skills, certifications, programming languages, or proficiency in application programs. Think again. An IT development manager can command a higher salary than a CIO!

IT systems have gotten more complex as ever-greater numbers of users expect more out of their applications, become more self-sufficient, and require more data analysis to make business decisions. On top of that, new technology emerges *every day*, requiring new product knowledge as well as legacy integration knowledge. Development managers are expected to know how to manage projects to time and budget constraints, provide leadership and motivation, and have complete understanding of business issues and processes.

The top IT positions go to candidates with great customer service, stellar project management, and effective team-building skills. These are classic "soft skills," and they can mean the difference between you and the next technically qualified candidate applying for your next promotion or job. Why? Because today's IT world isn't just about being technically savvy. With the increased shortage of IT professionals, the best jobs go to seasoned professionals who have a great combination of technical knowledge, general business skills, and great communication skills.

Soft Skills Defined

Simply put, soft skills are the ability to communicate with people. They are the skills that make customers feel happy. They are the skills that keep customers. And that makes individuals with these skills very valuable. So if you're wondering what the incentive is to brush up on this skill set—it's money, baby!

To a techie, anything outside of product and development skills could be considered soft skills, but here's an unofficial list of soft skills for techies and why they're important.

Project management   Project management goes beyond learning Microsoft Project. Success as a project manager depends on your ability to define, plan, organize, control, and complete a variety of complex and interdependent tasks.

Communication   Whether answering the phone, writing an email, or putting together a proposal, how well you put your point across will affect others' perceptions of your abilities. Make sure each interaction paints an intelligent picture.

Presentation   Forget the horror of high school Oral Communications classes. These skills are a must for any situation, from running a meeting to pitching a product or solution, or justifying why you should get that raise. It doesn't matter how many are in the audience; every time you open your mouth you are using these skills. Make sure you're presenting the image you want by mastering this skill set.

Selling   Face it, regardless of whether your title includes "sales," you're always selling. Whether it's yourself, your project, or your next position, you're always asking people to buy in on something. Learn how to do it more effectively.

Running meetings   Learning how to facilitate meetings and manage group interactions is an important first step to becoming a team leader.

Leadership   There are many keys to successful projects, including organizational buy-in, good project management, and proper resourcing. A strong leader understands these dynamics, harnesses the diverse energies within an organization, and pulls everyone together.

Problem solving   This is the skill you are probably most familiar with. To some, problem solving comes instinctively. To others, it's not so natural. The key is to find a process that works and apply it.

Customer service   Yes, people are difficult. But when they're customers, they come first and they're always right. They need to feel valued and important. Just remember: if you don't treat them right, someone else will.

Self-direction   This is the ability to do your job without having to be told how to do your job. It's extremely important because by the time your manager gets through telling you how to do it she could have probably done it herself.

Teamwork   No man is an island, certainly not in IT where there just isn't room for egos. With so many different operating systems, servers, networks, databases, and other things that need to be coordinated, no one can do it alone. Here's where those skills you learned in kindergarten come in: sharing, saying "please," and—more importantly—saying "thank you." Play nicely with others or take a time-out.

Unfortunately, as any five-year-old can tell you, knowing how to share isn't the same as doing it. You can't learn soft skills unless you practice them. And this top ten list is worth more than a few quick laughs—it can be your ticket to a highly successful IT career. Take a look at your current situation and see how you've managed to put these skills into practice. On your résumé, demonstrate how you use these soft skills—and you'll earn cold, hard cash.

TIP   *Online courses offer a great way for IT professionals to be introduced to soft skills. Some of the leading Web sites offering soft skills training include http://onlineanytime.newhorizons.com/, http://www.skillsoft.com/, http://www.smartplanet.com/, and http://www.youachieve.com/. Here's a sample list of the great topics on the market:*

- ▶ *How to excel at customer service*
- ▶ *Call center frontline skills*
- ▶ *Fast-tracking your career*
- ▶ *Problem solving and decision making in business*
- ▶ *Managing yourself through change*

The best place to feature these skills is as a part of a skills and qualifications summary section at the top of your résumé. Check out Figure 1-1 as an example.

Getting Past the HR Recruiter to the Hiring Manager

Your résumé is your calling card for an appointment to interview with a hiring manager. But like a king in his castle, the hiring manager is surrounded by gatekeepers: recruiters, HR managers, even the hiring manager himself as he sorts through stacks of résumés sent by his subjects. Your objective is to make it to the top of the stack that gets invited to an interview.

Jon Doe

34 Orchid Avenue

San Diego, CA 98455

(555) 555-5555

Qualifications

- Personable and articulate, skilled in handling customers with professionalism and courtesy.

- Highly perceptive, with proven ability to pinpoint problems, provide creative solutions, and follow through to resolution in a timely and cost effective manner.

- Exceptional communication and presentation skills, ability to interrelate with people at all levels.

FIGURE 1-1   Sample skills and qualifications summary

The trick here is to make it so easy for them to pick you as a natural choice that it won't even be an option not to.

Reading Between the Lines: Tailoring Your Résumé to the Job Ad

The job ad will tell you a lot about what the hiring manager is looking for from candidates. Depending on where the ad is posted, you will be able to get the details you need to target your résumé. Ads posted on job boards usually provide more information than newspaper ads and allow you to do a better job of targeting your résumé.

When you read a job ad, you should look for the following information about the position:

- ▶ Job title

- ▶ Responsibilities

- ▶ Industry

- ▶ Years of experience required

- ▶ Software/hardware experience required

- ▶ Education required

Obviously, you need to review this information to determine whether you meet the company's criteria. If you do, the information they've given you will tell you exactly how you should target your résumé to the specific skills the company needs.

The process is simple. Through the power of using interchangeable words, you will turn yourself into a highly desirable candidate. Here's a quick summary of the steps:

1. Print out the original job listing.

2. Underline the job title. Rephrase your career objective so it includes the job title as your desired position.

3. Underline the industry. If you have experience in this industry, make sure that you call out experience in this industry (and possibly other industries) in the description of your past positions.

4. Underline the particular job skills and responsibilities. Review your own résumé to see whether there is a direct match. If the employer calls for particular tasks that you may have rolled up into more general descriptors, break these tasks out again in your résumé. Also note when they are looking for additional experience that you may already possess but have not specifically listed on your résumé. Add it to your résumé. The goal is to have as many matches as possible with what is included in the job posting because job search engines are keyed off the original job description. The more exact matches, the better.

5. Look for any acronyms listed in the job description. Incorporate these acronyms in parentheses in your résumé.

6. Reread your résumé to ensure that it has not lost some of its power as a result of the edits.

In Chapter 4 we provide examples of how to perfect the art of tailoring your résumé.

Filling in the Gaps: What's Implied in the Job Ad

When you pick up a job posting out of a newspaper, it may not have all the information you need to properly target your résumé. You'll need to fill in some of the information based on common industry knowledge. Shorter job ads will list job titles and assume certain skills and qualifications. They may simply list years of experience as a measure of competency. Make sure that you meet these criteria. Tables 1-4 and 1-5 will help you assess what skill levels are assumed for various IT positions. More detailed job descriptions are available in Part II of this book.

 TIP *Before responding to a newspaper job ad, visit the company Web site. You'll often be able to find a more comprehensive ad for the same position there.*

TABLE 1-4   What's Expected Based on Years of Experience

Experience	Expectations of Skills
Under 1 year	Knows commonly used concepts, practices, and procedures in the field or with the technology.
	Relies on instruction manuals, outside resources, and pre-established guidelines to perform the job.
	Works under immediate supervision and generally requires little independent thinking.
1–2 years	Familiar with standard concepts, practices, and procedures to get the job done.
	Can work independently on assigned duties and can make decisions about what needs to happen.
	Able to multitask to accomplish multiple projects at the same time.
	Works under general supervision; typically reports to a project leader or manager.
2–4 years	Has worked on projects "outside the box."
	Has been the team leader on a variety of projects. Usually a point of escalation for junior team members.
	Considered relatively knowledgeable on best practices.
	Is comfortable with accountability of results.
4 years +	Plans, directs, and manages the daily operations of a computer operations department.
	Establishes department policies and procedures.
	Generally manages a team. Relies on experience and judgment to plan and accomplish goals.
	Typically reports to a senior manager.

TABLE 1-5   What's Expected Based on Job Titles

Network Engineer	Desired Skill Level
Level I	A+ certification desirable.
	Proficient in PC troubleshooting and basic network troubleshooting.
	Handle day-to-day operations of networks, including troubleshooting user access, software installation, printer setup, and system backup.
Level II	Network+ and Server+ certification desirable. MCSE or CNE certification a plus.
	Install servers and software applications.
	Analyze, design, develop, support, and troubleshoot networking issues.
	Work with users, manage basic file, print, and application services, perform backups, install and upgrade software of all kinds, and do what it takes to keep networks working.

TABLE 1-5 What's Expected Based on Job Titles (*continued*)

Network Engineer	Desired Skill Level
Level III	Manage multiserver environments.
	Manage a variety of hardware platforms.
	Administer security, troubleshoot to the protocol level, and perform network capacity planning.
Database Administrator	**Desired Skill Level**
Level I	Has knowledge of commonly used concepts, practices, and procedures within database administration.
	Has worked with common commercial database products, including Oracle, Microsoft SQL Server, and Access.
	Relies on instructions and pre-established guidelines to perform the functions of the job.
Level II	Design and build relational databases.
	Develop strategies for data acquisitions, archive recovery, and implementation of a database.
	Clean and maintain the database.
	Has a working knowledge of designing, developing, and manipulating Oracle databases, data warehouses, and multidimensional databases.
Programmer	**Desired Skill Level**
Level I	Work on existing applications, enhancements, debugging, and documenting.
	Is proficient in at least two common programming languages (VB, SQL, and so on).
	Is familiar with database structures and understands the fundamentals of programming, including conditional statements and loops.
	Has practical experience through real-world application development or college work.
	Has knowledge of commonly used concepts, practices, and procedures, but relies on instructions and pre-established guidelines to perform job functions.
Level II	Has 2–5 years of work experience.
	Has a strong understanding of programming fundamentals and object-oriented programming.
	Work with customers to create system specifications.
	Follow the development process from conception to deployment, including initial specifications, development, quality assurance, revisions, and deployment.
	May serve as project leader in small to medium-sized projects.

Reading the Hiring Manager's Mind

While the job ad will tell you a lot about the hiring manager's immediate needs, it doesn't reveal his deep, dark secrets. Relax—there's nothing illegal or illicit about this. We're just going to take a closer look at the dynamics of an IT environment.

IT departments are, almost by their very nature within the company structure, always short staffed. IT managers are constantly in recruiting mode for technicians, helpdesk staff, programmers, and project managers. There's a never-ending stream of projects to deploy, an always-full inbox, too much work, and not enough people to do it. And just when the poor guy has a handle on things—BAM! New technologies, new business directives, new management, heck, even a new flavor of coffee can throw a frazzled IT manager for a loop.

Change constantly influences an IT department's priorities. The dot-com crash is a direct example of how even a change in the economy can affect the priorities of an organization. For you, this change is good. Learn to view it as an opportunity to better position yourself based on the known and hidden needs of an IT manager.

Challenges for Employers

Employers are always at risk every time they make a new hire. Will the person be truly competent or did they just interview well? Will they stick around long enough for the company to receive a return on investments in training, company benefits, and so on? There are ways for you to alleviate some of these worries. Let's take a closer look at how.

Reducing the Time to Productivity

You know that downtime you have when you start at a new job? You don't know where the bathroom is, you don't have the password for your email, you can't even remember your phone number, and oh yeah, you have a job to do. Well, while you view ramp-up time as an inconvenience, your employer sees it in terms of dollars down the drain.

Every moment you take to learn your way around the company and its technology is money lost for the company. Clearly, IT managers favor candidates who bring with them industry experience and advanced systems and software skills. This isn't rocket science—the more experience you demonstrate having, the higher your résumé will rate. Your résumé should include a list of all the networking technology, operating systems, database systems, applications, processes, and procedures you can support.

If you do not have experience in a specific industry, you will want to include your transferable skills. Transferable skills are those skills that are important to employers regardless of the industry. Many times IT professionals think to include only their technical skills. Just as important are the soft skills they have mastered through their careers. When presenting transferable skills, you should be specific with how you exhibited these skills so that the hiring manager can see how they would apply within his or her organization.

TRANSFERABLE SKILLS

Transferable skills help round out your experience. They hint at what you are capable of without being specific to an industry or job. These work well in a qualifications summary section, open up possibilities for promotion, and position you as a better balanced and experienced professional. Try these out for size when you are building your list of skills:

- ▶ Learns technical information quickly.
- ▶ Proven history of improving operations and increasing profitability.
- ▶ Success-driven team player who continually meets and exceeds goals.
- ▶ Able to handle challenges, with proven history of increased productivity.
- ▶ Very detail-oriented with excellent analytical and project-tracking skills.
- ▶ Able to coordinate many tasks simultaneously.
- ▶ Strong communication skills.
- ▶ Team player interested in achieving overall department goals.
- ▶ Enjoys working as a team member as well as independently.
- ▶ Proven skills resolving problems and tense situations.
- ▶ Willing to do whatever it takes to get the job done.
- ▶ History of flexibility; able to handle constant change and interruption.
- ▶ Eager to perform work to maximize customer satisfaction.
- ▶ Able to lead others in high-demand situations.
- ▶ Self-motivated, hardworking team player.
- ▶ Able to motivate staff to meet project deadlines.
- ▶ Deals effectively with culturally diverse customer base.
- ▶ Excellent interpersonal, verbal, and written communication skills.
- ▶ Able to prioritize and work proactively.
- ▶ Quick learner.
- ▶ Proven ability to work in a fast-paced, challenging environment.
- ▶ Exceptional ability to quickly master new software/hardware and apply its full range of capabilities.
- ▶ Infectious enthusiasm for computers; gifted and inspiring PC trainer.
- ▶ Expert troubleshooter and problem solver.
- ▶ Team player with the ability to effectively coordinate; devoted to excellent service and customer satisfaction.
- ▶ 14+ years experience with numerous software and personal/business computers of various manufacturers.

Training Means Growth and Promotional Opportunities

IT managers like to make safe choices—it keeps their own jobs intact. So they look for clues that a candidate will be a good fit for the company. One of these clues is training history. It's evidence that you're willing to invest in your own self-improvement, and that you're open to change and to working with new technology. Remember, IT departments are change agents within corporations. If you're not flexible, you're in the wrong field.

Your résumé should include a list of all the certifications you have achieved. Table 1-6 provides a list of some of the most popular IT certifications. In addition, you should also include a list of well-respected seminars, workshops, and full-length courses that you have taken. This is not to be confused with a full historical transcript of your educational history, though. The examples below demonstrate how to incorporate your educational history with certifications earned and seminars attended. A short listing is sufficient to demonstrate that you take your career seriously and are open to additional training.

TABLE 1-6   Hottest IT Certifications that Build Credibility

Vendor	Certifications
CompTIA	A+ This certification is for entry-level (six months experience) hardware technicians. This is a popular first certification, especially for individuals switching from another career to computers.
	I-Net+ This certification is for individuals who are hands-on specialists responsible for implementing and maintaining Internet, intranet, and extranet infrastructure and services as well as development of related applications.
	IT Project+ This certification is for individuals who lead and manage IT projects.
	Linux+ This certification demonstrates vendor-neutral Linux knowledge. Still under development.
	Network+ This certification is for networking technicians with 18–24 months of experience.
	Server+ This certification is for individuals who wish to demonstrate expertise with advanced PC hardware issues such as RAID, SCSI, multiple CPUs, SANs, and more.
Microsoft	Microsoft Certified Database Administrator (MCDBA) This certification is for individuals who are responsible for the logical and physical design, implementation, maintenance, and administration of Microsoft SQL Server databases.
	Microsoft Certified Professional (MCP) This certification is for individuals who would like to demonstrate their expertise with a particular Microsoft product. This used to be called Microsoft Certified Product Specialist.
	Microsoft Certified Systems Engineer (MCSE) This certification is for individuals who plan, implement, and support business solutions with Microsoft Windows (NT and 2000) and Microsoft BackOffice.
	Microsoft Certified Solution Developer (MCSD) This certification is for developers who design and develop custom business solutions with Microsoft development tools, technologies, and platforms, including Microsoft Office and Microsoft BackOffice.
Novell	Certified Directory Engineer (CDE) This certification is for senior engineers and consultants involved in the design, implementation, optimization, and maintenance of directories and directory-enabled solutions.

TABLE 1-6 Hottest IT Certifications that Build Credibility (continued)

Vendor	Certifications
Novell	**Certified Novell Administrator (CNA)** This certification is for individuals who handle the day-to-day administration of an installed Novell networking product.
	Certified Novell Engineer (CNE) This certification is for individuals who provide high-end, solutions-based technical support for Novell products.
	Master CNE (MCNE) This certification is for individuals who provide solutions to complex networking problems that may span across several different platforms. Focused on Novell products.
Cisco	**Certified Cisco Systems Instructor (CCSI)** This certification is for individuals who want to teach authorized Cisco courses.
	Cisco Certified Design Associate (CCDA) This certification is for individuals who design simple routed LAN, routed WAN, and switched LAN networks with fewer than 100 nodes that utilize Cisco routers and switches.
	Cisco Certified Design Professional (CCDP) This certification is for individuals who design complex routed LAN, routed WAN, and switched LAN networks of 100 to more than 500 nodes that utilize Cisco routers and switches.
	Cisco Certified Internetwork Expert (CCIE) This program is designed to identify computer professionals with internetworking expertise. This top-of-the-line certification is for individuals who work specifically with Cisco products. It is currently one of the premier IT certifications.
	Cisco Certified Network Associate (CCNA) This certification is for individuals who install, configure, and operate simple-routed LAN, routed WAN, and switched LAN and ATM LANE networks that utilize Cisco routers and switches.
	Cisco Certified Network Professional (CCNP) This certification is for individuals who install, configure, operate, and troubleshoot complex routed LAN, routed WAN, switched LAN networks, and dial access services that utilize Cisco routers and switches. This is the next step after CCNA certification.
	Cisco Internet Solutions Specialist This certification is for individuals who are actively involved in developing e-business solutions, and designing and delivering the underlying network architectures. Focuses on Cisco hardware/services as they relate to Internet business solutions.
	Cisco Security Specialist 1 This certification is for individuals who wish to demonstrate proficiency in designing, installing, and supporting Cisco security solutions.
	Cisco SNA/IP Design Specialist This certification is for individuals who wish to demonstrate proficiency in designing and installing Cisco SNA/IP Integration solutions.
	Cisco SNA/IP Support Specialist This certification is for individuals who wish to demonstrate proficiency in supporting Cisco SNA/IP Integration solutions.
Oracle	**Oracle Certified Professional (OCP)—Application Developer** This certification is for individuals who develop Oracle applications.
	Oracle Certified Professional (OCP)—Database Operator (DBO) This track is primarily for database operators who have ideally completed Oracle Education's training for database operators and have hands-on work experience with Oracle databases before taking the Oracle8 Certified Database Operator exam.

TABLE 1-6   Hottest IT Certifications that Build Credibility (*continued*)

Vendor	Certifications
Oracle	Oracle Certified Solution Developer—Jdeveloper This certification is for individuals who use Oracle JDeveloper. This is part of the multivendor Certification Initiative for Enterprise Development.
Project Management Institute	Project Management Professional (PMP) This certification is for project management professionals.
Citrix	Citrix Certified Administrator (CCA) This certification is for individuals who work with Citrix application server software. Choose the MetaFrame or WinFrame track.
	Citrix Certified Enterprise Administrator (CCEA) This certification is for individuals who have extensive knowledge of Citrix products and experience installing and administering Citrix MetaFrame, WinFrame, and Management Services.
Check Point	Check Point Certified Infrastructure Engineer (CIE) This certification is for individuals who manage their company's IP infrastructure.
	Check Point Certified Network Traffic Engineer (CNTE) This certification is for individuals who handle network bandwidth and congestion issues.
	Check Point Certified Security Administrator (CCSA) This certification is for end-users and resellers who need a good technical understanding of FireWall-1 and need to install and set up simple configurations.
	Check Point Certified Security Engineer (CCSE) This certification is for network and security administrators who need to implement and maintain air-tight security with Check Point's FireWall-1. Includes use of multiple firewall systems and other advanced security techniques.
American Society for Quality (ASQ)	Certified Software Quality Engineer (CSQE) This certification is designed for those who have a comprehensive understanding of software quality development and implementation; have a thorough understanding of software inspection and testing, verification, and validation; and can implement software development and maintenance processes and methods.
Compaq	Accredited Compaq Technician (ACT) This certification is for individuals who work for Compaq service partners delivering post-sales service and support on Compaq products, as well as other individuals who provide similar services.
Help Desk 2000	Certified Help Desk Professional (CHDP) This certification is for individuals who administer front-line helpdesk support for their organization.
	Certified Help Desk Manager (CHDM) This certification is for individuals who implement helpdesk systems. Includes human resources and technical aspects.
	Certified Help Desk Director (CHDD) This certification is for senior management at the helpdesk who need to make a business case to represent helpdesk needs and benefits to the organization.

One caveat: If you're a recent grad with a lot of experience, you may want to leave dates off your résumé because most companies try to offer lower salaries to college hires.

The more advanced training you include on your résumé, the higher the hiring manager's comfort level in selecting you as their ideal candidate. Continuous learning demonstrates to the employer that you believe in improving your skills and will continue to develop yourself to become a more knowledgeable and productive employee.

TIP *Be sure to keep your résumé updated as you re-certify your skills and take additional professional development courses. Résumés should always be works in progress, even if you're not actively looking for a job.*

The following are samples of educational history sections.

Sample 1

Pamela has earned advanced degrees in computer science and is applying for a consultant position with a worldwide consulting firm.

Education and Professional Development

2000	M.S. Computer Science, Bingham Young University, Utah
1987	B.S. Computer Science, Lewis-State College, Idaho
	Project Management Institute (PMPI) Certification
	Microsoft Certified Engineer (MCSE) Certification

Professional Seminars:

1998	Developing the Leader in You, Dale Carnegie
1997	Franklin Covey Project Management

Sample 2

Jason has a two-year degree, is in the process of completing a networking certification, and has completed coursework online.

EDUCATION

A.S. Computer Science, Cypress College, Orange, CA   1999–2001
MCSE Windows NT Certification (four out of six courses completed)
A+ Certification

Additional coursework in:
Customer Service (online course), Element K
Call Center Frontline Skills (online course), SkillSoft

Sample 3

Hank has an undergraduate degree in computer science, has earned several networking certifications, is working on a high-level certification, and has completed coursework online.

EDUCATION

B.S. Computer Science, Rutgers University, Newark, NJ   1992

Certifications:
CCIE (in progress)

CCNP	2001
CCNA	2000
Network+	2000
A+	1999

The Hidden Challenges for IT Managers

IT managers have a tough job. On top of the normal hiring managers' dilemmas, IT managers face unique challenges because of the importance of their departments in today's organizations. Imagine having to remain customer service driven while constantly being told what a terrible job you're doing and you'll begin to understand the mindset of the IT manager.

To build an immediate rapport with a hiring manager, all you need to learn is how to read his mind. Relax, there's a trick here: empathy. Understand the challenges the manager faces. How does it work? Like this.

Remember that big project you spent every moment on for six months? Remember how it didn't get the results your company had hoped for? Think about why. From an outsider's perspective, what were the issues the organization had to contend with? What was being asked of the CIO and his IT manager? What were the expectations and deliverables, and how closely did the outcome come to meeting these?

If you had been the CIO or IT manager, how would you have managed the projects better? Of course, you have the luxury of 20/20 hindsight, but this exercise provides you with insight into the challenges of IT managers—and that can help you create a connection with the person who can give you your next job.

Top Five Management Challenges

The top five management challenges are really quite simple. They may be challenges you've faced yourself in which case you'll be able to address these with personal recounts of lessons learned. These challenges include:

▶ Ownership of the company's Web site

▶ Managing development teams

▶ Project managing for timely deliverables

▶ Managing outsourced vendors

▶ E-everything

To truly stand out from the crowd, you need to master the fine art of translating your understanding of and experience with these issues into result-oriented entries on your résumé. Here are some examples of how to address the top five IT manager's challenges:

Project-managed the development of the company's customer Web site, coordinating between the internal marketing department, information services, and an outsourced development company

Wrote detailed product specifications document based on results of company-wide joint application development sessions

More than five years in Web design and consumer marketing experience

Consulted with Fortune 100 companies on network design, implementation, and management using Novell and other vendor products

Published best-practice methodologies for knowledge sharing with customers and partners

Introduced a new revenue stream with sustained 30 percent revenue growth by implementing an e-commerce system

Managed outsourced development team, created new team, and brought development services in-house

Designed and implemented corporate network/intranet and satellite office connectivity and integration of technologies across acquired companies

Implemented a client management process focusing on more profitable customers

Cross-functional IT experience in areas of Web administration, IS systems analysis, technical support, and computer training

Developed standards for desktops, servers, notebooks, and PDA devices

Summing It Up

Hey, it's not natural for a techie to be a self-marketer, but that's what it takes to get noticed and get the job. Pull out all the stops. You've got to be confident. You have to know how to read the job ads, adapt your skills to what employers are looking for, and truly be able to present yourself in a way that makes employers sit up and take notice. The tips and tricks included in this chapter will get you started on the path to getting the job you want.

And speaking of that job you want… There are plenty of jobs out there, but they're going to those who make finding them a full-time job. Now, more than ever, is the time of opportunity for techies. But if you want to get ahead, you've got to take control of your career. Look for opportunities, and be prepared when they come. The best jobs go to the candidates who have the sharpest skills, know what they're worth, and have their résumés ready to go.

Chapter 2

The Anatomy of a Technical Résumé

Your experience and education will not make your job hunt easier if you don't nail the essential elements of your résumé. Your résumé is the showcase for your skills, and if your showcase is not attractive it will not get the attention it deserves. Fortunately, understanding how to best present your information is not that complicated.

First, evaluate what you bring to the table and keep that in mind as you lay out your skills and past experience. Begin with the basics: evaluate how your résumé looks. This can be almost as important as what your résumé says. The formatting and layout may come easier for a graphic artist than to a systems engineer, but by analyzing the components of your résumé you can identify the prime factors of your résumé's appearance.

In this chapter, we'll cover:

▶ The sections of your résumé

▶ Writing a powerful objective statement

▶ Saying you are a "people person"

▶ Using honest terminology

▶ Presenting your education and experience

▶ The differences between chronological and skill-based résumés

▶ Laying out your résumé

▶ Other information you *think* you want to include

▶ Choosing paper type, font size, and all the technicalities

▶ Presenting your references

The Sections of Your Résumé

The following are the standard sections of a résumé:

▶ Header

▶ Objective statement

▶ Education

▶ Experience

▶ Computer skills and certifications

We will attack these sections one at a time.

Header

This is the easiest part of your résumé. It is essential that you have all of this information correct and complete, or don't expect too many calls. Include the following information:

Line 1   Name (bold and a couple of points larger than the other lines)

Line 2   Street address

Line 3   City, state, and ZIP code (you can also combine your complete address on one line)

Line 4   Phone number and/or cell phone number

Line 5   Email address

You can center the header at the top of the page or place it flush to the right or left column. It is ideal to list a phone number where you can be reached during daytime hours. By including a cell phone number you may open opportunities that you would otherwise miss. If you are currently employed you probably cannot talk openly at work. Prospective employers understand this and are usually considerate of this fact. Try to check your cell phone or voice mail messages regularly throughout the day and return phone calls during your lunch or break time.

Objective Statement

This section is key. It is one of the first things an employer reads, and it's your best opportunity to grab their attention and announce you are perfect for this job. Unfortunately, many people do not utilize this opportunity.

Somehow the standard was set that the objective statement is used to explain the job you would like. What a waste of time and space! When you are applying for a job, you usually state the position in the cover letter. Why waste the prime location on your résumé to repeat it?

Not a believer? Take a look at the following two objective statements and decide which one is more likely to catch a hiring manager's eye:

To obtain a challenging position as a network engineer that utilizes my experience and knowledge of networking systems.

or

Network engineer with experience in design, implementation, and support for Ethernet and AppleTalk local and wide area networks. Additional experience includes purchasing, planning, and cost control. Background includes administration of Unix, PC, and Macintosh operating systems and software. Interpersonal skills with excellent problem solving skills.

Hopefully you agree that the second example is a more powerful statement to begin your résumé. Yet so many people still opt for the traditional objective statement. Isn't it obvious that every applicant would like to obtain a challenging position that utilizes his or her experience and knowledge?

There are also other reasons why you may not want to list a specific job. That position may have been filled or there may be several openings you are qualified for. You would be limiting yourself if you listed a specific job title. Instead, an employer can view your résumé, see your area of expertise through your alternative objective statement, and find you ideal for a job that you did not even know about.

What if you are applying with a large company that has several positions to fill? Couldn't it be confusing if you didn't state the job you would like on your résumé? You are in a unique situation since you are applying for an IT job. Your field of study is usually specified and your skill set reflects that directly. Your résumé is technical and will be directed to the IS department more easily than in other fields of work.

Writing a Powerful Statement About Yourself

Think of this space on your résumé as a commercial about yourself. Television commercials are brief, direct, and to the point with a specific purpose in mind. Your commercial needs to be the same way, emphasizing your strong points in a few concise sentences to sell your skills and experience to a potential employer. In your objective statement, you can effectively paint a picture of your personality and skills. The following are some guidelines for writing your objective statement:

▶ Use modifiers to describe qualities that are important to employers in the IT field.

▶ Highlight skills you have that are listed in the job description or advertisement, using slightly different wording.

▶ Make sure to avoid clichés such as "I am a hard worker" or "I am a nice person."

▶ Be creative with your descriptions of yourself, but do not lie.

▶ Include at least one sentence that describes your personal characteristics.

▶ Keep the length to three to four short sentences.

▶ Do not use the word "I."

▶ Do not sell yourself short.

You can write this as a paragraph or a list, whichever best serves your purposes. Here are two examples that show both styles:

Example 1: The paragraph objective statement

Energetic, self-motivated Microsoft Certified Professional skilled in Windows 95/98, Windows NT, and Macintosh environments with Linux/Unix and NetWare experience. Possesses knowledge of LAN and WAN technologies, protocols, and configurations, and expertise in PostScript printer hardware and software. Experienced in Internet technologies, Web page design, and marketing. A quick learner skilled in communication, problem solving, and conflict resolution.

Example 2: The list objective statement

KEY QUALIFICATIONS

▶ 10+ years in IT training and certification with relationships with key IT vendors, training providers, and learning and assessment companies

▶ 5+ years in Internet consumer marketing to the IT professional

▶ Comfortable working in a fast-paced environment, building and leading cross-departmental integration teams, and working with cutting-edge technologies

The list format in Example 2 is especially beneficial when quantifying your experience. By leading the statements with a number of years, your background is exemplified at a glance.

How to Say "I Am a People Person"

Even though you are searching for a technical position, your technical skills may not be your biggest asset. Hiring managers want someone who can work well with the team to achieve objectives. A position where you would be working solely on your own at all times is extremely rare.

For example, in networking and helpdesk positions, you are in the business of customer service whether it is for internal or external users. With programming and database design, you will need to work closely with team members to plan and implement projects. As a Web designer, you may interact with other IS members or even other departments, such as a marketing manager or art director.

Employers might not only be looking for the necessary technical skills, but also the personality and the people skills to fulfill this role. So what are some of the terms you can use that signify these characteristics?

Approachable	Personable
Conflict management skills	Positive motivator
Customer service oriented	Professional
Effective communicator	Receptive
Interpersonal	Sales and marketing skills
Leadership	Strong soft skills
Outgoing	Team player, team leader, team work

Honest Terminology

The Politically Correct movement increased the likelihood of *spin doctoring* a job title or job responsibilities. While it is okay to rephrase some of the details of your experience, remember to keep it honest or else it might come back to bite you later on—either in the interview or on the job.

Compare it to explaining your knowledge of a foreign language. You can be *fluent*, meaning you can speak, read, write, and comprehend the language in its entirety. You can be *conversational*, able to carry on a basic conversation, but not necessarily able to read or write the language. Or you can be *familiar with* the language and capable of recognizing phrases or words. Now translate this analogy into the IT world. Let's use Microsoft Office as an example. What is the degree to which you know the applications?

Basic understanding or familiar with   You can use the basic functions.

Well-versed or proficient in   You know and can use every major function.

Expert in or master of   You know every feature and function of the program inside and out, possibly possessing the ability to train others on the application.

When you are describing your knowledge or abilities, make sure that you are portraying them accurately.

Education

If you attended a prestigious college, list the name of the college first, as shown here:

Harvard University, B.S. in Computer Science, 1992 – 3.7 GPA

If you did not, list the degree first, as shown here:

B.S. in Computer Information Systems, University of Kentucky, 1989 – Cum Laude

If your GPA was not 3.5 or above, it is best to leave it off. If you graduated several years ago, you can also drop the mention of your GPA.

If your education history falls into another scenario, you can present it on your résumé, as follows:

If you attended college but did not receive a degree   Present this by categorizing your studies that are applicable to the job, but do not include courses that are not related to the field. For example, the following:

Web Programming and Design, Essex Community College, 1992–1994

is more impressive than:

Essex Community College, 1992–1994

- ▶ Java Programming
- ▶ Web Fundamentals
- ▶ Adobe Photoshop
- ▶ Communications

> ▶ Political Science

> ▶ Biology

College with no degree, many years ago   When it is more than ten years since graduation, it is better to list the number of years rather than the specific years—for example, "three years" instead of "1965–1967."

Attended several colleges   Only list the most recent college you attended or the institution you graduated from. An exception may be if you attended a prestigious university and would like to include this in addition.

Master's degree   List this prior to undergraduate education.

High school education   This should only appear if you did not attend college, do not have certifications, and recently graduated from high school. With these exceptions, most individuals seeking an IT position will not place their high school education on their résumé. If you do, use the same format as when presenting college education.

Studies in progress   These are appropriate to list in your résumé along with your education. List the information the same as you would with completed college education or certifications along with the anticipated finishing date. This is common practice, as many people start to look for jobs prior to finishing school or taking a certification exam.

Certifications

Here is one place where abbreviations are appropriate and even preferred, but make sure you are using the correct ones. (If you have the certification, let's hope you know the proper abbreviation.) Sometimes these abbreviations are crucial.

If a Human Resources manager is evaluating the résumés, he or she may have been instructed to only pass along a candidate who is MCSE certified. If those letters are not on your résumé, it may not go anywhere. You hope that everyone in that position would know that a "Microsoft Certified Systems Engineer" is MCSE certified, but you never know who is dealing with your résumé. This is especially true if the company is not a technology company, but another type of industry looking for a computer technician.

Using the proper terminology for your certifications is also imperative when companies use electronic scanners or résumé posting, such as at monster.com. Electronic searching will look for specific phrases or terms such as *A+* or *Java*.

If you do not have many certifications and would like to write out the certification titles to take up space, it is a good idea to include the abbreviation in parentheses.

Experience

When displaying your work experience, what do you include? How long should your work history go back? As a rule of thumb, only include experience that is relevant to the job you are applying for. Don't go back more than ten years unless there is a position from that time that is directly relevant to the desired job.

You also don't have to list recent jobs that are not relevant to the one you are applying for. If you were in a management role for ten years, then took a part-time receptionist job to be home more with your children, don't feel you need to include it on your résumé. You can explain that in the interview.

One important factor to remember when writing your résumé is *consistency*. If you are bolding the names of companies, make sure you do it to every one. If you are abbreviating states, do it in every instance. You want to keep your writing style to the point, but do not over-abbreviate. Use standard abbreviations where appropriate, such as with states and dates, but don't assume that everyone knows that HSI stands for Hightech Solutions International.

Chronological Order Is Not Mandatory

One résumé myth is that experience needs to be listed in chronological order, beginning with the most recent. This is not true. If you are in the industry, have a stable work history, and are searching for a similar job, this layout is ideal for you. But if you are changing careers or changing industries, you don't need to adhere to that hierarchy.

Evaluate your experience and make judgment calls about your unique situations. If you performed similar job responsibilities in a past position and believe that it will cast you as a more qualified candidate, list that job first. Simply de-emphasize the dates in your job listings. This would be in the format of a skill-based résumé (see sidebar).

If you are a recent grad or a career changer, you may have several jobs that are not appropriate to the position you are applying for. If you were in a position of management, it is acceptable to keep that job on your résumé if you don't have other experience, as it demonstrates some of the other qualities a company may be looking for. If the non-IT related job was not a management position, it is usually best to leave it off. Focus on your skills more than your experience.

SKILL-BASED IT RÉSUMÉ

A skill-based résumé may benefit anyone in the following situations:

▶ Lack of experience in the industry

▶ Many technical skills acquired in a short amount of time

▶ Skills are more impressive than job titles or past positions

▶ Older job experience needs to be highlighted

▶ Gaps in employment history

This format is appropriate for many job seekers in this relatively young IT industry. In this type of résumé you focus on your computer skill set, and possibly your certifications, more so than your experience. There are several examples of skill-based résumés in Part II. In an upcoming section we will also discuss formatting the layout depending on your experience.

Job Titles and Locations

If your job titles are more powerful than the companies you worked for, present your title first. Then remember to keep it consistent and format the rest of your experience the same way. Don't make your résumé more difficult to read by switching the format from one listing to another.

This is an excellent place to make judicious use of bold, italics, and regular fonts, as shown here:

IBM, *Systems Engineer*, January 1999–Present

Or reverse the layout if you would like to highlight your job title:

Systems Engineer, *Competitive Enterprises*, January 1999–Present

If you have held several positions within the same company, list the company as a heading and the various positions below, with bulleted points about each one. If you have held a lot of positions, don't list them all. It will appear as if you were not able to do any of the positions successfully and needed to be replaced. Instead choose the most significant positions and only include them.

Listing the location of your past employment is optional, but it does not add anything to your employment history. It takes up space and makes your eye search more for the relevant information. If you have moved around a lot, listing locations may hurt you. You do not want to give the employer that idea that you are a flight risk and will only be with their company until you are ready to move on. As part of an interview, you may need to fill out an application where you will list your complete history and you would disclose that information then.

Dates and Gaps in Employment

When should you include dates? With employment and education history, include dates if they are profiling you appropriately for the job you are applying for. If you fear an employer may think that you are too old or too young, omit dates all together or de-emphasize them.

Consistency is important here too. If you are spelling out the month followed by the year, use the same format throughout. Don't use March 2001 and then later use 5/99. And there is no need to be exact, such as pinpointing the day you left your last job.

If you have large gaps in your employment history, you will probably prefer to use the year only. A comparison of the two styles is shown here:

Month to Month	Year to Year
8/1994–Present	1994–Present
2/1989–1/1994	1989–1994
2/1982–5/1988	1982–1988

Using the month-to-month format, it is easy to see those gaps, but the year-to-year format makes this issue less obvious. Don't feel this is misleading, as it is commonly used in writing résumés. Again, those details will be disclosed in the interview or if you are required to fill out an application. Your goal now is to get the interview and then make the employer realize those gaps are not a deciding factor.

Volunteer and Internship Experience

If you have volunteer or internship experience *that is relevant* to the job you are applying for, list this in the same format you would use for work experience. Give yourself a title and support it with your list of accomplishments. Don't downplay this experience just because you did not get paid. Instead use it as a stepping-stone to obtain a better position.

Salary History

Do not include your salary history on your résumé. Sometimes an advertisement or job posting may request or require this. If so, you can put it in the cover letter, but never on the résumé itself. Even then, you will best serve yourself by stating that your salary is negotiable.

The Layout of Your Information

A common dilemma—what information do I display first on my résumé? My experience, education, or certifications? It depends on your level of experience and varies case by case, but here are a few guidelines for recent graduates, candidates with certifications only, and experienced computer professionals.

Recent Graduate

After your objective statement, list your education followed by your computer skills. If you have a computer degree, list your courses that are related to the job.

Be sure to leave off skills that can be assumed. If you are a computer programmer, it is likely that you know how to use Internet Explorer, and a hiring manager is not going to want to see that. This looks like you are trying to make your list of skills longer, and in the process you look less credible.

With your list of courses, keep it relevant to the job. You may think that the fact that you took Controversial International Conflicts makes you a more well-rounded candidate, but the hiring manager will not.

The layout for recent graduates should be as follows:

▶ Education

▶ Computer skills

▶ Related courses

The following is an example of a layout for recent graduates:

EDUCATION
B.S. in Computer Information Systems
Hawaii University, Honolulu, HI, 1999

COMPUTER SKILLS

Programming: C++, Java, HTML

Word Processing: Microsoft Office 2000, Corel WordPerfect, Office 2000, Lotus SmartSuite

Other: Windows 95/98/ME/NT, MS SQL Server 7, Microsoft IIS, PVCS Version Manager, PVCS Tracker, New Atlanta Servlet Exec

RELATED COURSES

Data and File Structures; Advanced Information Systems; Data Communications and Networking; Systems Design and Systems Analysis; Software Engineering; Database Management; Software Project Management

Candidate with Certifications Only

If you do not have a computer degree and do not have work experience, your certifications and your computer skills are definitely your strong points. If you have several certifications, list those first followed by your computer skills and a section about your experience with computers. If you only have one or two certifications, lead with your skill set.

The following is the layout for several certifications and little experience:

▶ Certifications

▶ Computer skills

▶ Experience with computers

Here is an example:

CERTIFICATIONS

MCSE, A+, Network+, Linux, MOUS

COMPUTER SKILLS

NT Server	Windows 95/98/2000	DHCP
NT Workstation	Windows NT 4.0	LAN/WAZ
NT Server/Enterprise	TCP/IP Protocol	PC Assembly/Repair
Exchange Server 5.5	LINUX	MS Office Suite

EXPERIENCE

List experience

For one or two certifications and little experience, use this layout:

▶ Computer skills

▶ Certifications

▶ Experience with computers

Here is an example:

TECHNICAL SKILLS

Operating Systems: Installation and repair of Windows 95/98 and Windows NT Workstation 4.0. Applications: Microsoft Office 97/00, Norton Antivirus, pcAnywhere, modem software such as Internet Explorer and Netscape Navigator.

TECHNICAL KNOWLEDGE

Partitioning and formatting hard drives, assembling and disassembling desktops, demonstrated troubleshooting skills, installation of applications.

CERTIFICATION

CompTIA A+ Certification

EXPERIENCE

List experience

Experienced Computer Professional

You have many options for the layout and presentation of your information. Often the most difficult part is summarizing the information that is most relevant to the job. Most importantly, you need to utilize the objective statement to summarize your qualifications for that specific job. Then list the information that is emphasized in the description followed by your education, certifications and possibly your skill set if space permits. You can find several examples in Chapter 12.

Other Information You Think You Want to Include

You probably are thinking of including a lot of information in your résumé that we haven't discussed yet. Before you do, take the following recommendations into consideration:

Don't overdo it   You want to leave some surprises for the interview. Think of your résumé as the preview to a movie. You are showing the main plot, but you don't want to give away the entire storyline.

How does this relate to the job?   Before you add any additional information, ask yourself how this relates to the job you are trying to get. Does an IT manager care that you are CPR certified? Probably not. But if you are fluent in Japanese and applying to an international company, this is a definite asset. You not only need to look at the job, but also at the company.

Skills from the past   Be especially careful when considering adding items that are too far in your past. If you took a weekend workshop on Photoshop five years ago and haven't touched it since, you probably don't want to list this program under your computer skills. If you get hired, your boss may ask you to use that skill at a later date. You won't look quite as impressive as when you wrote it on your résumé.

Extracurricular Activities and Achievements

Depending on where you are in your career, you may or may not want to include your extracurricular activities and achievements. If you are a recent grad, it may be a good idea to include leadership roles and honors received, as you don't have much experience to put on your résumé.

So when should you take these items off? As your work experience becomes greater, this section will become smaller and you will probably drop all references to being the chess club president. And even as a new grad, keep this section to a minimum.

Some appropriate extra topics to include in your résumé are:

▶ Foreign languages

▶ Memberships in technical associations

▶ Recent leadership positions

▶ IT-related volunteer work, such as providing networking support for a charity organization

▶ Publications, if you have worked on any books, articles, or journals

▶ Recent awards and recognition for work related to the desired job

The Technicalities

As you are laying out the following areas of your résumé, ask yourself, "Will Human Resources be able to easily read and scan my resume?" If you can't get by them, it is doubtful that you will ever have an opportunity to impress the CIO.

The résumé layout essentials are as follows.

Paper

Keep it simple. Use white, off-white, or a light cream-colored paper. Do not try to impress with flashy paper or crazy combinations of colored font. That will not get you the positive attention you are shooting for. Plus, your résumé is likely to be faxed or photo copied, and colored paper will not reproduce well. A slightly thicker paper, such as 24 pound bond or résumé paper, will withstand the shuffling from desk to desk, but don't use anything heavier.

Number of Pages

If you are just beginning your career, try to keep it to one page. Do not extend your résumé to that second page to include your part-time waitress job or to list your ten college extracurricular activities. If you are trying to keep it to one page, you will be more likely to focus on precise skills and assets, keeping the unnecessary details out.

A two-page résumé may be appropriate for someone who has more experience and expertise. If you go to two pages, make sure that you mention your strongest points on the first page or at least highlight them. If you don't, employers may not be motivated to turn the page. Going beyond two pages will almost ensure that it doesn't get read.

Font

Times New Roman or Arial are two of the most used fonts, and this is not the time or place for creativity. Variation in fonts makes your résumé more difficult to read and doesn't impress anyone in the technical field.

Use either a 10-point or a 12-point font. Anything smaller is difficult to read and anything larger appears that you do not have experience to fill up the page.

Avoid excess use of italics, as they are difficult to read. You may want to use them in a title or to distinguish one field from another.

Keep all text black. Black on white is most common for a reason: it has a punch. Why else would every newspaper in America be written on white paper with black ink? Even changing to gray can lose some impact.

White Space, Margins, and Alignment

One of the most overlooked components of résumé layout is the use of white space. In the process of overloading a résumé, many people do not leave enough space between lines or sections, congesting their résumé more than the L.A. freeway. Make yourself look professional and organized by simply allowing for more white space. It makes it easier to read and lets the main points of your résumé stand out more.

It is okay to use smaller margins, such as a half-inch all around. Using narrow margins saves space and it looks okay as long as you leave ample white space between sections.

Also make sure you are using proper alignment. Do not center all of the information on your résumé; left-align the main content. If you indent a section, be sure to indent the entire section to the exact same place and then use that indent as the standard for the rest of your résumé.

Let's take a look at the difference attention to such details can make. The résumé shown in Figure 2-1 is a good use of white space.

Now look at the same information that is presented without consistent indentation or additional line spacing shown in Figure 2-2.

Without making a good use of white space, your résumé becomes more difficult to read and the information gets lost.

To increase readability, utilize bullets wherever appropriate, especially when highlighting your experience. These bulleted statements stand out much more than a paragraph that includes all of your accomplishments in prose format.

Nicole Ruhn

8142 Green Orchard Rd. Apt. 507
Grand Rapids, MI 37281
W (541) 547-3883, H (541) 746-6738
Nicole.Ruhn@hotmail.edu

Network Engineer with experience in design, implementation, and support for Ethernet and AppleTalk local and wide area networks. Additional experience includes purchasing, planning, and cost control. Background includes administration of Unix, PC, and Macintosh operating systems and software. Interpersonal skills with excellent problem solving skills.

TECHNICAL SKILLS

Operating Systems

Windows NT Server 4.0, Windows NT Workstation 4.0, Windows 95/98, DOS, Novell 3.12/4.11, SCO Unix 5.0.5, Novell 4.11.

Applications

SQL Server 7.0, Goldmine 4.0, MS Office 97/00, Unidata, Richter, Support Magic 3.31, Lotus Notes 4.6, Norton Antivirus.

Technical Knowledge

DHCP, Winds, routers, switches, PBX, POP3, TCP/IP, NetBIOS, NetBEUI, SNMP, and other networking protocols. HTML 4.

EXPERIENCE

Director of MIS, HealthNetwork.com   March 99 to June 00

- Engineered and supported a copper 10/100 switched Ethernet network, which included a Cisco 1720 router, T1, and managed switches.
- Integrated a Macintosh AppleTalk/TCP/IP network for a design department of 7 Macs and a Mac Server with OS 9.

FIGURE 2-1   Good use of white space

Presenting Your References

References should never be included in or attached to your résumé. Another great résumé myth is that the bottom of your résumé should contain the phrase "References available upon request." There is no reason for this—it does nothing for you except take up space. All employers assume you are going to be able to provide them with references when appropriate. In addition, you cannot be sure who will get a copy of your résumé, and you don't want just anyone calling your references.

Nicole Ruhn
8142 Green Orchard Rd. Apt. 507, Grand Rapids, MI 37281, W (541) 547-3883, H (541) 746-6738
Nicole.Ruhn@hotmail.edu
Network Engineer with experience in design, implementation, and support for Ethernet and AppleTalk local and wide area networks. Additional experience includes purchasing, planning, and cost control. Background includes administration of Unix, PC, and Macintosh operating systems and software. Interpersonal skills with excellent problem solving skills.
Technical Skills

Windows NT Server 4.0, Windows NT Workstation 4.0, Windows 95/98, DOS, Novell 3.12/4.11, SCO Unix 5.0.5, Novell 4.11, SQL Server 7.0, Goldmine 4.0, MS Office 97/00, Unidata, Richter, Support Magic 3.31, Lotus Notes 4.6, Norton Antivirus, DHCP, Winds, Routers, Switches, PBX, POP3, TCP/IP, NetBIOS, NetBEUI, SNMP, and other networking protocols. HTML 4.
Experience

HealthNetwork.com, Director of MIS   March 99 to June 00
- Engineered and supported a copper 10/100 switched Ethernet network, which included a Cisco 1720 router, T1, and managed switches.
- Integrated a Macintosh AppleTalk/TCP/IP network for a design department of 7 Macs and a Mac Server with OS 9.

FIGURE 2-2   Bad use of white space

Prepare a list of references as a separate document (see Figure 2-3). Bring this with you to every interview. You can't predict when an employer will ask for them, and you don't want to be caught looking unprepared. If they don't make the request, offer your references when you are fairly advanced in the interview process.

Include three professional and three personal references. Put them in order of your strongest reference first, as the employer may only contact the first person on your list.

Before you add someone to your list of references, make sure that you get their permission. Also make sure they will give you a favorable reference. Aside from your skills, a prospective employer may ask them about your work habits, punctuality, temperament, reliability, and weaknesses. If you feel comfortable with your reference, ask them what they would say when asked about those questions. If their answer is not favorable, remove them from your list.

When you are starting your job hunt, notify all of your references. Ideally it is also best to let them know just before they may be contacted so they will be prepared to give you a good recommendation.

As important as what you include in your résumé is what you should not include. Here are the highlights:

▶ Elaborate fonts, pictures, or outlandish paper stock

▶ Too much or not enough information; give enough but not irrelevant information

TARA MASTERSON
101 Cross Road Drive
Atlanta, GA 93241
(634) 522-9134

_____ PROFESSIONAL REFERENCES _____

Ephrem Rufael, Director of MIS
Smart IT Solutions
Baltimore, MD
(410) 634-8121
ephrem.rufael@smartITsolutions.com

Bobbi Conley, IT Manager
Creative Publishing
Washington, DC
(202) 584-9910
bobbi.conley@creativepublishing.com

Dr. Chad Spence, Professor of Computer Science
American University
Denver, CO
(624) 512-5932
chad.spence@american.edu

_____ PERSONAL REFERENCES _____

Jessica Waxman
11 Bear Creek Parkway
Freehold, NJ 21201
(212) 443-7171
jwaaxman@excite.com

Andrea Sendroff
1877 Towson Drive
Newport Beach, CA 10332
(213) 884-5692
andrea.sendroff@newyork.edu

Jana Seifarth
1742 20th Street SE
Dundalk, MD 21034
(443) 574-9912
jseifarth23@hotmail.com

FIGURE 2-3 Sample references document

▶ Misspellings, typographical errors, or poor grammar

▶ Outdated information

▶ Unrelated experience or accomplishments

▶ References

▶ Names of past supervisors

▶ Past compensation

▶ Personal information such as health, sex, marital status, weight, height, Social Security number, citizenship, date of birth, or race

▶ Unprofessional email addresses or personal Web sites

▶ Salary history

▶ Reasons for leaving past employment

By keeping these technical details of the anatomy of your résumé in mind, you will create one that is more likely to get noticed and get you results.

Chapter 3

Résumés for the eWorld:
Electronic Résumés that Get Noticed

Recruiting and hiring new employees can cost a company thousands of dollars and a ridiculous number of man-hours, especially when they become engulfed in paper résumés. To save money and time, many companies use electronic methods to review candidates. These include 1) accepting email résumés, 2) having applicants complete online résumé forms, and 3) scanning résumés.

When you are creating your résumé you need to consider how you will submit it, as this will affect the layout and design you use.

In this chapter, we'll cover:

▶ Emailing your résumé

▶ Online résumé forms

▶ Scannable résumés

▶ Keywords and buzzwords

▶ The biggest mistake of electronic résumés

▶ Example of an electronic résumé

Emailing Your Résumé

When you email your résumé, follow the instructions given by the hiring manager. If none are given, it is a good idea to insert an ASCII version in the body of the email. Many recruiters and employers will request that you submit it in this format only. Unfortunately, many people don't even know what ASCII means!

Since you are a techie, you probably already know that ASCII is the abbreviation for American Standard Code for Information Interchange. This is a format that can be easily understood by most computers around the world and ensures that any employer will be able to access your résumé.

Résumés as Attachments

You can also attach your Microsoft Word résumé for those hiring managers who might prefer the "pretty" version. If you do this, still include your ASCII résumé in the body of the email just in case the recipient is not able to open the document.

If you create your résumé in a program other than Word, such as Word Perfect, you increase the likelihood of employers and résumé-listing services being unable to view your attachment. Some employers even say *do not* send attachments, but this is rare.

Send your attachment in the lowest-common-denominator version, such as Word 6.0 for Windows 95/98. If you do not have the capability of saving in this version, it is worth the trip to Kinko's or the local library to ensure that your résumé can be viewed.

Creating an ASCII Résumé

The following is an exercise to create an email-friendly résumé in ASCII format:

1. In your word processor document, set your margins so you have 6.5 inches of text displayed.

2. Open your existing résumé or create a new one.

3. Select all of the text, and then select a font that is fixed-width 12 point, such as Courier 12. This will give you 65 characters per line, which will accommodate most email programs.

4. Save your résumé as a text-only file with line breaks. If you have been instructed to use hard carriage returns at the end of paragraphs instead of at the end of lines, save as text-only without the line breaks.

5. Open this new file in Notepad or any other text editor that you have on your system.

6. If your traditional résumé is longer than one page and contains your contact information or page numbers on every page, remove that information. On the computer screen your résumé will read as one continuous page.

7. Review the appearance of your résumé in the text editor. This is exactly how most recipients will see it.

8. Replace all characters that are not supported by your text editor. For example, bullets may appear as question marks in Notepad. You can replace the bullets by using asterisks or dashes. You can create a horizontal line for effect by using a series of hyphens or other characters.

9. If there are long lines of text in your editor, use Notepad's Word Wrap feature under the Edit menu. This feature inserts hard returns, allowing you to format the résumé to meet your specified margins.

10. Copy and paste the text of the résumé into the body of an email when you are satisfied with the way it looks.

11. Create a short cover letter using the same steps described above. Insert the cover letter above the résumé within the email message.

12. Send a copy of this email to yourself and to a friend who is using a different email program *before* sending this text résumé to the recruiter or employer.

Online Résumé Forms

Many of the popular job-seeker sites allow you to post your résumé using an online form that can then be searched by employers or emailed out to job postings that interest you. Some individual companies also have an online form on their Web site that you can use to submit your information.

Sometimes the form will be a simple, open field where you cut and paste your entire résumé. In electronic online forms, the data is automatically converted to ASCII and entered into a searchable database.

Other online forms, such as the forms at Monster.com, may require you to enter your information line by line in a guided format. You are asked questions and enter your information into the fields one at a time.

When completing an online résumé form, you can make this process easier by using your eWorld résumé to extract what is appropriate. In this situation, you will not have any control as to how your résumé is displayed. The power of your résumé will be in the words that you use. An employer can search on different criteria, so you want to make sure that you cover all of the bases.

Scannable Résumés

Many companies scan your résumé upon receiving it. This does not mean they read it super-fast! Scanning a résumé transforms a paper résumé to electronic data that can be read, searched, and tracked by a computer system.

What Is Résumé Scanning?

Your résumé is placed on the scanner and an OCR (optical character reading) program reads the résumé. All of your information is converting into text files, stored in a database, and then graded by your qualifications.

When an employer is ready to hire someone, he or she can specify the type of experience, skills, or education needed for a particular position and sort all the résumés in their database. Any résumés that match are selected and printed.

If the employer uses this technology, a computer will read your résumé before a human does. When applying for a job with a mid-size to large company, it is a good idea to ask them if they would like both a scannable and a traditional résumé. It is not as common for a small company to make the investment in a résumé scanning system, but try to check with Human Resources before you send your résumé.

Tips for Creating a Scannable Résumé

The main difference between a traditional résumé and a scannable résumé is that the latter is much simpler. To make your résumé scannable, use standard fonts, dark type, and plenty of facts for the computer to extract.

The following are some tips on how you can enhance your résumé's scannability:

▶ Use white or light-colored paper, 8.5" by 11", printed on one side only.

▶ Provide a laser-printed original, not a photocopy.

▶ Use a large font size (10 to 14 points) and a standard font style, such as Times New Roman.

▶ Left-align all information in your résumé.

▶ Avoid italics, underlining, vertical and horizontal lines, graphics, and boxes.

▶ Use boldface and/or capital letters for section headings as long as the letters don't touch each other.

▶ Avoid compressing space between letters, as it becomes unreadable when scanned.

▶ Avoid two-column formats that look like a newspaper, as many scanners read left to right across an entire page.

▶ Put key information in the top third of the résumé. That corresponds to one screen on a computer.

▶ Do not fold or staple the paper.

▶ When faxing, set the fax machine to "fine mode" or "detailed mode" so the recipient will receive a better quality copy.

Keywords and Buzzwords

The secret to making your résumé effective in the eWorld is to use as many valid keywords as possible. When an employer is searching for experience they'll often use keywords that are nouns, such as programmer, HTML, B.S., or network engineer. So make sure you describe your experience with concrete words rather than vague descriptions.

Maximize the use of industry jargon and abbreviations. You can logically assume that recruiters will instruct the search-engine dictionary to look for all the buzzwords in your field. You may want to both write out terms and abbreviate since you do not know what search will be done—for example: MCSE (Microsoft Certified System Engineer). The clearer you can be with your qualifications, the more often your résumé will be hit in searches.

One way to identify keywords is to underline all skills listed in the job description and then incorporate those words into your résumé.

The Biggest Mistake of Electronic Résumés

Many electronic résumés contain one similar problem: they look just like a traditional résumé pasted into another format. The spacing and alignment are not consistent, which makes an electronic résumé ineffective, disorganized, and difficult to read. You need to make sure your résumé is delivering the punch that you want when using these other forms of technology.

Look at the sample résumés shown in Figures 3-1 and 3-2. Which résumé is easier to read and why? It isn't going to be too hard to figure it out.

```
Michael Davis
8142 Green Orchard Rd., Apt. 507, Glen Oakes, CA 37281, W (541) 547-
3883, H (541) 746-6738, michael_davis21@email.com

Network Engineer with experience in design, implementation and support
for Ethernet and AppleTalk local and wide area networks. Additional
experience includes purchasing, planning, and cost control. Background
in administration of Unix and Linux, PC and Macintosh operating
systems. Interpersonal skills with excellent problem-solving skills.

Education    B.S. in Computer Information Systems
        Hawaii University, Honolulu, HI, 1999

Computer Skills   TCP/IP protocols, hubs, routers, switches,
Workstations/Server setups, Windows 95/98/ME/NT/2000, LAN/WAN,
Microsoft Office 2000, Corel WordPerfect, Lotus SmartSuite

Certifications   MCSE, Cisco CCNA, Net+, Novell CNE, Linux/Unix
Administrator

Related Courses   Networking Essentials; Data Communication and
Networking; TCP/IP Protocol

Experience  Network Engineer, Health Network, May 1999 to present
Engineered and supported a copper 10/100 switched Ethernet network,
including a Cisco 1720 router, T1, and managed switches.
Integrated a Macintosh AppleTalk/TCP/IP network for a design department
of seven Macs and a Mac Server with OS 9.

        PC Technician, Hawaii University, September 1996 to May 1999
Installed and configured all PCs and Macs in seven computer labs.
Performed maintenance on all servers including software and hardware
upgrades.
Set up the network environment in four of the computer labs.
```

FIGURE 3-1 Comparison of bad and good formatting with electronic résumés: Example 1

```
MICHAEL DAVIS
8142 Green Orchard Rd., Apt. 507
Glen Oakes, CA 37281
W (541) 547-3883
H (541) 746-6738
michael_davis21@email.com

NETWORK ENGINEER -- KEY QUALIFICATIONS
-----------------------------------------
* Experience in design, implementation and support for
Ethernet/AppleTalk.
* Local and wide area networks.
* Additional experience includes purchasing, planning, and cost
control.
* Background in administration of Unix and Linux, PC and Macintosh
operating systems.
* Interpersonal skills with excellent problem-solving skills.

EDUCATION
-------------------------------------------
B.S. in Computer Information Systems
Hawaii University, Honolulu, HI, 1999

COMPUTER SKILLS
-------------------------------------------
* TCP/IP protocols
* Hubs, routers, switches
* Workstations/Server setups
* Windows 95/98/ME/NT/2000
* LAN/WAN
* Microsoft Office 2000, Corel WordPerfect, Lotus SmartSuite

CERTIFICATIONS
-------------------------------------------
* MCSE (Microsoft Certified Systems Engineer)
* Cisco CCNA (Certified Cisco Network Administrator)
* Network+ (Net+)
* Novell CNE (Certified Network Engineer)
* Linux/Unix Administrator

RELATED COURSES
-------------------------------------------
* Networking Essentials
* Data Communication and Networking
* TCP/IP Protocol

EXPERIENCE
-------------------------------------------
NETWORK ENGINEER
Health Network, May 1999 to present

* Engineered and supported a copper 10/100 switched Ethernet network,
including a Cisco 1720 router, T1, and managed switches.
* Integrated a Macintosh AppleTalk/TCP/IP network for a design
department of seven Macs and a Mac Server with OS 9.

PC TECHNICIAN
Hawaii University, September 1996 to May 1999

* Installed and configured all PCs and Macs in seven computer labs.
* Set up the network environment in four of the computer labs.
* Performed maintenance on all servers including software and hardware
upgrades.
```

FIGURE 3-2 Comparison of bad and good formatting with electronic résumés: Example 2

At the risk of sounding cliché, it is the little things that make the difference, such as alignment and spacing, the use of special characters and capitalization, and inclusion of keywords. The information is basically the same in these two examples, but by modifying the format and layout, your qualifications and skills are more easily noticed.

Transforming your traditional résumé into one that is going to be a showstopper in the eWorld is just that easy.

Chapter 4

· ·

Uncovering Your Hidden Talents

It's tough to evaluate your own skills honestly. If you yammer on and on about the things you're great at, it sounds too much like bragging. If you harp on what you're not good at—well, really, who wants to do that? But an honest evaluation of your skills is a crucial step in résumé writing. Skip this one and you could be stuck in the same dead-end job forever, or never even land that first job in your field.

Once you've accepted the inevitability of a self-evaluation, the process can seem overwhelming. Not to worry—we've broken it down into several manageable steps for you.

In this chapter, we'll cover:

▶ Identifying your technical skills and accomplishments

▶ Plugging information you've gathered about yourself into your résumé in three sections: summary, technical skills, and work experience

▶ Tailoring your résumé to *any* job posting—including the one for the job of your dreams

Discovering Yourself

Self-discovery can be grueling work. In many IT jobs, daily deadlines mean you barely have time to breathe, let alone time to reflect on the job you've done and what a terrific person you are. But you *have* to make time to reflect on your accomplishments if you want to better your situation. Think of it as an incredibly cheap alternative to therapy.

To identify your skills and abilities, we'll follow a three-step formula:

1. Identify technical skills and operational abilities.

   Our goal is to end up with a concise list of operating systems, applications, hardware systems, and other technical capabilities. (Managers will list operational experience rather than technical skills.) Why a list? It's an effective, eye-catching way to present a lot of information clearly. Skim through this book and you'll see what we mean!

2. Create a complete work/experience history.

   Here, we'll gather the information that will make up the bulk of your résumé. We'll identify your job responsibilities and accomplishments. This is the section that'll make Mom proud, even if she still doesn't have a clue what you do.

3. Work the magic.

   This is the crucial step that will set you apart from every other candidate. We'll show you how to turn run-of-the-mill IT skills into highly sought-after performance-impacting skills. The result? You'll stand out as the leading candidate for any position.

   Set aside about two hours for this task. It doesn't have to be all at once—break it up into four 30-minute sessions if that's easier. But do put in the necessary time if you want to have a résumé that stands out from the crowd.

Step 1: Identify Your Technical Skills

Your résumé should start with an overview of your technical skills. A bulleted list is an effective way to present this information. It lets recruiters and hiring managers quickly scan your skills and match them with the position they need to fill. If a hiring manager has a stack of résumés, he won't waste time trying to dig out hidden information. Make it easy for him to choose you.

Use Worksheet 4-1 as a jumping-off point for listing your skills. You may have skills not covered here; if so, add them in. Be sure to note software versions where applicable as well as your level of expertise and when you last used the product, according to the key that follows this list.

WORKSHEET 4-1 Technical Skills Inventory

Skill	Version	Self Rating	Years Experience	Last Used
Hardware				
____ PC				
____ MAC				
____ Sun				
Operating Systems				
____ Windows				
____ DOS				
____ Unix				
____ Linux				
____ IBM AIX				
____ Solaris				
Network Operating Systems				
____ NetWare 4/5				
____ Windows NT Server				
____ Windows 2000 Professional				
____ Unix				
Networking				
____ TCP/IP				
____ SSL				
____ SMTP				
____ SIP				
____ RTP				
____ DNS				
____ NIS				
____ NFS				
____ Cisco IOS				
____ Legato				
____ EMC				
____ SMS				
____ Lotus Notes				
____ Lotus Script				
____ Lotus Domino				
____ Cisco				

WORKSHEET 4-1 Technical Skills Inventory (*continued*)

Skill	Version	Self Rating	Years Experience	Last Used
Networking				
____ Netscape Enterprise Server				
____ OSPF				
____ BGP				
____ ISIS				
____ MPLS				
____ GRE				
____ Citrix MetaFrame				
____ MS Exchange				
____ Novell GroupWise				
Web Development				
____ HTML				
____ DHTML				
____ ColdFusion				
____ ASP				
____ Java				
____ JavaScript				
____ VBScript				
____ XML				
____ IIS				
____ Commerce Server				
Development				
____ C++				
____ Visual C++				
____ Visual Basic				
____ XML				
____ Java				
____ Servlets				
____ Applets				
____ Active X				
____ MFC				
____ COM				
____ ADO				

WORKSHEET 4-1 Technical Skills Inventory *(continued)*

Skill	Version	Self Rating	Years Experience	Last Used
Development				
____ ATL				
____ SQL Server				
____ CORBA				
____ ASP				
____ Interdev				
____ VBScript				
____ J2EE				
____ WebLogic				
____ Active Directory				
____ Visual Studio				
____ Microsoft .NET				
____ NEON				
____ Vitria				
____ BEA Tuxedo				
____ MQSeries				
____ BizTalk				
____ WinCE O/S				
____ COBOL				
____ CICS				
____ Perl				
____ Unix Shell Scripts				
____ IBM WebSphere Application Server				
____ VisualAge for Java				
____ WebSphere Studio				
____ iPlanet Web Server				
____ LDAP				
Web Designer/New Media				
____ HTML				
____ Dreamweaver				
____ Photoshop				
____ JavaScript				
____ SMIL				

WORKSHEET 4-1 Technical Skills Inventory *(continued)*

Skill	Version	Self Rating	Years Experience	Last Used
Web Designer/New Media				
___ RealText				
___ RealPix				
___ Flash				
___ FrontPage				
___ Adobe Illustrator				
___ Macromedia Fireworks				
___ Macromedia Flash				
___ Allaire HomeSite				
___ Macromedia Director				
Database Development				
___ Oracle Database 7/8 or 8i				
___ RDBMS				
___ JBuilder				
___ PL/SQL				
___ SQL*Plus				
___ SQL*Net				
___ CA-Easytrieve Plus				
___ DB2				
___ Visual FoxPro				
___ PowerBuilder				
___ JDBC				
___ Crystal Reports				
___ OLAP				
___ Informix				
___ ADO				
___ OLE DB				
___ Relational databases				
Telecom				
___ Octel				
___ PBX				
___ ISDN				

WORKSHEET 4-1 Technical Skills Inventory *(continued)*

Skill	Version	Self Rating	Years Experience	Last Used
Telecom				
___ VoIP				
___ CTI				
___ IVR				
___ WAN				
___ Voice				
___ Video				
___ Definity				
___ Cable				
___ DSL				
___ IVR				
___ Mosaix				
___ Telephony systems				
Applications				
___ Windows 95/98				
___ Windows 2000				
___ Microsoft Office				
___ Microsoft Word				
___ Microsoft Excel				
___ Microsoft PowerPoint				
___ Microsoft Access				
___ Microsoft FrontPage				
___ Internet Explorer				
___ Netscape Communicator				
___ Lotus Notes				
___ WordPerfect				
___ ACT				
___ FileMaker				
___ GroupWise				
___ Microsoft Project				
___ QuickBooks				
___ Quattro				

WORKSHEET 4-1 Technical Skills Inventory (*continued*)

Skill	Version	Self Rating	Years Experience	Last Used
Hardware				
___ Installation				
___ Troubleshooting				
___ Repair				
___ Maintenance				
___ PC support				
___ Remote administration				
Operating Systems				
___ Installation				
___ Troubleshooting				
___ End-user training				
___ Beta test				
___ Rollout product				
___ Customer support				
___ Field service maintenance				
Network Operating Systems				
___ Administration				
___ Installation				
___ Supporting				
___ Planning				
___ Security administration				
___ Configuration management				
___ User management				
___ Administer print services				
___ Security planning				
___ Protocol analysis				
___ Systems backup				
___ Security management				
___ System troubleshooting				
___ Login scripts				
___ Client configuration				

WORKSHEET 4-1 Technical Skills Inventory *(continued)*

Skill	Version	Self Rating	Years Experience	Last Used
Networking				
____ Network cabling				
____ Router configuration				
____ WAN design				
____ Intranets				
____ Extranets				
Development				
____ User requirements gathering				
____ Flowcharting				
____ Product specifications				
____ Application development				
____ Interface design				
____ Product development				
____ Program debugging				
____ Quality assurance				
____ Program testing/analysis				
____ Developing algorithms				
____ Data storage techniques				
____ Logic structures				
____ Structure programming methodology				
____ Object-oriented programming				
____ CPU memory addressing				
____ Client/server programming				
____ Event-driven programming				
____ Advanced access programming				
____ OLE automation				
____ ODBC integration				
____ Integration				
____ Dynamic data exchange				
____ System analysis				
____ JAD				

WORKSHEET 4-1 Technical Skills Inventory (*continued*)

Skill	Version	Self Rating	Years Experience	Last Used
Database Administration				
____ Transact–SQL				
____ Server administration				
____ Database programming				
____ Performance and optimization techniques				
____ Transactions and record locking				
____ Database design				
____ Relational database design				
____ Database permissions				
____ Database migration				
____ Data analysis				
____ Report creation				
Web Development				
____ Web page development				
____ E-commerce				
____ Searching				
____ Web site management				
Web Design				
____ User interface development				
____ Graphic design				
____ Information architecture				
____ Web page development				
____ HTML development				
____ Scripting				
Applications				
____ Antivirus security management				
____ User support				
____ Installation				
____ Configuration				
____ Optimization				
____ Training				

WORKSHEET 4-1 Technical Skills Inventory (*continued*)

Skill	Version	Self Rating	Years Experience	Last Used
Helpdesk				
____ Internal customer support				
____ Escalation support				
Technical Writing				
____ Documentation				
____ Technical manual development				
____ User training				
____ Help support				
Engineering				
____ Resource planning				
____ Infrastructure design and planning				
____ IT planning				
____ LAN architecture				
____ Software engineering/design				
____ Standards planning/compliance				
____ Integration				
____ Systems design				
Systems Analysis				
____ JAD				
____ Project management				
____ Team leader				
____ Develop system specifications				
____ Systems analysis life cycle				
Quality Assurance				
____ Product testing				
____ Scalability testing				
____ UI testing				
____ Quality control				
____ User assessment				
Management				
____ Departmental coordination				
____ Team leader				
____ Project management				

WORKSHEET 4-1 Technical Skills Inventory *(continued)*

Skill	Version	Self Rating	Years Experience	Last Used
Management				
____ Contractor managing				
____ Project leader				
____ Quality control				
____ Resource allocation				
____ Scheduling				
____ Service-level agreements				
____ Site supervision				
____ Product specifications				
____ Strategic planning				
____ Systems design				
____ Technical presentations				
____ Technical staff supervision				
____ Vendor management				
____ Budgeting				
____ Staff supervision				
____ Interfacing with upper management				
____ Asset management				

Self-rating Key

0   Heard of the product (doesn't really count)

1   Know what the product does (covered it in a college course or read about it in a magazine) and have seen a demonstration of the product (do not list this as a skill)

2–3   Use the product occasionally (basic functions; not a primary job responsibility), or have not used the product in the last year

4–5   Continue to use the product/skill on a daily basis

6–7   Can provide frontline support for the product

8   Have trained others on how to use the product

9   Am the person people turn to for help when they can't figure it out

Last Used Key

<6 months

6–12 months

1–2 years

2+ years

As you go through the list, take a moment to jot down major projects you have completed using a particular software package, hardware setup, or operating system. Get everything down on paper at once, while it's all fresh in your mind. Otherwise, you risk forgetting something important.

Don't worry about presentation as you fill out the table—we'll pretty it up later. For now, all that matters is creating a written record of your skills.

Look at the following examples to see how the checklist translates to a robust, easy-to-read experience section.

Software Engineer

TECHNICAL EXPERIENCE:

REPORTING TOOLS
SQR 4.3/4.0, Crystal Reports 5.0

DATABASES
Sybase v 11, Oracle v7.x, SQL Server 7.5/6.0, SQL Base 5.0

GUI TOOLS
PowerBuilder 5.0/4.0/3.0, X-PATH, ObjectSmith, Data Junction

CASE TOOLS
S-Designer 5.0/4.0, InfoMaker 5.0/4.0

LANGUAGES
C, SQR 4.0, SQL, SQL*Plus, PRO*C, Pascal, Fortran, PeopleCode, PowerScript, Transact-SQL, PL/SQL

HARDWARE
IBM-PC, Sun Workstation, Macintosh

OPERATING SYSTEMS
Windows NT 4.0/3.5, Unix, Sun OS, MS-DOS, Windows for Workgroups, Windows 95

QA Tester

TECHNICAL SKILLS:

Testing Tools: WinRunner 5.01/6.02, TestDirector 6.0, LoadRunner 6.0/6.5, QAPartner/Silk Test, SQA Suite, PVCS Tracker (bug reporting and analysis)

Software: SQL, PL/SQL, C, C++, VB5.0/6.0, Java 1.1/1.2, JavaScript, VBScript, HTML, 4Test-script, TSL (Test Script Language)

GUI: Visual Basic 5.0/6.0, Developer 2000 (Forms 4.5, Reports 2.5)

Databases: Oracle 7.x/8.0, MS Access 97, FoxPro, MS SQL Server 6.0/7.0

ERP: SAP R/3 version 3.x

Applications: MS Office, MS Word, MS Excel, MS PowerPoint

Internet: Java, JavaScript, VBScript, ASP, JSP, HTML, JDK1.2.2, JDBC, Internet Explorer 5x, Netscape 4.x

Operating Systems: Windows 95/98, Windows NT 4.0, Windows 2000, MS DOS 6.22, HP/Sun Solaris-Unix

SPECIAL CONSIDERATIONS FOR IT MANAGERS

When you make the move to management, the rules change a bit. Your technical skills take a backseat to your experience with managing policies, procedures, forecasting, budgeting, space planning, vendor relationships, team building, documentation, infrastructure design, and resource planning. Employers do still want to know about the technical environments you've worked in previously, but not in the amount of detail you're used to giving.

When you apply for a management position, your Technical Skills section will evolve into a Qualifications section. We'll show you how to showcase your expertise in that section and provide you with examples you can see and put to work for you in Part II of this book.

Step 2: What Have You Accomplished?

Once you've defined your areas of expertise, it's time to get specific. As before, we'll break things down into manageable bits of information and rebuild it in a results-oriented, benefits-loaded format.

Start by simply listing your previous employment experience. Use the form we've provided in Worksheet 4-2. List employers (and relevant information), the positions you've held, and the dates of employment. Next, using the skills checklist from the previous section, note specific skills used in each position. Also jot down special responsibilities and other projects that really gave you a chance to shine.

WORKSHEET 4-2 Employment History

Job Title: _____

Employer: _____

Employment dates: _____

Skills: _____

_____

_____

_____

_____

_____

_____

Take your time on this section. Look for documentation to help jog your memory—were you given written performance evaluations? Read them over and excerpt any information that you can.

Uncovering Your Special Talents and Skills

Want to really shine? Use the following questions to uncover your own special talents and skills. You'll be surprised by just how much you have to contribute to your next organization.

▶ Your boss always counts on you for something you're especially good at. What is it that he always counts on you for?

▶ Think of a problem that came up that had other people stumped but that you were able to resolve. What did you do? What does that say about your abilities?

▶ What's your best "trick of the trade"? What do you do better than anyone else in your organization? What keeps you successful?

▶ When did you go above and beyond your job description, and more than earn your pay that day?

▶ If your friends were to praise your skills, what would they say?

▶ If you felt totally comfortable bragging about yourself, what would you brag about? What are you most proud of?

▶ List ten qualities other people have that you most respect or admire. Go through the list and apply each of these qualities to some aspect of yourself or your work.

▶ If you suddenly had to leave the area for a while, how would your coworkers' jobs be tougher or less enjoyable when you're not there to help?

▶ What professional award would you most like to receive? For what? How close are you to getting it?

▶ How many of your professional goals have you achieved so far? Five years ago, did you think you could be where you are today?

Step 3: Making Magic Happen

If you've properly completed the previous section, you probably have a straightforward list of skills, tasks, and responsibilities. Here's where the magic comes in. But our magic gives you much more than a rabbit in a hat. Used correctly, it'll land you the opportunity of a lifetime. We're going to take your résumé and turn it into reasons why an employer should choose you over any other candidate who applies for a position.

So how does our magic work? We'll follow a three-step procedure to create a résumé that is guaranteed to generate results.

PAR

PAR—problem, action, and results—is a widely used method for quantifying your skills. PAR statements are powerful because they show clear examples of you making a difference for your past employers. Job seekers who develop achievement statements and use them almost always find work faster than those who don't.

Why? It's simple, really: achievement statements give potential employers a chance to see your professional competencies, strengths, and skills. It's almost like giving them a sneak preview of what you can do for them. They'll want to interview you—and make you an offer—quickly, before someone else takes advantage of your skills.

Remember, it's all about presentation. We're taking *skills you already possess* and marketing them in an entirely new way to get you the best opportunity possible. Here's how it works:

▶ What **problem** did you solve for your employer?

▶ What **action** did you take to resolve the problem or situation?

▶ What were the beneficial **results** of your action?

Having trouble determining how your skills fit into this model? Run down the following list of questions to help jog your memory as you begin writing your career achievements:

▶ Did you solve a recurring problem for your department?

▶ Did you suggest any new procedures or programs for your company?

▶ Did you make your job easier or more efficient?

▶ Did you train anyone?

▶ Did you implement a new procedure or system?

▶ Did you do a job with fewer people or in less time?

▶ Did you help increase sales?

▶ Did you save the company money?

Here are some examples of PAR statements:

Developed scripts to replace outdated backup system and automate backup processes, saving company over $10,000.

Cut requisition costs by 20%, saving the company $100,000 for the fiscal year.

Reduced the cost of purchased computer systems by 40% by finding alternative suppliers.

Worked extended hours when the company experienced a shortage of resources.

Implemented configuration control standards to streamline helpdesk center operations.

Ideally, you'll be able to come up with several PAR statements for each job on your résumé. They can be presented in a bulleted list beneath your job description to allow employers quick, easy access to the information they need.

Recognition

In this section, we'll seek out the work you've done that has been recognized—the stuff that sets you apart from the rest of the crowd.

▶ Were you asked to take on more responsibility?

▶ Were you asked to lead or participate in a special project?

▶ Did you create or assume new responsibilities?

▶ Did you receive any rewards or special recognition?

▶ Did you receive a bonus for exceeding your goals or objectives?

▶ Did you do anything for the first time at your company?

▶ Were you promoted?

▶ Were you praised or acknowledged by customers, coworkers, or vendors you worked with?

▶ Did you receive perfect scores on standard industry or college examinations?

The following examples are recognition statements:

Invited to head product development division for new company product created in response to customer demand.

Served as technical consultant to committee formed to assess customer satisfaction.

Created new tracking system to monitor response time on customer calls.

Selected as the spokesperson by the American Association for the Advancement of Science for Engineers and Software Developers.

So What?

The "So what?" technique, when properly applied, is what makes your résumé a true winner. Too many people fill their résumés with boring job descriptions. Potential employers are busy people. They don't have time to sift through endless terminology and long-winded language. They want to know what you can do for them.

To get at that information, you need to explain not only what you did, but *why it mattered*. After each statement written in response to the questions above, ask yourself, "So what?" That will help you come up with the difference your action made.

Think of it as the difference between features and benefits, for example:

Microsoft Word has macro functionalities.

So what?

Microsoft Word offers users macro functionalities that enable quick, easy customization of documents and reports.

See the difference?

We'll look at some of the statements just mentioned and apply the "So what?" method to strengthen them.

Before	After
Worked double shifts as a result of understaffing	Preserved customer response time by working extended hours when the company experienced a shortage of resources
Implemented configuration control standards	Implemented configuration control standards to streamline helpdesk center operations; reduced manpower needs by 20% and improved overall customer satisfaction levels
Technical consultant	As technical consultant to committee formed to assess customer satisfaction, provided technical expertise in creating and implementing automated online helpdesk functionality
Head of new product development division	Headed product development division for new company product; brought product to market ahead of schedule and under budget

Summing It All Up

The Summary or Qualifications section of your résumé is designed to give hiring managers a "big picture" view of who you are. Especially if you are applying for your first management position, you must get inside the employer's head. Think benefits, not features. You want the employer to recognize and become interested in the competitive advantage you bring to the position.

The job posting itself is your best clue. Use it to your greatest advantage: pick out the keywords and focal points, and stress those in your summary. Include keywords likely to be entered in a searchable database.

Although it sounds simple, this is a difficult section of your résumé to write. Do not attempt it until the rest of your résumé is complete. It's a summary, and you can't summarize information you haven't yet written or seen.

Some additional tips:

▶ Aim for about five bullet points, using nouns and adjectives, not action verbs. Save your action verbs for the body of your résumé.

▶ Draw upon your work experience, volunteer time, and/or extracurricular activities in terms of duration, scope, accomplishments, and so on. If you lack relevant experience, emphasize interpersonal, organizational, and supervisory skills you have developed.

▶ The first statement summarizes the experience you have related to your job objective (for example, one year experience in helpdesk support).

▶ The second statement describes your working knowledge of the various components or aspects of the position, such as customer service, troubleshooting, or project management.

▶ The third statement outlines the various skills you possess to do the work effectively, such as problem solving, customer service, or project management.

▶ The fourth statement may refer to any academic background you have that complements your practical experience, such as machine design, resource assessment, or marketing.

▶ The fifth statement lists your personal characteristics and attitudes as required on the job, such as reliable, able to work under pressure, and creative.

Not sure how to put it all together? The following is an example of a project manager's qualifications:

Holly Smith, Project Manager

Qualifications

▶ 18+ years experience in IT supporting technologies in the oil and gas, financial, banking, medical, insurance, legal, government, education, and telecom (GSM) sectors.

▶ Excellent project management, business analysis, and technical writing skills.

▶ Sound understanding of application development methodology from the perspective of a user, designer, and developer.

▶ Experience includes five years of programming/analysis/QA within a Tandem mainframe environment.

▶ Effective communication skills with all levels of management, customers, development team members, and vendors.

Of course, the Qualifications section is still relevant even if you're not yet at the management level. The following example gives you a look at how a programmer's summary might appear:

Sam Gill, Programmer

Summary of Qualifications

▶ Extensive experience of six years in business systems analysis, database, and applications design.

▶ Experienced in different business systems, including credit card systems, insurance, banking, public utilities, warehouse maintenance systems, manufacturing, human resources, and technology groups.

▶ Experienced in database designs and performance tuning of DB2 applications.

▶ Excellent communication and interpersonal skills.

Obviously, people at different levels need to stress different skills. An IT manager could follow the example shown here:

Henry Rocks, IT Manager

Qualifications

▶ Accomplished IT professional with over ten years experience in the accounting and consulting industries.

▶ Broad knowledge and experience in matching appropriate technologies, designs, and systems development techniques with organization needs, capabilities, and resources.

▶ Ability to plan and implement information technology strategies and develop user teams for large-scale technology transitions.

▶ Keen ability to develop operational plans to meet organization goals.

▶ Detail oriented with a commitment to high standards.

Tailoring Your Résumé

Once you've invested a significant amount of time perfecting your résumé and cover letter, you may be tempted to simply send it off again and again without changing a word. Resist the urge. We'll show you just how to tailor your résumé perfectly to each individual job posting. With a small amount of effort, you can maximize your results and snag multiple offers.

Why is it important to tailor your résumé to specific job postings? In general, people are lazy and set in their ways. A hiring manager who has to replace an employee who is leaving or who needs to fill a new position typically has a prepared job description. The first thing this person will do when considering the stack of résumés that pour in within minutes of placing the job posting is to compare the information presented by the candidates against the specific skills needed for the job.

Remember, the hiring manager may not be a technical person and may not realize that your seven years of SQL experience mean you are obviously a database expert. You want to use terminology *from the job ad* in your cover letter or résumé (or both) to maximize your chance at getting the interview.

Sample Job Listings and Résumés Made to Fit

Following are several sample résumés tailored to specific job ads. Notice that even when a candidate doesn't have all the required skills, as many matches as possible are made between the résumé and the ad text.

Director of IT

As Director of IT, ensure technology leadership in the marketplace and provide internal support to drive quality, productivity, and innovation.

TECHNICAL DUTIES AND RESPONSIBILITIES

- Responsible for the development and oversight of business applications, which run on Digital Equipment Corporation (now Compaq) Alpha computers running the OpenVMS operating system.
- Responsible for overseeing the design and development of software applications. The development language is Synergy.
- Provide oversight of the Technical Services group, which manages the local area network (LAN). The LAN employs NT servers.
- Provide oversight of the Technical Services group, which manages desktop applications. The applications are standard Microsoft products.
- Negotiate contracts, determine future capacity, and manage telecommunications equipment, which is a PBX switch, "Definity" model G3R.
- Provide oversight of the Technical Services group, which manages the wide area network (WAN). The WAN communicates with 6 remote sites and supports approximately 50 remote users.
- Provide oversight of the Operations group, which includes helpdesk, EDI transmissions, and disaster recovery.
- Bring innovative ideas and systems to support business strategies.

OTHER DUTIES AND RESPONSIBILITIES

- Provide oversight of Computer Operations, Technical Services, and Programming areas within the IT department needed to support the 24/7/365 organization.
- Manage the day-to-day activities, relationships, and resources necessary for the continued support of the division's business information system.
- Coordinate with the Web Services group to ensure that the web applications integrate with mainframe applications.
- Assist the Business Planning team to ensure that all IT services (equipment, data, phone services) are coordinated and managed.
- Responsible for developing and maintaining disaster recovery plan.
- Provide oversight for all data and network security.
- Responsible for developing and maintaining a corporate-approved IT operating budget.

COMPETENCIES

- Leadership skills
- Communication skills
- Project management
- Analysis and reporting skills
- Customer focus
- Interpersonal skills

EDUCATION AND/OR EXPERIENCE

College degree in computer sciences (or related academic field) and a minimum of ten years of progressively responsible and diverse IT experience, or equivalent education and experience in a service environment. Ability to communicate with all levels of the organization is critical. Demonstrated leadership and problem-solving skills. Familiarity with numerous aspects of the computing environment, including applications development cycle, PC operating systems, PC architecture, network architecture, voice/data communications environment, and EDI processes.

FIGURE 4-1 Job listing for director of IT position

Thomas Banks
2343 High Road
Catonsville, MD 23433

(410) 455-5678
tbanks@aol.com

Summary of Qualifications

- Innovative and dynamic Director of IS with 13 years of diversified IT experience, including applications development, network architecture and operations, security, voice/data communications, and EDI processes
- Responsible for an IS operations team of 20 with a $10 million operating budget
- Direct oversight of computer operations, technical services, and development departments to support a 24 x 7 business environment
- Responsible for proper capacity and disaster recovery planning as well as all data and network security
- Proven success in solution providing, project management, systems analysis, designing, development, pre-sales technical support, implementation and post-implementation support and maintenance
- Customer focused, with excellent communication and interpersonal skills

Experience

Director of IS   11/1998–Present
Data Processing Institute, Baltimore, MD

- Outsourcing systems consulting company supporting client network infrastructure, voice communications, security management, email, VPNs, and web sites. Serviced 50 clients with typical installations of 200–500 distributed users. Services provided included:
    - Hosting and maintenance of global web sites
    - Intranet and VPN installations to support partners and remote users
    - MS Exchange email services supporting corporate and remote users
    - Network security (Checkpoint firewall/VPN)
    - Ecommerce transactional capabilities
- Managing procurement and lease programs for all desktops, laptops, servers, and networking equipment (Dell, GE Capital, Cisco) on behalf of all clients in order and leveraged aggregate buying power for deeper discounts.
- Managing 18 full-time staff members, an outsourced helpdesk, in-house and consultant development groups to support a 24 x 7 operations environment.
- Responsible for business recovery and capacity planning for internal and client systems and networks.

IT Manager, Development Services   8/1997–10/1998
Blue Streak Utility Services Inc., Baltimore, MD

- Managed outsourced development team, created new team, and brought development services in-house for overall cost savings and increased productivity.
- Assisted in logical application development and systems architecture of online energy management and profiling service.
- Managed all Internet-based systems and equipment, including Web, email, ftp, application, SQL, ColdFusion, SMS servers, and all routers, switches, and redundant connectivity.

FIGURE 4-2   Director of IT résumé

- Designed and implemented corporate network/intranet and satellite office connectivity and integration of technologies across companies that were acquired.

QA Consultant   1/1997–7/1997
OptiMark Technologies Inc., Jersey City, NJ

- Developed the test plan and test script to allow the QA department to validate a new market data interface (DEC Alpha, HP Unix).

Manager, Development   6/1990–12/1996
Dow Jones Markets, New York, NY

- Member of a cross-functional team (12 people) set up to assist a strategic partner (OptiMark Technologies Inc.) develop and deploy a new automated order match and trading system.
- Responsible for development, operations, and networking interfaces between OptiMark and Dow Jones' systems (ActiveX, Java, CORBA, TCP/IP, NT4.0, Web Server, Lotus Notes).

Education

B.S. in Computer Science, University of Maryland, Baltimore, MD   1988
Minors: Math and Business

FIGURE 4-2   *Continued*

Director of IT Position

Figure 4-1 is a sample job posting for a director of IT position, and Figure 4-2 is an example of a résumé optimized for this position.

IT Manager

Figure 4-3 shows a posting for an IT manager position, and Figure 4-4 demonstrates how to target a résumé based on this posting.

Internet Security Analyst

Figure 4-5 shows a job ad seeking an Internet security analyst. In Figure 4-06, we've targeted the résumé to meet its required qualifications.

Systems Administrator

Figure 4-7 gives an example of a job listing for a systems administrator with four years experience. Figure 4-8 is a sample résumé that has been targeted to those requirements.

IT Manager

- Responsible for planning, administering, and reviewing the acquisition, development, maintenance, and use of local computer and telecommunications systems within the Dallas offices.

- Responsible for the overall scheduling, controlling, and directing of resources, people, funding, and facilities for IT projects. These projects may involve major modifications to existing systems or the implementation of discrete new IT facilities, systems, or subsystems.

- Reports to the Senior Director of Administration.

- Consult with personnel across all organizational levels to determine current and future IT needs and to identify areas for improvement.

- Analyze the information needs of the company and develop technological solutions to satisfy those needs.

- Prepare and direct IT policy and plan strategy regarding security aspects of IT systems and overall IT growth.

- Oversee planning and implementation of all systems within company's overall IT framework. This includes interface with the on-site US SAP team.

- Direct activities to select and install technology as approved by management.

- Oversee the provision of training for internal users.

- Direct the integration of IT operations, computer hardware, operating systems, communications, software applications, and data processing.

- Establish priorities for systems development, maintenance, and operations.

- Provide advice to senior managers regarding IT-related issues.

- Prepare guidelines and evaluate IT systems against given standards and performance criteria.

- Provide day-to-day product or system support to users via the helpdesk.

REQUIRED SKILLS

- MCSE and CNE certification.

- Advanced Novell and Windows NT installation and administration skills.

- Lotus Notes and Domino Server Admin.

- MS product certifications.

- TCP/IP, VPN, and firewall working knowledge.

FIGURE 4-3 Job listing for IT manager

Jon Duffy
11 Cardinal Place
Reading, PA 19610

jon@yahoo.com

SUMMARY

- Six years experience managing IT projects and systems, development teams, and customer service centers using in-house and outsourced resources.
- Experienced network infrastructure and capacity planner.
- Internet technology skills, including TCP/IP, VPN, and firewall setup and administration.
- Excellent communication and interpersonal skills, including helpdesk skills.
- Detail oriented, with very strong organizational and planning skills.

TECHNOLOGIES

Windows 2000/NT 3.1–4.0 Server Administration
Internet Information Server 3.0+ Administration
Microsoft Project
Microsoft Office 97, 2000, and XP
IBM Netfinity Manager
Visual Studio 6.0
Networking/IP Technologies
Internet Technologies (DNS, FTP, POP3, SMTP, WWW)
Windows 3.1, 3.11WFW, 95, 98, ME

EXPERIENCE

Blue Streak Utility Services Inc., Concord, Ontario   1/2000–7/2001
Manager, Technology Division

Managed outsourced development team, created new team, and brought development services in-house. Outsourced web design and e-branding. Assisted in logical application development and systems architecture of online energy management and profiling service. Managed all Internet-based systems and equipment, including web, email, ftp, application, SQL ColdFusion, site minder servers and all routers, switches and redundant connectivity. Designed and implemented corporate network/intranet and satellite office connectivity and integration of technologies across companies that were acquired.

YourHome.com Inc., Toronto, Ontario   9/1998–5/2000
IT Manager

Project and technical management of a large home-based web portal. Included logical design and systems/network architecture. Managed development staff of 6 (DBA, Programmer x 2, Web Developer, Web Designer, HTML coder). Acted as technical liaison representing the organization to investors and clients.

Interlog Internet Services Inc., Toronto, Ontario   10/1996–9/1998
Manager, On-Site Support

Helpdesk/call center management covering telephone and on-site support with a staff of 20 employees.

EDUCATION

Humber College, Canada-Ontario-Rexdale   1996
Certified Electronics Engineering Technician, two-year program

FIGURE 4-4   IT manager targeted résumé

Internet Security Analyst

- Support the implementation, operations, administration, and maintenance of the corporate Internet infrastructure (firewalls, proxy servers, intrusion detection systems, web servers, news servers, VPN servers, etc.).
- Respond to critical firewall alarms and take corrective measures. Keep abreast of CERT advisories, firewall product announcements, and new Internet technology to improve the protection of the corporate network and information systems.
- Provide assistance in Internet-related issues to internal customers.
- Monitor the corporate firewalls and Internet servers' components and provide input into the performance and capacity planning for effective operation of the Internet connection.
- Develop, maintain, and implement procedures to generate and distribute Internet access usage reports.

REQUIRED SKILLS

Support the implementation, operations, administration, and maintenance of the corporate Internet infrastructure (firewalls, proxy servers, intrusion detection systems, web servers, news servers, VPN servers, etc.)

DESIRED SKILLS

Firewalls, proxy servers, intrusion detection systems, web servers, news servers, VPN

NON-TECH SKILLS

Good communication skills and presentation skills

FIGURE 4-5 Job listing for Internet security analyst

Shawna Kvislen

MCSE, CNE, Network+, A+
1632 Prairie Drive ~ Sioux City, IA 58474 ~ (443) 782-5512
shawna_kvislen21@yahoo.com

KEY QUALIFICATIONS

- **Internet Security Analyst** with 2+ years of experience managing corporate Internet infrastructure, systems, and network security, specifically operating systems, databases, interfacing, and data privacy.
- Excellent ability to identify system vulnerabilities and possible threats, and then apply prerequisite safeguards (technical and administrative) to defend against potential attacks.
- Detailed experience performing risk assessments, configuring, and monitoring firewall systems, and monitoring network for unexpected behavior.
- Professional knowledge and hands-on experience with Windows, Novell, and Unix; up to date on new Internet technologies.
- Function well in a team environment while being self-motivated to work effectively without supervision. Excellent organizational, interpersonal, and communication skills with the flexibility to adjust to changing work priorities.
- Hands-on helpdesk experience; highly effective communication skills.

TECHNICAL SKILLS

Operation Systems: Windows 2000 Advance Server, Windows 2000 Server, Windows 2000 Positional, Window NT 4.0 Server/Workstation, Windows 95/98/Me, Sun Solaris Unix, Novell 4.2.

Hardware: PC hardware, HP printers, 3COM switches, Nortel Switches, Cate5, Cabletron SSR2000 router, Cabletron SS2200, Tigris, ATM switches, Ethernet, fiber optic.

Application and Software: Exchange 5.5, IIS Server, TCP/IP, HTML, MS Office 98 Professional, MS Project Manager, MS Office 2000, Visio 2000, Terminal Server, MS FrontPage 98, Adobe Photoshop.

EXPERIENCE

Internet Security Analyst, VistaInfo, 4/2000–Present

- Over two years experience in administering and creating secure Unix (Solaris, Linux, OpenBSD, FreeBSD) and Windows NT environments.
- Extensive knowledge of firewall setup and administration of Checkpoint FW-1, Linux iptables, NATs, and VPNs.
- Experienced in bandwidth management, monitoring, and ensuring quality of service.
- Projects included centralizing 70+ company domain names hosted at different ISPs to the company's own name servers running OpenBSD and BIND 8.x/BIND 9.x.
- Also migrated 20+ company nationwide locations to one namespace. Configured DNSSEC, multiple views, zone delegation, multiple nameservers, DHCP and host registration with DNS via dynamic updates and TSIG signed zone transfers. Tested interoperability with Microsoft DNS servers.

FIGURE 4-6 Internet security analyst targeted résumé

- Integrated Active Directory with BIND, including handling zone transfers, dynamic updates, SVR records, BIND as engine for AD nameservices, WINS integration, and migration from WINS to DHCP/DNS.
- Additional responsibilities included maintenance of the firewall rule-base, overall network security, development of VPN connections between company and customer locations, firewall monitoring and alert, and monitoring the corporate network for possible network intrusion.

Network Administrator, Trinity College, 10/1998–4/2000

- Manage and perform the statistical and tactical aspects of disaster recovery, auditing, and security policies, procedures, and guidelines.
- Perform security administration functions (maintaining users, groups, IDs, and passwords) for HP, Unix, and FileNet systems at corporate and field office locations.
- Implement and oversee the installation and configuration of 25+ computers with Windows (95, 98, NT Workstation, NT Server), Novell (4.x, 5), and Unix (SCO UnixWare 7) operating systems.
- Assisted the network administrator in administrating, troubleshooting, and maintaining the network with over 200 client computers while ensuring top security.

CERTIFICATIONS

MCSE, CNE, Network+, A+

EDUCATION

Bachelor of Science, Computer Science, Cal Tech University, 1997

Figure 4-6 *Continued*

Systems Administrator

EDUCATION

Bachelor's Degree in Computer Science or equivalent technical certifications.

EXPERIENCE

- Minimum 4+ years of experience administering and maintaining optimized secure LANs in NT.
- Capable of installing complete network operation environments, including the operating system, service packs, server products, and supporting companion products.

JOB SUMMARY AND MAJOR RESPONSIBILITIES

- Duties include, but are not limited to: installing and administering Microsoft line of server products; developing, documenting, and maintaining server SW configuration and standardization; providing workstation assignments, remote dial-up, email, printer services; assisting network engineers in evaluating SW, patches, and fixes for security bugs and networking degradation; providing remote storage for data security and integrity; restricting unauthorized access of network resources; reviewing server loads and recommending load balancing for optimization.
- Provides 24x7, 365 days a year ownership of all NT infrastructure gear.
- Provides complex tier III troubleshooting and support services.

BREADTH AND DEPTH OF SKILL LEVEL AND PROJECT ROLES

- Senior level professional.
- Provides leadership for his/her systems administrators.
- May direct work of others.
- Leads medium-to-large projects.
- Acts as a role model to other systems administrators within group.
- Provides technical guidance and training to other systems administrators.
- Plans, conducts, and may supervise projects.
- Operates with substantial latitude for self-directed action and decision.
- Possesses and applies in-depth and specialized NT administration skills.
- Understands the interactions between various critical skill areas.
- Applies knowledge to the most complex technical challenges.
- Uses full technical knowledge of all phases of NT system administration.
- Holds 100% accountability for all NT infrastructure gear and system administrators.
- During system failures and outages, devises game plan and resolution.
- Coordinates the team to resolve issues and informs manager of situation and tasks to be accomplished.
- Participates in on-call pager rotation for NT system administrators and abides by company policies.

FIGURE 4-7   Job listing for systems administrator

Scott German
119 N. 12th St.
Guelph, MI 58447
(701) 522-8591 ◆ sgerman@dtel.com

SUMMARY

- Systems Administrator with six years experience administering and maintaining optimized secure LANs on Windows NT
- MCSE Certified
- Extensive experience installing and administering all Microsoft server products
- Able to coordinate and optimize backup strategies to ensure data integrity
- Strong helpdesk background; able to resolve technical problems and provide support across system and company
- Hands-on experience in purchasing, planning, and cost control
- Excellent communication skills

TECHNICAL SKILLS

Operating Systems

Windows NT Server 4.0, Windows NT Workstation 4.0, Windows 95/98, DOS, Novell 3.12/4.11, SCO Unix 5.0.5, Novell 4.11

Applications

SQL Server 7.0, Goldmine 4.0, MS Office 97/00, Unidata, Richter, Support Magic 3.31, Lotus Notes 4.6, Norton AntiVirus

Technical Knowledge

DHCP, WINS, routers, switches, PBX, POP3, TCP/IP, NetBIOS, NetBEUI, SNMP, and other networking protocols, HTML 4

EXPERIENCE

Systems Administrator, Rufael Enterprise Inc., May 96, 1995–Present

- SCO Unix Administrator for 47 remote servers.
- Performed regular maintenance via modem and dedicated lines as needed. Created users, reset passwords, reset ports, tape backups, and restores.
- Installed and configured hardware, including hard drives (SCSI and EIDE), tape drives, Digiboards, MUXs, printers, and network adapters.
- Built many servers, including IBM and Compaq. Installed and configured software and operating systems; SCO Unix 5.0.0, Unidata.
- Identified LAN/WAN problems covering 60 leased lines (56K frame relay), CSU/DSU, modems (async and sync), and dial-up servers.
- Database Administrator for Support Magic, a SQL database used to log support calls and generate reports. Ran daily, monthly, and yearly statistical and graphical reports for the support desk, management, and budgeting, respectively.
- Purchased all PCs and equipment, reducing the cost allocated for equipment by 40 percent.
- Wrote backup scripts to save the company $15,000 in backup software.
- Resolved application conflicts through experience and a high level understanding of memory usage, DLL files, operating system deficiencies, and application limitations.

EDUCATION

Bachelor of Arts in Economics, Lafayette College, 1994
Microsoft Certified System Engineer (MCSE), 1999

FIGURE 4-8 Systems administrator targeted résumé

Using the Right Words

You may not be a professional writer, but you'll need to learn the importance of choosing the right word if you want your résumé to make an impact. Whenever possible, write your job description with strong action words. Instead of the long-winded "Was responsible for maintaining database..." try the more concise—and powerful—"Maintained database..." In general, whenever you see an "-ing" construction, ask yourself if you could jazz it up a little if it were rewritten.

Short bullet points pack a punch and leave the hiring manager with important details she can find in a hurry and remember later on.

Here's a list of action words you can use to replace "-ing" constructions in your résumé.

achieved	acted	adapted
addressed	adjusted	administered
advised	altered	analyzed
arranged	assembled	assessed
audited	balanced	broadened
budgeted	built	calculated
calibrated	catalogued	categorized
chaired	changed	charted
checked	classified	coached
collated	collected	combined
communicated	compared	compiled
completed	composed	computed
conceived	concluded	conducted
configured	considered	consolidated
constructed	contracted	contrasted
controlled	converted	coordinated
corrected	corresponded	counseled
created	critiqued	cultivated
cut	decided	decreased
defined	delegated	delivered
demonstrated	described	designed

detected	determined	developed
devised	diagnosed	differentiated
directed	discovered	dispensed
displayed	dissected	distributed
diverted	documented	doubled
drafted	drew	edited
eliminated	empathized	encouraged
enforced	enhanced	enlarged
ensured	established	estimated
evaluated	examined	expanded
expedited	explained	expressed
extracted	facilitated	filed
finalized	financed	fixed
followed	forecasted	formulated
founded	gathered	gave
generated	guided	hired
hosted	identified	illustrated
implemented	improved	improvised
incorporated	increased	informed
initiated	inspected	installed
instituted	instructed	integrated
interacted	interpreted	interviewed
introduced	invented	investigated
itemized	judged	launched
learned	lectured	led
liaised	listed	located
maintained	managed	marked
marketed	measured	mediated
met	minimized	modeled

moderated	modernized	modified
monitored	motivated	narrated
navigated	negotiated	observed
obtained	opened	operated
ordered	organized	oriented
originated	oversaw	painted
patterned	performed	persuaded
photographed	piloted	planned
predicted	prepared	prescribed
presented	printed	processed
produced	programmed	projected
promoted	proofread	proposed
protected	provided	publicized
published	purchased	raised
received	recommended	reconciled
recorded	recruited	redesigned
reduced	referred	refined
rehabilitated	related	rendered
reorganized	repaired	reported
represented	researched	resolved
responded	restored	restructured
retrieved	reviewed	revised
revitalized	saved	scheduled
searched	secured	selected
separated	served	serviced
set	sewed	shaped
shared	showed	simplified
sized	sketched	sold
solved	sorted	specified
spliced	split	spoke

started	streamlined	strengthened
studied	summarized	supervised
supplied	talked	taught
tended	tested	traced
trained	transcribed	transformed
translated	traveled	treated
trimmed	troubleshot	tutored
uncovered	unified	updated
upgraded	used	utilized
verified	weighed	welded
widened	wired	won
wrote		

Getting It Right

Starting to get your skills down on your résumé is the hardest part. The worksheets and samples in this chapter should provide a shortcut to uncovering your hidden talents. You won't get it all the first time so make sure you keep refining how you present yourself. Once you have it down, let others provide feedback. Running your résumé by impartial parties will help you continue to refine it and make it better.

Chapter 5

· ·

The Cover Letter

When seeking out cover letter advice you will find a lot of cute, overly imaginative, amusing, and arrogant examples. Some begin with a quote about Kermit the Frog, and some close with "I will come to your office next Friday to take you to lunch." What are these people thinking?

That will not get employers to bite. Most IT hiring managers are going to throw that letter in the trash. They will not be impressed that you are making their lunch plans, and they will only remember your name because they think you're ridiculous. Some of those stunts might work when applying for a position in marketing, sales, or advertising, but you need to take a different approach in the technical arena.

In this chapter, we'll cover:

▶ The purpose of your cover letter

▶ Hooking the employer

▶ Getting to the point

▶ The content of your message

▶ Fatal mistakes of the cover letter

▶ Types of cover letters and how to write them

▶ Sample IT cover letters

The Purpose of Your Cover Letter

The purpose of your cover letter is to get your résumé read. Period. It is not to summarize all of your skills and experience—that's what your résumé is for. It is not to merely introduce you and direct the reader to the enclosed résumé.

So how will your cover letter accomplish its main goal? By enticing an employer and making a dynamite first impression. It needs to show a little about who you are and why you are the best person for the job. It is the warm handshake that puts a "face" to your name, highlights your strong points, and presents non-résumé details that set you apart from the next closest candidate.

For this to happen, you need to do three things:

▶ Hook the employer into reading your résumé

▶ Get to the point quickly and concisely

▶ Reveal some of the positive aspects of your personality

Hook the Employer

Your cover letter can capture the interest of the employer by telling them specifically what you can do for their company. It needs to be personalized, not generic, and it needs to demonstrate why you are going to make an impact on their company in particular.

To hook the employer, you need to find out as much about the company as possible, starting with the name of the hiring manager.

Personalize Each Letter

If the job posting does not list the name of the hiring manager, do some research:

▶ If there is a phone number, call and ask for the name of the hiring manager for that position. You may need to use some investigative skills, and turn on the charm!

▶ If there is only an email address, try to figure out the company from that address and then contact them by phone.

▶ If there is only a mailing address, get creative. Drive by the address and find out the name of the company. You can then call for the name of the hiring manager. If it is only a post office box, that probably won't be possible.

▶ If there is only a fax number, try dialing numbers that are close to that and see if you get the number of someone who works there. For example, if the fax number is 431-5015, try dialing 431-5000, 431-5016, or 430-5015. This one might be a stretch, but you could get lucky.

If you are unable to find a specific name to address your cover letter to, the best alternative is to use "Dear Hiring Manager." Avoid more formal salutations such as "Dear Sir" or "Madam."

Next, you want to do some research on the company. The easiest way is to visit their Web site or talk to someone you know who works there. Try to get an idea of what the company is all about, their motto, and their history, and take that into consideration when writing your cover letter. If you can incorporate some of their philosophy into your cover letter without sounding cheesy, go for it.

Get to the Point

Your cover letter needs to be less than one page. Any longer and you are lessening your chances of getting it read. Keep in mind that an employer usually spends less than 30 seconds reading a cover letter. If you fill the entire page, you may already be saying too much. Condense, condense, condense. Long sentences with colorful, obscure words are not impressive in a cover letter.

Reveal Positive Aspects About Yourself

It is acceptable to show some personality in your cover letter, but you don't want to cross that line and come off as unprofessional. If you have checked out books about writing cover letters, you have probably seen many examples of this.

To be effective, you want to use positive action words and keywords to reflect your positive aspects. And you want to write in a tone that projects confidence, professionalism, and experience.

On the other hand, here are some examples that indirectly reveal *negative* points:

Lose the attitude If you are looking for the best programmer you could possibly hire, look no further, because here I am! My unbelievable skill set and ability to work with others far exceed that of anyone you have employed before.

Get some confidence Although I don't have the experience you are asking for, I can probably step up to the challenge. I would just need some time to adjust to the work environment and develop my skill set further.

Don't be so blunt; they do not have to know this from the get-go I was recently laid off and am looking to get into the work force again.

The Content of Your Message

The body of a traditional cover letter basically covers these areas:

- ▶ Introduction
- ▶ Self-promotion
- ▶ Call to action
- ▶ Thank you

Introduction

In the first paragraph, you need to state why you are writing. A hiring manager or recruiter does not want to waste time trying to figure out the purpose of this letter. Be direct, concise, and to the point. State the title or type of the job you are applying for and why the position interests you.

Stay away from the common "I am writing in response to your ad in the Washington Times for a _____," but there is no need to try to come up with a catchy quote or crazy introduction. Just get to the point.

The following are some examples of effective opening statements:

I have been closely following the progress of Target Communications over the past year and am impressed with the growth of your organization.

I am A+ and Network+ certified and currently working toward my MCSE certification.

Sharon Bymers recommended that I contact you regarding the design position with Total e-Packages.

As a C++ programmer of four years, I have worked with all aspects of the language and found this field to be stimulating and challenging.

If your staff could benefit from the addition of an eminently qualified quality assurance professional, we should meet to discuss my credentials.

Self-Promotion

The next section needs to outline why *you* alone are ideal for this job. If you are responding to a job posting, you know what the company wants, so exploit that. Use the main points of the job description to explain how you could best satisfy their needs, incorporating your relative skills, experience, and training. Use the keywords that are listed in their ad and hone in on specifics related to them.

Keep in mind that no one likes a pushy salesman. Be careful not to exaggerate your skills or sound too boastful. No one wants to hear that you are the greatest person ever, and most employers do not want to hire someone with that attitude.

In addition, your résumé needs to be an *overview* of your relevant qualifications and experience, not a paraphrased summary of your résumé. For example, if they are looking for someone with networking experience, don't write the whole letter about your last job doing this. Just introduce the fact that you have this experience, with a supporting fact or two. Further details are contained in your résumé.

Call to Action

This closing paragraph requires some assertiveness, but not over-aggression. As mentioned earlier, it is not a good idea to suggest that you will see them on Friday when you pick them up for lunch. This is simply over the edge, arrogant, and inconsiderate of the hiring manager's schedule. Wouldn't you be offended if someone said this to you?

That said, you do want to make a call to action at the conclusion of your cover letter. Although you should make respectful follow-ups, you still want to prompt them to contact you. This would suggest a closing such as, "I look forward to hearing from you about my suitability for this position." This is less pompous than "I will call you on Thursday at 11:00 A.M."

Watch out for employers that state "no phone calls." You don't want to disregard these requests.

Thank You

Ending your cover letter with a gesture of thanks is proper job-hunting etiquette. If the Human Resources director or hiring manager is taking the time to read your correspondence, you want them to know you appreciate it. This ending can positively affect their impression of you.

Fatal Mistakes of a Cover Letter

After you have written your cover letter, solicit the advice of others and proofread.

The following are some fatal mistakes to avoid when writing your cover letter:

► Grammatical, spelling, or formatting errors.

► Salutations such as "Dear Sir" or "To Whom It May Concern." It is best to personalize the letter with a name, but if that is not possible, "Dear Hiring Manager" or "Dear Employer" are acceptable.

► A handwritten cover letter. Some people think this is more personal, but that couldn't be more wrong.

► Specific salary figures, even if they are requested. State that your salary is negotiable and can be discussed in the interview. You don't want to count yourself out before you have a chance to prove what you are worth. Even if an employer has a maximum dollar amount they want to spend, you might change their mind.

► Summarizing your résumé. Don't be redundant.

► Exaggerations of qualifications or experience.

► Negative or controversial subject matter such as political or religious topics, or insults to your previous employer or company.

► Revealing too much about *why* you are looking for a job. That can come out in the interview.

► Personal issues or feelings.

► Overly aggressive sales pitch about yourself.

► Excluding the cover letter. Some Human Resources personnel do not even accept résumés without cover letters.

► Personal or cheesy closing such as *Yours truly, Eagerly waiting,* or *Your next employee.*

Emailing Cover Letters

When emailing your cover letter, use the same writing guidelines. Then follow the formatting guidelines, as discussed in Chapter 3:

▶ Create your emailable cover letter using the guidelines for writing an ASCII résumé.

▶ Make sure that all information is left-aligned.

▶ Use characters such as asterisks and hyphens to highlight information.

▶ You may want to shorten your letter slightly as it is more difficult to read from a computer screen than from a piece of paper.

▶ Paste the cover letter into the email; do not send it as an attachment.

▶ Write a descriptive subject line, such as "My assets for PC technician position" or "Software engineer résumé, referred by Larry Thorpe."

▶ If you are using Outlook or another email program, you can set an *auto reply* to notify you when the recipient opens your message. This may work to prompt a response.

Types of Cover Letters and How to Write Them

There are different types of cover letters that can be used depending on the situation:

▶ Traditional cover letter

▶ T-letter

▶ Networking letter

▶ Thank you letter

▶ Recommendation letter

Traditional Cover Letter

The traditional cover letter accompanies your résumé when you are responding to an advertisement or job posting. Figure 5-1 illustrates an outline of the sections of the traditional cover letter.

The T-Letter

The T-letter is a straightforward cover letter that lists the *employer's wants* in one column and *your qualifications* in the adjacent column. For busy hiring managers, this layout is a quick read and easily points out a great match.

A T-letter is perfect if your skills and experience match most or all of the employer's requested qualifications. If that is not the case, do not use this type of cover letter. You would be highlighting your weaknesses before the employer even has a chance to see your strengths. See Figure 5-2 for a sample of the body of a T-letter.

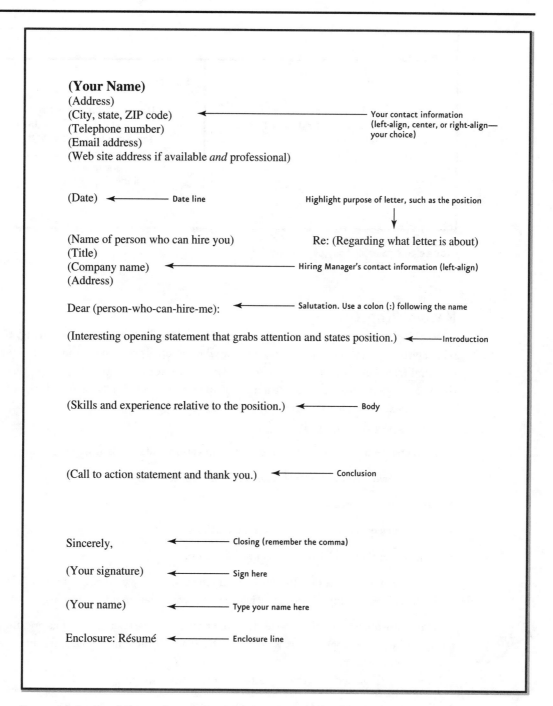

(Your Name)
(Address)
(City, state, ZIP code) ←——————————— Your contact information
(Telephone number)   (left-align, center, or right-align—
(Email address)   your choice)
(Web site address if available *and* professional)

(Date) ←——————— Date line   Highlight purpose of letter, such as the position
                                                              ↓
(Name of person who can hire you)   Re: (Regarding what letter is about)
(Title)
(Company name) ←——————————— Hiring Manager's contact information (left-align)
(Address)

Dear (person-who-can-hire-me): ←————— Salutation. Use a colon (:) following the name

(Interesting opening statement that grabs attention and states position.) ←——— Introduction

(Skills and experience relative to the position.) ←——— Body

(Call to action statement and thank you.) ←——— Conclusion

Sincerely, ←——————— Closing (remember the comma)

(Your signature) ←——————— Sign here

(Your name) ←——————— Type your name here

Enclosure: Résumé ←——————— Enclosure line

FIGURE 5-1 Sample layout for a traditional cover letter

You want:	I have:
• A computer degree • Basic understanding of Java and JavaScript • Attention to detail	• **B.S. in Computer Science** • Thorough knowledge of **Java** and **JavaScript,** as well as **SQL** • **Attention to detail**, as well as expert organization and logical thinking skills

FIGURE 5-2 Sample body of a T-letter

Networking Letter

Networking is not limited to asking the people you know if their company is hiring. You can send a letter to someone you do not yet know who could help you in your job search. By utilizing a mutual friend or acquaintance, you can make connections with potential employers. In addition to asking for a job, you can use a networking letter to solicit advice and ideas, or job leads and referrals. A sample networking letter is shown in Figure 5-3.

Your networking letter can:

▶ Help you get a job by making a personal connection and establishing rapport.

▶ Prioritize you over applicants who don't have connections.

▶ Provide information on a target employer.

▶ Help you acquire referrals or recommendations.

▶ Help you gather advice on your course of action.

▶ Enable you to become familiar with an employer who may be hiring later on. To save time with their recruiting efforts, they may contact you when that time comes.

Make sure your networking letter is well written and does not come off as presumptuous or pushy. If the person does not know you or probably won't remember you, state that openly at the beginning of the letter.

When writing your networking letter, mention the following:

▶ How you came to write this letter, such as from a referral of another lead.

▶ The credentials you have in the field, such as your education or background.

▶ Your knowledge about issues the employer is facing. Be careful not to sound like you are telling them how to do their job. Using phrases like "as you know" can set the proper tone.

Melissa Spellman
11 South Ferry Way
Springfield, MI 91120
515-645-2727
spellmanm@excite.com

October 17, 2001

Matt DeWitt
Vice President of Technology
eBusiness International
2121 Broadway
St. Louis, MI 91343

Dear Mr. DeWitt:

I am not sure if you will remember, but we met when your department was attending IT training in Springfield this summer. I assisted you and your employees with their workstation setups and MCSE lab sessions at the Technology Institute. I was very impressed with you and your team, and have a small request.

I have been with my company for some time, and I am interested in leaving to further my career in the networking field. You seemed to know a lot about the industry as well as who's who in St. Louis, and I would like to ask your advice about corporations there. I am planning on moving to the area soon and would appreciate any insight you could provide.

I will call you next Thursday to try to set up a couple of minutes to talk. Don't worry, I only want some advice, and if you have the time I would love to take you to lunch. I am enclosing my résumé to remind you of some of my qualifications.

Thank you in advance for your time and assistance!

Sincerely,

Melissa Spellman

Melissa Spellman

Enclosure: Résumé

FIGURE 5-3   Sample of a networking cover letter

Thank You Letters

You may not necessarily sway an employer's decision with a thank you letter, but there are no disadvantages to sending one—pre- or post-interview.

Before the Interview

You can send a note or an email to thank the interviewer for the appointment, confirm the time and place, and add a selling point to increase the interviewer's anticipation of your meeting.

After the Interview

Send a thank you letter or email to immediately remind the interviewer of you, make another good impression, add information that was not covered in the interview, and provide another reason for the interviewer to contact you.

Although your thank you letter is more casual than an initial cover letter, do not forget about professionalism. Type and proofread just as you would with other correspondence to potential employers.

Others Who Deserve a Thank You

If someone gives you a recommendation or refers you to a job opening, send them a thank you letter (see Figure 5-4). Keep them in your good graces, as you may need their help again later on.

Recommendation Letter

After meeting with a hiring manager, you may receive a request for letters of recommendation. While it is best to get letters of recommendation when you are directly involved with your references, don't panic if you do not have any when you are asked.

Contact your references and, if they are willing to praise you, offer to write a draft letter. Tell them that you know they are busy, that you would like to save them some time, and that they can fine-tune the letter.

When you do get a recommendation letter, keep an electronic copy and a paper copy to ensure you have them for future reference.

Sample IT Cover Letters

Figures 5-5 through 5-9 are sample cover letters for several different IT positions and experience levels.

Rebecca Fellows
13 Cherry Court
Freehold, NJ 71180
(213) 452-9900
rfellows32@hotmail.com

July 3, 2002

Nicole German
IT Manager
World Perks Inc.
52 Gallow Way, Suite 502
Aberdeen, SD 52009   **Re: Desktop Support Technician position**

Dear Ms. German:

Thank you for taking the time to speak with me yesterday about the exciting **Desktop Support Technician** opportunity with World Perks Inc. As I mentioned, I am extremely interested in working for an organization of this caliber.

(Insert a paragraph summarizing any strong points that were not discussed in the interview. If everything was covered, summarize the top qualifications of theirs that you meet.)

Thank you for your concise explanation of your needs. I know that my experience and knowledge of desktop applications and your networking system will be a great benefit to your organization.

I look forward to hearing from you soon to continue our discussion.

Sincerely,

Rebecca Fellows

Rebecca Fellows

FIGURE 5-4 Sample of a thank you letter

The following numbered list of points corresponds to the numbers in Figure 5-5, indicating the highlights of the cover letter.

❶ Todd researched the company and mentioned that in the first paragraph. This shows his interest in the organization, not just in the position. He then stated how he could help the company.

❷ Todd used headings to point out important qualifications from the job description. He did this because he is not experienced and he wants to draw attention away from that and toward his abilities.

❸ Todd created "experience" by discussing work he has done for friends and family, such as setting up a network.

❹ Todd mentioned traits of his personality that would be beneficial in this position. He tied that into how this will help with nontechnical aspects of this position, such as training new employees.

Todd Hagen
3645 Lake Trail Rd., Apt. 301
Grand Rapids, MI 30221
412-631-8802
toddlhagen@email.com

September 5, 2002

Harvey Waletzko
Director of Engineering
Target Communications
7712 Commerce Ave., Suite 410
Detroit, MI 31882   **Re: PC Technician position**

Dear Mr. Waletzko:

❶ I have been closely following the progress of Target Communications over the past year and am impressed with the growth of your organization. I am particularly impressed by your recent expansion and hiring of 100 employees that increased your need for additional **PC technicians**. I am interested in showing you how I can help make this transition smoother for your company.

Certified and Experienced ❷

I am **A+ and Network+ certified** and currently working toward my **MCSE certification**. I have an ample amount of hands-on experience, which includes installing and configuring operating systems on both PCs and Macs. I also set up a home network of an NT server and several ❸ workstations, as well as performing consultant work troubleshooting and repairing systems.

Dedicated to Customer Service

❹ My dedication to precision and customer service will benefit your company as you introduce new employees to your network. Having an outgoing and detail-oriented personality, I will be very effective in training new hires on the essentials of their system, as well as providing time-saving computing tips and increasing productivity by facilitating an easy transition.

Thank you for considering me for the PC Technician position at Target Communications. I am interested in setting up a time to further demonstrate how I can bring the positive attitude and knowledge you need for your networking team.

Sincerely,

Todd Hagen

Todd Hagen

Enclosure: Résumé

FIGURE 5-5 Sample cover letter for a PC technician with no experience

Helen Rufael
1900 Foxhill Court
Spokane, WA 55021
321-563-0091
hrufael2@excite.com

May 30, 2002

Scott Clausson
Technical Services Manager
IT Training Corporation
648 Battery Avenue
Seattle, WA 55762   **Re: Helpdesk Analyst**

Dear Mr. Clausson:

① Customer service is something that comes naturally to certain people, and I am one of those people. I excel as a **Helpdesk Analyst** because I have the technical skill set combined with the personality to deliver solutions and solve problems quickly, with an upbeat attitude.

② My experience at the General Electronics helpdesk included servicing 300 **③** franchise locations in desktop applications and proprietary software support. While there, I researched, implemented, and administered a call tracking system used by the helpdesk, development team, and training department. Within two **④** months the average call time went down by nearly 50 percent.

⑤
Statistically, **my average performance ranks number one** or two each week in regards to number of calls, average call time, percentage of closed calls, and customer appreciation rating.

⑥ Thank you for considering me as a top candidate. I would like the opportunity to meet with you to discuss my background further and share my ideas about making the helpdesk at the IT Training Corporation more productive and more successful.

Sincerely,
Helen Rufael
Helen Rufael

Enclosure: Résumé

FIGURE 5-6   Sample cover letter for a helpdesk analyst with minimal experience

The following list points out valuable tips found in Figure 5-6 for writing a cover letter to reflect your personality and key accomplishments, even when your experience is minimal.

1 Helen used the first paragraph to demonstrate her understanding of the importance of customer service in the helpdesk profession.

2 She highlighted past experience in a similar position to create credibility.

3 She quantified past experience by using specific numbers to explain the size of the helpdesk in her last position.

4 Helen highlighted a major accomplishment to show initiative in improving the company, aside from performing normal duties.

5 She added bold highlighting to a fact about personal performance to show her dedication to job responsibilities.

6 Helen concluded by thanking the hiring manager for his consideration. She included a statement about helping the company.

The following details highlight the cover letter in Figure 5-7, illustrating an excellent way to write a cover letter that incorporates a referral.

1 Melissa name-dropped right away by referring to the current employee who recommended the position.

2 She used the company's motto to draw attention to the message in the letter, as well as to show familiarity with the company.

3 She bolded key points, such as the company's motto, years of experience, and job title.

4 Melissa summarized key accomplishments in bulleted form as her qualifications matched the job description very closely.

The following numbered list corresponds to the numbers in Figure 5-8, pointing out key examples of personal traits, work experience, and professional skills maneuvered into the cover letter.

1 Molly highlighted her key qualifications for this position: C++ programming and management experience.

2 She plugged some of the other skills mentioned in the job description and highlighted her education.

3 Molly emphasized her teamwork abilities as well as independent work capabilities.

4 She included a personal statement about having an open mind and the ability to adapt to new projects easily, both valuable characteristics to an employer.

Melissa Johnson
1463 19th Street SE
Fargo, ND 58102
701-563-8221
Melissa.Johnson@email.com

July 30, 2002

Heather Molnar, MIS Manager   **Re: Web Page Designer position**
Total e-Packages   **Referred by Kevin McMahon**
17 Technology Drive
Santa Ana, CA 92701

Dear Ms. Molnar:

❶ Kevin McMahon recommended that I contact you regarding the design position with Total e-Packages. As a **Web Page Designer**, I was impressed by your organization's widespread public visibility with recent design projects. I was especially interested when Kevin showed me the innovative work you are doing with FedEx and NationsBank.

I want a role with Total e-Packages—and with me on your team, Total e-Packages will be even more able to deliver **the total package for e-business success. ❷**

My experience at Smyth and Turner Agency includes:
                          ❸
- **Three years in graphic design** and layout for major accounts, including Burger Time and Hudson Bay Inc.
- Utilization of my **B.S. in Web Design and Development** from the Baltimore Institute
❹   of Art.
- Assisting in the design of Smyth and Turner's recently launched Web site, in addition to working on sites for various other **large, national clients**.

My graphic design expertise combined with my solid skill set has prepared me for handling large accounts such as those you service at Total e-Packages. I look forward to discussing how my contributions can assist in marketing your company for bigger profits and higher visibility.

Thank you for your consideration and for an opportunity to further demonstrate how I can help you deliver the total package for e-business success.

Sincerely,

Melissa Johnson

Melissa Johnson

Enclosure: Résumé

FIGURE 5-7 Sample cover letter for a Web page designer, including mention of a referral

Molly Skandalis
153 Rolling Avenue
Bel Air, FL 40214
410-803-7171
mskandalis@yahoo.com

January 15, 2002

Ms. Paige Boyle
IT Manager
Raven Enterprises
162 Main Ave., Suite 451
Ft. Lauderdale, FL 30201

Dear Ms. Boyle:

As a **C++ Programmer** ❶ for the past four years, I have worked with all aspects of the language and found this field to be stimulating and challenging. I am able to produce work of a high standard in coding, testing, debugging, and writing documentation.

Recently I moved into a **position of management** ❷ and enjoy using my experience to guide the development team to many successes, in addition to working independently on high-level projects. Although my **B.S. in Computer Science** focused on C++, I have been ❸ fortunate to work with a range of other programming languages, including **Java**. My open-mindedness and easy adaptability make the transition to other languages relatively simple.

❹

I can be available for an interview at short notice and look forward to meeting you to discuss how my combination of management and technical skills can benefit the IT department of Raven Enterprises. Thank you for your consideration.

Sincerely,

Molly Skandalis

Molly Skandalis

Enclosure: Résumé

FIGURE 5-8 Sample cover letter for an experienced computer programmer

Jeff Kloos
72 Guelph Avenue
Mound, MN 93225
605-523-9821
jeff_kloos@aol.com

February 26, 2002

Mindy Thompson
Quality Assurance Manager
Stanley Morgan Financial Institute
5523 106th Avenue SE
Minneapolis, MN 93218   **Re: Quality Assurance position**

Dear Ms. Thompson:

If your staff could benefit from the addition of an eminently qualified Quality Assurance
professional, we should meet to discuss my credentials.

①

You want:	I have:
▪ A computer degree ▪ Basic understanding of Java and JavaScript ▪ Attention to detail	▪ **B.S. in Computer Science** ▪ Thorough knowledge of **Java** and **JavaScript,** as well as **SQL ②** ▪ **Attention to detail**, as well as expert organization and logical thinking skills **③**

In addition to meeting all of your primary qualifications, I also have knowledge of defect
tracking tools, such as **PVCS tracking**, and automated test tools through my experience **⑤**
with **IBM. ④**

I look forward to talking with you soon about how I can effectively contribute to the
Quality Assurance team at Stanley Morgan Financial Institute. Thank you for your
consideration.

Sincerely,

Jeff Kloos

Jeff Kloos

Enclosure: Résumé

FIGURE 5-9   Sample cover letter for a quality assurance professional with no experience

The following list of points refers to the cover letter in Figure 5-9, demonstrating how to project yourself as an ideal candidate even though you have little experience.

❶ Jeff is using a T-letter because the employer's qualifications and Jeff's profile match well. This format easily points out why Jeff deserves consideration.

❷ The employer said SQL was a plus, but not a requirement, so Jeff only listed this in his column and presented this skill as a bonus.

❸ Jeff added some personal characteristics that are relative to a quality assurance specialist.

❹ He highlights IBM because of the credibility of the company.

❺ His experience at IBM was actually a three-month internship, but Jeff is leveraging this to let the employer know that even though he is just graduating, he does have some working knowledge.

Chapter 6

· ·

Common Résumé Dilemmas

After reading this far, you're probably itching to write the perfect résumé. Well, we have a secret for you: it doesn't exist. Before you march off to the bookstore to demand your money back, let us clarify. We all have experience we want to highlight—and other experience we'd rather downplay. In this chapter, we'll show you how to handle four of the most common résumé dilemmas faced by IT professionals. We'll give you practical examples you can put to use immediately. Chapter 12 will provide you with additional résumé samples that will teach you how to develop your own strategy for facing these challenges.

In this chapter, we'll cover:

▶ Recent college graduates

▶ Paper certifications

▶ Career changers

▶ Problem histories

Recent College Graduates

Do any of these statements describe your situation?

▶ Your résumé lists your college extracurricular activities.

▶ Your parent's address is listed as your permanent address.

▶ You list every job since you started working at 16.

▶ Your uncle is listed as a reference.

If you answered yes to even one of these, you're most likely a recent college grad, and the prospect of writing your first professional résumé may seem daunting. The biggest challenge is to fill the page so that it doesn't just include your name, address, and college degree. (And increasing the font to 16 points is not an option!)

As you sit down to draft your résumé, keep one thing in mind: you are most likely competing for entry-level jobs whose other candidates are faced with the same dilemma. No employer will expect you to have the track record of a 40-year-old if you are only 23 and just out of college. Don't worry about your lack of real-world experience. Focus instead on the skills you've learned and the knowledge you've attained. Let's take a look at how to approach each section of your first résumé.

A special note for IT professionals-in-process: The final semester of your senior year is not the time to start on your résumé. It is extremely important to start building it as soon as you get into your heavy-duty IT courses. Your projects will be fresh in your mind and describing them will be easier when it's time to put them to good use. You never know when that great internship is going to come along—you want to be prepared!

Defining Your Career Objective

Forget the flowery language that you find on most résumés. Very simply put, recent college graduates need not include anything beyond the position they seek. Why?

▶ No one expects recent college graduates to know what they want in the long term from their career.

▶ Traditional career objective statements are usually ignored by employers scanning résumés in response to job ads.

No Plan Required

Employers know that most recent college graduates have spent the last two to five years earning their degree, taking general classes that will provide the foundation for thinking logically and methodically (in theory, at least). They may be familiar with local college programs that offer more practical and hands-on programs, but they are primarily interested in finding candidates with working knowledge in IT systems and who appear trainable.

Your first post-graduation résumé is used to apply for your first "real" job in IT. College grads with a career plan are the rare exception. Truly, no one expects recent college graduates to know what their career will look like five to ten years out. Fortunately, a career is built one job at a time, and many of the most successful and rewarding careers take unexpected detours that no one could have predicted at age 22. So define the type of job you want as your first entry-level position and *describe your qualifications for that job.*

Objective Ignored

If you've spent hours perfecting the career objective portion of your résumé, you may be disappointed to learn that most employers won't take the time to admire your carefully crafted sentences. But you should understand why employers don't bother to read this statement.

▶ It is so generic that it could apply to any position in the company.

▶ It describes every other candidate applying for the position.

▶ Employers are reviewing résumés for very specific job postings.

There's a double-edged sword, though. Even though your objective statement will probably be ignored, you still need to include it. Look at it this way: the hours you've invested won't go to waste. You just need to learn to maximize the effectiveness of your objective statement. The next section will show you how to do just that.

I'm Trainable!

Employers are looking for candidates who have a base set of IT skills and who are trainable. The top of your résumé is precious real estate for effectively addressing the question "Why should you hire me?" It is space that should be devoted to selling your credentials—both your educational and practical experience. Use this space to *imply a job objective* and *advertise credentials and strengths as a potential employee.*

Check out the example shown here:

Qualifications

▶ Self-motivated, customer-focused recent college graduate with an exceptional ability to quickly master new software/hardware

▶ MCP, A+, and Network+ certified as part of earning undergraduate degree

▶ Six-month internship supporting a multiple server Windows NT environment servicing 200 users for an accounting firm

▶ Hired full time post-graduation as the network administrator

▶ B.S. in Computer Science, Montclair State University, 2000

Jennifer recently graduated from college and has been working for the past six months as a networking technician. She earned A+ and Network+ certifications as part of her undergraduate work and has gained valuable experience with on-the-job training through an internship program with a local accounting firm. It is important to highlight her capacity to handle multiple important projects at the same time (completing her coursework and holding down a full-time job) and her readiness to keep her skill set current with industry demands.

Defining Your Experience

Many recent IT college grads obsess over describing relevant, interesting, and impressive background experience. Some are so intimidated by their lack of hands-on experience that they resort to exaggerating or fabricating their personal histories.

Don't give in to this temptation. Stretching the truth on your résumé is always a mistake, particularly with IT positions. Most IT hiring managers include peer interviews as part of the interviewing process to help assess candidates' experience. A few simple questions by an experienced IT professional will uncover just how much you really know. Exaggeration can mean automatic disqualification.

Relax. You actually have learned quite a bit in college. And once you write this section of your résumé, you'll be able to tell your parents that they got their money's worth. The following section will help you uncover your relevant experience. It involves two steps:

1. Uncovering your knowledge

2. Uncovering and applying your practical experience

What Have You Learned?

Ever wonder what exactly you learned from those endless theoretical college courses? A lot, in fact. Theory, design, and analysis courses go a long way on your résumé. First of all, these classes show that you are trainable. You can learn. Employers like this. They also like knowing that you know the basics—decision trees, logical operations, redundancy planning, or whatever.

A simple way of discovering how much you know is to make a list of all the IT, math, and business courses you took in college and then look up the descriptions of these courses in your school's course catalog as a refresher of what you've learned. Luckily, most course catalogs are available online these days, so it's not hard to copy and paste the descriptions into an impressive list. Table 6-1 is an example of the information you should look for and list.

TABLE 6-1   Skills Learned from College Courses

Course Title	Skills and Knowledge Gained
Introduction to Computer Science	Computer operating system architecture
	Hardware interfaces and operating system software of computers
	Software engineering methodologies, including initial system specification, development, quality assurance, revisions, and deployment
	Data structures, arrays, records, files, pointers, linked lists, trees, graphs, stacks, queues, and heaps
	Application programming in Pascal
	Algorithm design, induction, recursion, and complexity
Unix Operating System	Unix system administration, including tools and utilities, shells, and mail and news administration
C Programming	Structured techniques, pointers, structures, classes, declarations, tools and libraries, I/O and file manipulation, application compilation, and abstract programmer-defined objects

TABLE 6-1   Skills Learned from College Courses *(continued)*

Course Title	Skills and Knowledge Gained
Java Programming	Java object-oriented programming principles, graphical user interface programming, SQL databases, and client/server programming techniques
Operating Systems and Computer Architecture	Systems structure and systems evaluation
	Memory management and process management
Programming Fundamentals	FORTRAN and LISP
	Pascal
	C
Relational Databases	Relational algebra, views, queries, normal forms, optimization, and incrementality
	Other models for databases: hierarchical and network models
	The entity-relationship model, knowledge bases and exceptions
	Distributed databases
	Applications
	Programming in SQL and Oracle
Software Engineering and Object-Oriented Development	Large-scale application design using entity-relation and object-oriented models
	Management of large-scale projects, including version control, document traceability, distributed development
	Testing, validation and verification
	Introduction to formal methods, simulation as a tool
	Large-scale, team-oriented project
RPG Programming	RPG computer programs to solve business problems, including payroll, general ledger, and inventory applications
Business Applications Using COBOL I	COBOL to solve a variety of business problems, including projects using calculations, report formatting, data validation, control breaks, and sequential file processing
Systems Analysis/Design Theory	Fundamentals of development of successful computer-based information systems, with an emphasis on the roles of systems analysts, programmers, users, and management
	Definition of user requirements
	Systems analysis life cycle
Database Theory	In-depth coverage of the content of database management systems (DBMS), including physical and logical database structures using Oracle
Introduction to SQL	Foundations of SQL commands for business applications
HTML Programming	Web design, HTML, FrontPage, Dreamweaver, JavaScript

TABLE 6-1   Skills Learned from College Courses (*continued*)

Course Title	Skills and Knowledge Gained
AS/400 Programming	Control Language (CL) for message handling, data queues, data areas, logic statements, program calls, and asynchronous jobs
Web	Email, HTML basics, telnet
Oracle	Database design, objects, data integrity, security, and performance tuning
Networking Essentials	Networking architecture, transmission concepts, and management
	OSI model
	TCP/IP, server installation, applications, user management, workgroup management, printing, and security
	Windows NT
	Client/server
	Network cabling
VB Programming	VB, database creation and access, inter-application communication, advanced printing techniques, graphics
	Event-driven programs
	Advanced access programming
	GUI design
C++ Programming	Object-oriented programming
	Microsoft Foundation Classes
	GUI programs
	Pointers, memory management, user-defined types
	OLE automation
	DDE
	Large application design and development

Uncovering Your Practical Experience

Most computer science or MIS programs include hands-on projects. Some come in the form of course projects, others in senior projects and, best of all, internships.

Course projects and senior projects are practical applications of your theoretical knowledge. With the fast-paced IT environment out there, it is difficult to find a computer science program that teaches the latest and greatest of the commercial applications and languages used in today's business environment. It is next to impossible to hire leading-edge developers to teach in a college environment or to find college professors who are truly involved in real IT business projects. Nonetheless, your college projects offer a lot of experience that can be represented as practical experience on your résumé.

Make a list of the experience that you accomplished. The things to pull out of this list include:

▶ Real-world application languages that you can program in (C++, Visual Basic, Java, HTML, XML)

▶ Use of commercial applications (Microsoft Excel, Microsoft Word, Macromedia Flash)

▶ Use of real-world processes for planning, design, and project management (Microsoft Visio, Microsoft Project, Microsoft Interdev)

▶ Management of networking systems (Windows NT, Novell NetWare, Sun Solaris)

▶ Operation of computer operating systems (Windows NT, Windows 2000 Professional, Unix, Linux)

▶ Development of databases using commercial software (Microsoft SQL, Oracle, Sybase)

▶ Understanding of ERP systems (PeopleSoft, SAP)

Internships are more common with IS degrees from business management schools. They offer an excellent opportunity to gain hands-on experience in a true business environment. Most last only a single semester, so you can't expect to get a lot of real experience, but you do get a sense of what it means to work within a team of IS people.

If you've completed an internship, it shows you have initiative. Hiring managers value that more than the actual experience you may have gained. The key things that employers look for from internships are:

▶ Application of basic skill set

▶ Introduction to real-world applications, programming languages, development processes

▶ Accountability

▶ Ability to perform under a deadline

▶ Project planning and documentation experience

▶ Project ownership and responsibility

▶ Ability to work as part of a team

Pulling It All Together

The best way to describe the skills you've picked up from course projects and internships is to use a skills-based résumé or functional résumé layout. A skills-based résumé works best when your skills are more impressive than your job titles. As the name suggests, it highlights skills while de-emphasizing actual employment dates by presenting a condensed work history at the bottom of the résumé. This is a great way to present significant skills gained from a position that lasted a short period of time—like an internship.

A skills-based résumé organizes your skills into categories and allows you to list your knowledge under these headings, like the ones that follow:

▶ Programming and Analysis

▶ Database Design

▶ Computer System Administration

▶ PC Support and User Training

▶ Network Analysis and Documentation

▶ Customer Support

▶ Computer Math

▶ Data Integrity

▶ Computer Applications

▶ Systems Analysis

▶ Internet Development

▶ Business Management

▶ Operations Management

The next step is to review the job posting that you're applying for. Identify the key skills they're seeking and pick out the relevant skill headings that you should include. Any other knowledge and skills that you feel would make you a better candidate for the position should be categorized under a functional heading of "Additional Skills." Practical experience should be interspersed with the knowledge and skills you have acquired. Look to include three to six supporting statements under each skills heading, including examples of your practical experience.

Figure 6-1 shows a sample résumé that doesn't maximize college experience very well. Figure 6-2 shows the same information presented differently to create a much more effective résumé. Without a lot of editing, we were able to draw attention from the fact that Nick has only been working as a helpdesk technician for three months, has yet to earn his B.A. degree, and had previous unrelated experience. Here's what we did:

▶ Removed the objective statement. It had too many buzzwords and was too generic.

▶ Moved up and renamed the "Special Skills" section to "Summary of Qualifications." Listed skills in bulleted format and included a reference to helpdesk support skills.

▶ Removed irrelevant job titles that did not support position being sought.

▶ Removed irrelevant majors that may have caused hiring manager to question focus.

▶ Rewrote major to be more focused.

▶ Eliminated "Interests" section, which is irrelevant to employers.

NICK RUHN
6108 Rosemont St.
Long Beach, CA 90888

Residence: (555) 555-6666   E-mail: nlruhn21@hotmail.com

OBJECTIVE   To obtain a challenging position in a progressive company,
                  utilizing abilities developed through experience and education,
                  with the opportunities for professional growth based on
                  performance.

EDUCATION   California State University, Fullerton. B.A. degree expected 12/01
                  Major: Business Administration
                  Concentration: Management Information Systems
                  GPA in major: B average
                  Humboldt State University, Arcata, CA. 1995–1997
                  Major: Oceanography
                  Long Beach City College, 1991–1995
                  Major: General Education

EXPERIENCE   Cool Fuel Incorporated, Paramount, CA. 9/2000–Present
                  Position: Technical Support Analyst
                  Duties: Assisted in the transition from a Novell to an NT network.
                  Performed administrative duties on the network, provided technical
                  support on the network and user level, wrote programs for
                  company reports in Visual Basic, Excel, and Crystal Reports.
                  Trader Joe's, Long Beach, CA. 1997–2000
                  Position: Cashier
                  Duties: Customer service, order writing, stocking, and
                  coordinating employees in distributing work duties.

SPECIAL SKILLS   Visual Basic 6.0, SQL, Microsoft Access, C++, Mas90, Microsoft
                  Office, Windows 95/98, Windows NT Server 4.0, knowledge of
                  networking and TCP/IP, the ability to learn software, strong
                  written and oral communication skills, strong organizational skills,
                  and a team player.

INTERESTS   Snowboarding, surfing, mountain biking, running, and a love for
                  the outdoors.

FIGURE 6-1   An example of an ineffective résumé

NICK RUHN
6108 Rosemont St.
Long Beach, CA 90888

Residence: (555) 555-6666   E-mail: nlruhn21@hotmail.com

SUMMARY OF SKILLS

- Programming/Databases: Visual Basic 6.0, SQL, Microsoft Access, C++, ASP, VBScript, HTML
- Applications: Microsoft Office product suite, Crystal Reports
- Networking/Operating Systems: Windows 95/98, Windows NT 4.0, TCP/IP
- Excellent communication and problem-solving skills for resolving user issues quickly and courteously
- Highly motivated, fast learner, and a team player

EXPERIENCE   **Technical Support Analyst**   2000–Present
Cool Fuel Incorporated, Paramount, CA
- Assisted in the migration from Novell NetWare to Windows NT
- Administered Windows NT Server, including user creation, system backup, security administration, and network printing configuration
- Provided networking technical support to 50 corporate users
- Developed company-wide reporting using Visual Basic, Excel, and Crystal Reports

Trader Joe's, Long Beach, CA.   1997–2000

EDUCATION   B.A. in Management Information Systems, anticipated Dec. 2000
California State University, Fullerton, CA

Humboldt State University, Arcata, CA   1995–1997
Long Beach City College, Long Beach, CA   1991–1995

FIGURE 6-2   Pulling it all together

Striking the Right Balance

As you can see, a recent college grad's résumé needn't appear skimpy or unimpressive. Draw upon the knowledge you've acquired, the practical projects you've worked on, and your internships and part-time jobs. Demonstrate your ability and willingness to handle a responsible full-time position, even if it is your first such job.

Be careful, not to go too far. Don't exaggerate or stretch the importance and degree of responsibility of your past jobs. Depending on the breadth of your background, a one-page résumé may be long enough. This is the rule especially if you have never held a full-time position.

You will strike a bargain when applying for your first post-college job. You will offer your talent, knowledge, and hard work in exchange for a salary and benefits on the assumption that the value you'll create for your employer will be worth at least as much as the income you'll receive. You'll offer an extra measure of enthusiasm, energy, and dedication in exchange for the opportunity to learn and grow on the job. You must be willing to "pay your dues." You are starting at the bottom and will be working your way up. Always keep in mind that this is your first job and it will be an extension of your learning experience. Keep your expectations in check and you will be successful.

Paper Certifications

Paper certifications are a hot issue with IT professionals—those who have certification but no experience, and those who don't have certification but have years of on-the-job experience.

About ten years ago, certifications were a sure-fire way of getting your foot in the door. Companies desperately needed knowledgeable professionals to get the job done. But as the number of certifications granted has increased dramatically over the years, the value of a certification has decreased—and so has the cost involved in earning it.

IT professionals who are "paper certified" or have earned a certification without previous work experience face the same issues as recent college graduates. Without hands-on credentials, employers look at these candidates as entry-level professionals whom they will have to train.

Of course certifications are valuable. Formal technology education provides crucial knowledge, something employers value greatly. If you do not have the experience to back up your certification, your résumé must stress your foundation knowledge and skill set *and* how trainable you are. Certainly, you will have an edge over other candidates applying for entry-level positions.

The hottest certifications in the marketplace today are Cisco and Oracle. These certifications are hard to get, and the number of certified professionals out there is low. In addition, these certifications require a lot of lab time, which can only be gained from commercial work experience.

Figures 6-3 and 6-4 provide an example of how to turn a run-of-the-mill résumé into an effective résumé for candidates with a paper certification. There is nothing wrong with admitting you have just earned your certifications, especially if you don't have relevant job experience. Admit it up front and focus on your strengths. Here's what we did to alter the original résumé shown in Figure 6-3 to make it much more effective:

▶ Strengthened the "Summary of Qualifications" section by combining technical and soft skills under one section.

▶ Changed the job titles to show career progression with increased job responsibilities. Trimmed down on elusive job functions.

▶ Substantiated certification and college experience with actual dates and course hours.

Tracy Foye
13840 Riviera Street
Los Alamos, CA 88788
(555) 555-1590 ♦ tfoye@cna.com

COMPUTER SKILLS:

- Windows 95
- Windows 98
- Windows 2000
- Windows NT 4
- DOS
- MS Office
- WIN 3.1
- Novell NetWare 5
- HTML
- Internet
- FrontPage 98

SUMMARY OF QUALIFICATIONS:

CNA – Certified Novell Administrator
MCP – Microsoft Certified Professional
A+ Computer Technician
Training and supervisory skills
Excellent presentation, oral, and written communication skills

PROFESSIONAL EXPERIENCE:

FADZ Entertainment, Fullerton, CA   3/97–1/00
Manager

- Analyzed and provided production reports to the management team
- Increased efficiencies through in-depth operational analysis
- Forecasted and planned financial position
- Interviewed and selected sales staff
- Advised and supported senior-level management on financial operations and performance

Flynn Signs & Graphics, Long Beach, CA   7/94–1/97
Sales

- Generated sales of $200,000 of $2M annually
- Implemented and integrated revenue generating programs
- Increased revenue through market research and promotion
- Established customer requirements, schedules, and ground rules for numerous projects

Insight Design, Cerritos, CA   10/91–4/94
Account Representative

- Performed pricing and bid analysis for sales team
- Utilized information technology to meet company and customer requirements
- Generated new customer base and achieved production standards
- Investigated and provided timely solutions to customer problems
- Sold and demonstrated products

EDUCATION:

New Horizons Computer Learning Center, Irvine, CA
   CNA – Certified Novell Administrator
   MCP – Microsoft Certified Professional
   A+ Computer Technician
Cypress College, Cypress, CA
   Two years of full-time general education coursework

FIGURE 6-3 The original paper certification example

Tracy Foye
13840 Riviera Street
Los Alamos, CA 88788
(555) 555-1590
tfoye@cna.com

SUMMARY OF QUALIFICATIONS:

- Recently A+, CNA, and MCP certified professional seeking an entry-level technical support position.
- Experience with Windows 95/98/2000, NetWare 5, Windows NT 4, MS Office, FrontPage, HTML
- Highly motivated, fast learner with excellent verbal communication skills
- Six years operations, management, and sales experience

PROFESSIONAL EXPERIENCE:

Sales Manager, **FADZ Inc., Fullerton, CA**   3/97–1/00
- Managed sales staff of 12, including recruitment and hiring
- Managed an operating budget of $500,000
- Provided financial report and analysis to senior management for improving company-wide efficiency

Account Executive, **Flynn Signs, Corona, CA**   7/94–1/97
- Generated sales of $200,000 of $2M annually
- Increased revenue through market research and promotion

Account Rep, **Insight Design, Cerritos, CA**   10/91–4/94
- Supported sales team of 12 outside sales reps by providing pricing, customer demonstrations, and customer support

EDUCATION:

A+	1999
Certified Novell Administrator (CNA)	1999
Microsoft Certified Professional (MCP)	2000
Cypress College, CA	1997–99
60 credit hours in general education coursework	

FIGURE 6-4   From paper certification to professional résumé

Career Changer

Just a couple of decades ago, job-hopping was practically unheard of. People almost always stayed in the same careers and rarely even left the company that first hired them, potenially working for one company for at least 30 years! Today, pension plans have given way to 401(k) plans, which transfer from company to company, and there's a reason: job-hopping is the reality. And career changing isn't at all uncommon today.

The IT industry has opened up opportunities over the last 20 years that were unavailable to previous generations. With the gamut of jobs available in this industry, it continues to be a very popular alternative to military careers, bartending, and construction work. It is also an upgrade path from traditional office work, marketing, and sales. The many different areas of specialization means there's sure to be something for everyone—from programming and systems analysis to sales, support, project management, and even recruiting.

The perks are great—potential for six-figure salaries with a few years under your belt, flexible working hours, exciting travel—but as technology becomes more complex, it gets harder to make the transition. The learning curve is longer than it was 15 years ago when networking was in its infancy, the de facto programming language was COBOL, and there was only one real database system to learn. There is simply more to learn to be qualified for entry-level positions. But the prognosis is good for career changers, as there are still hundreds of thousands of IT positions that will go unfilled in the United States alone over the next few years because of the lack of IT professionals to fill them.

Non-IT companies expect their IT workers to remain on staff an average of 36 months. IT companies expect their IT workers to remain on staff an average of 30 months (ITAA [International Technology & Trade Associates, Inc.]).

Setting Realistic Expectations

Making a dramatic career change, such as moving from a blue-collar job to becoming a programmer, takes a long time. In many ways, career changers will be in the same position as recent college graduates—facing a résumé with a recently granted certification but not much in the area of practical experience. Unfortunately, it will be magnified by the need for immediate returns on putting that certification or two-year degree to work. Career changers are typically older individuals who have families to support and loans for their training to repay. This intensifies the need to find a good paying job as quickly as possible.

You may also come face to face with some harsh realities when looking for your first IT job. Because career changers are typically older workers, they may face age discrimination. How well will you fit in with a team of considerably younger recent college graduates? Will you have the energy to go the extra mile? Will your family obligations allow you to put in the longer hours? How much more will your benefits cost the organization? These questions are not here to discourage you, but rather to heighten your awareness. You need to address these issues in your résumé to increase potential employers' comfort with hiring you over someone younger.

You will also have to face your own expectations of what jobs are available to career changers. What probably sold you to change your career was the opportunity of earning a high paying salary, job security, and the availability of a lot of jobs. This is all true within the IT industry, but the common disclaimer applies: your results may vary. A career changer who has just earned his certification will have some difficulties in landing a job that meets all the above expectations without practical, hands-on experience.

Even doctors need to go through a residency period before they are allowed to go out on their own. The same is true with IT professionals. Your first job will be tough. The money may not all be there, and the hours will be grueling, but you will learn what you need for your next job. Don't be fooled by the thousands of job openings. Take a look at your local paper to see what's really available in your area. Most likely, the job openings are for mid-level IT positions for workers with at least two or three years of experience. These are the realities that most people face once they enter the job market. If you are aware of these realities and have planned for them, you won't be disillusioned and will have a more successful time with your job hunt.

Your first job may not be your dream job, but with two to three years of experience you'll be on your way to greater opportunities.

What You Have to Offer: Transitioning Your Skill Set

Career changers often have plenty of job experience—in the wrong kind of jobs. IT is specialized. Hiring managers are looking for candidates with specific technical skills. Much of your hard-earned experience is completely irrelevant. But every cloud has a silver lining. Careful presentation of your past experience will set you ahead of college grads who have never been in the workforce before.

Unlike people seeking new positions in their current fields who want to present specific experience, career changers need to present a generic background—that is, emphasize skills rather than the specific responsibilities of current or former positions. Feel free to drastically simplify the job listings from your former life.

In addition, depending on how dramatic your career change is, you may want to de-emphasize your previous employers. Force people to pay more attention to the skills you have to offer than to the names of your former employers. There are different ways to accomplish this.

Skills Over Function

It is said that the average adult will change careers at least three times in their lifetime. Does this mean that they start all over again each time? Probably not. Much experience can carry over from one job to the next and one career to the next. A career change is an opportunity to apply lessons learned in working in one environment to the next. Career changers have a leg up on recent graduates. The trick is to write your résumé so that it focuses on the skills rather than on the job titles you've had.

To do so, we recommend that you create a skills-based résumé rather than a chronological résumé. A skills-based résumé draws out your knowledge and skills and makes them more prominent on paper. Job history is downplayed by simply listing your employment history at the end of the résumé with little information about the actual company and job.

In Figure 6-5 we have included a sample cover letter and résumé for this over-50 career changer candidate. Jan has lots of experience, but none of it is directly supporting a position in IT. The goal is to demonstrate how he can be a valuable asset to any organization. In Figure 6-6, the skills-based résumé we created eliminates the outdated and irrelevant history and now highlights his ability to apply his general business knowledge to an IT position and his entrepreneurial experience, management, and sales skills. The possible positions that he can immediately pursue include technical sales and technical customer service positions.

Jan Holmes
1654 234th St.
Laguna Hills, CA 90734
jholmes@aol.com
home: (555) 345-5555

February 19, 2002

Dear Sirs,

With my 24 years of being in the work force and the experience that I have acquired, I would be an asset to your company. I have been a business owner for 12 years, and have held management positions in different fields.

I have been involved with computers for over 15 years. I have experience with building and upgrading computer systems for standalone as well as LAN systems. I am A+ certified and am currently pursuing NT and CCNA certificates. I have been attending Cerritos College on weeknights and Saturdays. I have, to date, completed Network Fundamentals, LAN, WAN, and Cisco TCP/IP. The Cerritos Computer Lab was moved to a different location in which I helped. This involved OS installs, mostly NT 4.0, setting up of routers, hubs, and switches, and manufacturing RJ45 cables. I have had hands-on experience with Cisco routers. I am very familiar with Windows 95, 98, NT 4.0, ME, 2000 Pro, MS Office 97–2000 Pro, and working knowledge of Linux/Mandrake 7.4. Due to my continual usage of upgrades and trial version software, I am well versed with a broad platform of software being used with cutting-edge companies.

I would like to meet with you to discuss your opportunity in more detail. I am available for a personal interview at your earliest convenience.

Sincerely,

Jan Holmes

Jan Holmes

FIGURE 6-5 Sample cover letter and résumé for an over-50 career changer candidate

Jan Holmes
1654 234th St.
Laguna Hills, CA 90734
jholmes@aol.com
home: (555) 345-5555

Objective

I am eager to utilize the skills and experience that I have acquired in the positions I have held in the last 24 years. I have been on both sides, having worked as an employee and a business owner. I am very motivated, dependable, professional, and a self-starter who enjoys challenges. I am looking for a position with both growth potential and long-term opportunities.

Experience

1999–Present   Shower Walls, Branch Office
                  San Gabriel, CA

Manager

- Responsible for entire branch operation.
- Increased sales by 40% in the first year.
- Hired and trained installers.
- Controlled all inventory and production.
- Built and reviewed weekly, biweekly, monthly reports with the owner.
- Set up a network in our main office.
- Made several databases using Access for direct marketing.

1998–1999   Self-employed
                  Modesto, CA

Owner

- Established and built up custom shower wall business.
- Responsible for entire business operation.

1998–1998   IRM Corporation
                  Concord, CA

Property Manager

- Responsible for eight apartment buildings, totaling 850 units.
- Trained and supervised 26 employees ranging from managers to leasing agents and maintenance personnel.
- Prepared and submitted budgets. Stayed within budget constraints while improving our properties and clientele.
- Managed advertising in newspapers, as well as magazines.
- Controlled all bids for work needed and signing of contracts.
- Reported on a weekly basis to the president and vice-president of the corporation.

FIGURE 6-5   *Continued*

1997–1998   Self-employed
                   Modesto, CA

Sales and Service

- Serviced grocery food chain stores with organic whole bean coffee. Dealt directly with store managers and serviced displays.

Computer Skills

Proficient

- DOS, Win95, Win98, Win2000Pro, NT 4.0, Windows for Work Groups
- MS Office 97–2000 Pro, Outlook, IE5
- Netscape 4.75, Netscape 6
- WinZip, WinRar, WinAce
- Norton Software
- Various anti-virus programs

Working Knowledge

- Novell NetWare, Adobe Photoshop, Hot Dog Pro, Linux/Mandrake, MS PowerPoint.

Education

Valley Christian High School – Graduated 1978, Cerritos, CA
Cerritos College, Cerritos, CA

- Fundamentals, LAN, WAN, Cisco TCP/IP. January–May 2000.
- I am A+ certified.
- Currently pursuing NT and CCNA certificates.

Interests

Computers, flying, snow and water skiing.

FIGURE 6-5 *Continued*

For IT professionals, the most important skills to present first are your technical skills. These should appear at the beginning of your skills section. Next, list all your other skills, whether they are management, project management, or sales. Chapter 4 provides detailed information on how to discover your hidden talents and skills to feature in a skills-based résumé.

Jan Holmes
1654 234th St.
Laguna Hills, CA 90734
jholmes@aol.com
home: (555) 345-5555

February 19, 2002

Dear Hiring Manager,

I am submitting my résumé for consideration for the channel sales position listed in the Sunday *Los Angeles Times* on February 3, 2002. After 24 years in sales and management as an independent business owner, I believe that I bring a well-rounded set of skills that meet the requirements advertised for this position. I'd like to highlight some in particular that fit well with the position advertised.

- Entrepreneurial spirit from having owned and managed my own business for over 12 years
- Experienced in solution selling
- Technically knowledgeable
- Broad software knowledge
- Customer service focus

I have been involved with computers for over 15 years and have experience with building and upgrading computer systems for standalone as well as LAN systems. I am A+ certified and am currently pursuing NT and CCNA certificates. I have been attending Cerritos College on weeknights and Saturdays. To date, I've completed Network Fundamentals, LAN, WAN, and Cisco TCP/IP courses. As testament to my diverse capabilities, I was instrumental in helping the Cerritos Computer Lab move to a different location during the past year. This involved OS installs, mostly Windows NT 4.0, setting up of routers, hubs, and switches, and manufacturing RJ45 cables. I have also had hands-on experience with Cisco routers. I am very familiar with Windows 95, 98, NT 4.0, ME, 2000 Pro, MS-Office 97–2000 Pro, and have working knowledge of Linux/Mandrake 7.4. Due to my continual usage of upgrades and trial version software, I am well versed in a broad platform of software being used with cutting-edge companies.

I would like to meet with you to discuss your opportunity in more detail. I am available for a personal interview at your earliest convenience

Sincerely,

Jan Holmes

Jan Holmes

Enclosures: Résumé

FIGURE 6-6   Skills-based résumé for career changers and the accompanying cover letter

Jan Holmes
1654 234th St.
Laguna Hills, CA 90734
jholmes@aol.com
home: (555) 345-5555

Objective

I am seeking to apply my 24 years of sales and management experience to a position selling technical solutions.

Summary of Qualifications

- Seasoned sales and management professional experienced in solution selling
- Entrepreneurial spirit with over 12 years experience in running own businesses
- Technically knowledgeable with over 15 years computer experience and broad software knowledge

Technical Skills

Networking:	LAN/WAN, Windows NT 4.0, Novell NetWare, Linux, Cisco, TCP/IP
Software:	DOS, Windows 95/98, Windows 2000 Professional, Internet Explorer 5, Netscape 4/6, Access, PowerPoint, Photoshop, Norton Utilities, and various anti-virus software
Certifications:	A+ certified, pursuing MCSE and CCNA

- Set up a network in our main office
- Made several databases using Access for direct marketing

Experience

PC/Networking

- Hands-on experience in the installation of the Cerritos College computer lab, including installation of Windows NT servers, configuration of Cisco routers, hubs, and switches, and cabling installation
- Management of Windows NT, including setting up and configuring user accounts, printing environment, and security
- PC software installation and upgrades

Small Business Sales and Operations

- Independent organic coffee distributor servicing grocery food chain stores working directly with store managers
- Established and built up custom shower wall business
- Four years experience in managing all business operations
- Proven ability to drive sales (40% increase in the first year of operation)
- Personnel management, including hiring and training installation team
- Effective inventory control and production

FIGURE 6-6   *Continued*

Property Management

- Managed eight apartment buildings totaling 850 units.
- Trained and supervised 26 employees ranging from managers to leasing agents and maintenance personnel.
- Prepared budgets and stayed within budgets while improving properties and clientele.
- Managed property advertisements in newspapers and magazines.
- Oversaw all outsourced bids and contracts for work needed.
- Provided weekly revenue and operations reports to executive management.

Work History

1999–Present	Branch Office Manager, Shower Walls, San Gabriel, CA
1998–1999	Owner, Holmes Showers, Modesto, CA
1998–1998	Property Manager, IRM Corporation, Concord, CA
1987–1998	Self-employed, Coffee Distributorship, Modesto, CA

Education

A.S. Network Administration, Cerritos College, Cerritos, CA

FIGURE 6-6   *Continued*

Masking Your Previous Employers

If you are making dramatic career changes, de-emphasize the names of your previous employers. As hiring managers sift through the pile of potential candidates, don't leave it up to them to have to make the connection between how your previous work experience relates to the job you are applying for. If a potential employer sees the name of an employer that is clearly in a different industry, they are likely to have preconceived notions of what your responsibilities were.

To avoid this dilemma, you can do several things. Keep to a functional, rather than chronological, format that will allow you to present work history as the last part of your résumé. There, list employer names and employment dates only.

The next thing is to find alternative ways of listing the employers' names. Consider listing only the name of the company or parent organization without references to departments or divisions. You might also abbreviate the name of the company.

Many career changers are making the transition from military careers to the private sector. Private employers without military experience often have a hard time transferring military skills to the private sector. Unfamiliar with leadership and technology skills acquired in a military environment, they don't understand the similarities in the use of technology, project management, and leadership. This is unfortunate, because military candidates often possess a highly developed set of skills that lend themselves well in a corporate environment. Figure 6-7 provides an example of how you can transfer military experience into experience and examples that will deem valuable by the shirts and ties of the corporate world.

CORY CRAIG
34 Warrior Street
San Angelo, TX 76904
555-555-1212
cory.craig@hotmail.com

KEY QUALIFICATIONS

- Decorated Gulf War veteran with over 18 years experience in leadership and information technology.
- **Major skill areas:** Management, network development and administration, training, and a belief in strong computer security policies.
- **Certifications:** Microsoft Certified Systems Engineer + Internet (MCSE + I), Microsoft Certified Systems Engineer (2000), Microsoft Certified Trainer (MCT), Certified Cisco Network Administrator (CCNA), Certified Cisco Design Administrator (CCDA), Certified Novell Administrator, A+.
- B.S. in Liberal Arts, graduate of the Master Analyst Course and a governmental TS/SCI security clearance.

CAREER HIGHLIGHTS

NETWORK DEVELOPMENT AND ADMINISTRATION

- Administered several Windows NT 4.0, Novell NetWare, and Unix LANs supporting 40 remote sites. Also supported Cisco routers and switches, FDDI concentrators and Gigabit Ethernet server connections with 100 Mbs to the desktop.
- Annual budget exceeded 2 million dollars.
- Established Unix-backed network for Warrior system in Saudi Arabia, dealing with numerous logistical and environmental problems.
- Led the Y2K project, including modifying and testing more than 1,000 computer systems and backbone structural systems.
- Consultant for New Horizons for several Maryland-based firms.

MANAGEMENT AND LEADERSHIP

- Served as a team project leader in six different national-level exercises.
- Required to administer the affairs of up to 50 individuals.
- Headed project team responsible for the creation (from the ground up) of seven independent networks. Networks were implemented under budget and in less than 50% of projected timelines.
- Received "Exceeds Course Standards" in both the Primary Leadership Development Course (PLDC) and the Basic Non Commissioned Officers Course (BNCOC), two military leadership and management courses.
- As a district manager in the Hartmarx Corporation, responsible for the hiring and firing of personnel, as well as the management of resources and finances.

TRAINING

- Worked as a Microsoft Certified Trainer for New Horizons, Stevens College in Maryland, and Howard Community College in Texas. Trained more than 600 IT professionals within a three-year period.
- Honored as a senior instructor for the Advance Individual Training Course at Goodfellow Air Force Base for dedicating over 2,000 instructional hours in an Instructional Student Development (ISD) arena. Primary training and development revolved around the All Source Analyst System (ASAS), the primary tactical Unix-based system used by the military.

FIGURE 6-7 Transferring military experience

- Awarded the Army Commendation Medal for the creation of numerous training scenarios, including a Gulf War-like scenario, directed by the Secretary of Defense.
- Selected ahead of peers to train more than 100 senior-level executives of the Saudi Ministry of Defense in collection management techniques, traffic analysis, and computer manipulation.

COMPUTER SECURITY

- First soldier selected to be a part of the U.S. Army's Computer Exploitation Unit.
- Worked with several Tiger teams in support of strengthening computer network security.
- Developed numerous Standard Operational Procedures documents detailing computer security measures, computer virus isolation and prevention techniques, and password protection criteria.

PROFESSIONAL EMPLOYMENT

Staff Sergeant, U.S. Army	1987 – present
MCT for Windows 2000, Stevens College, San Angelo, TX	2000 – present
MCT for Windows NT 4.0, Stevens College, Columbia, MD	1997 – 1999
Consultant and MCT, New Horizons, Columbia, MD	1997 – 1998
District Manager for Hartmarx Corp., Dallas, TX	1984 – 1987

FIGURE 6-7 *Continued*

Transition to Management

Making the transition from technician to technical management is the next step for some IT professionals. Again, beware the double-edged sword: management moves you beyond the helpdesk and earning additional certifications, but it may mean an end to the hands-on work that brought you to IT in the first place.

When you make the move to management, you may lose the "cool factor"—the opportunity to apply your creativity by maximizing the potential of software and hardware for new product releases. But new doors may open. As chief information officer or chief technology officer, you may help determine just what the next big thing will be.

If you're ready to make the switch, you may wonder just how you get from here to there. It's critical to demonstrate that you have acquired the skill set to effectively lead a department and manage a business. Downplay your technical background, and emphasize your managerial potential. The skills sets that you will want to demonstrate are:

► How to hold effective meetings

► How to conduct performance evaluations

► How to write a proposal or report

► How to put together a project plan

► How to deliver a presentation to various audiences

- ► How to deal with difficult employees
- ► How to effectively plan your resources
- ► How to build and motivate a team of technical professionals
  Figure 6-8 provides an example of a management résumé.

Problem History

It would be nice to graduate from college, find a great entry-level position, then move up the corporate ladder from one wonderful job to the next without a glitch along the way. Unfortunately, life doesn't quite work this way. We all have to face challenges in careers and our personal lives that affect our professional history. Some face these challenges voluntarily, such as the personal choice to start a family, while some are a circumstance of health or family issues. Even if you are able to cope with these issues, they may still come back to haunt you and your résumé. Perspective employers may see disruptions in work history as potential problems and may eliminate you from consideration.

The types of issues we'll address in this section include:

- ► Missing years of work
- ► Too many jobs
- ► Too few jobs
- ► Lack of formal education
- ► Being laid off, fired, or having been involved in a scandal

Missing Years of Work

Many people have, for one reason or another, unemployment gaps in their work history. Whether it is six months or six years, an employment gap may raise questions from the hiring manager. Depending on the length of time you were out of work, you may want or need to camouflage these gaps so they are not prominent on your résumé.

Looking for Work

It is common to take a few months off in between jobs. The easiest way to prevent any questions from being raised regarding any time off is to represent the number of years of employment with each company rather than being specific about months and years. For example:

Implementation Consultant, KPMG, New York, NY	December 1995–April 1999
Software Engineer, AMA, New York, NY	January 1992–April 1995

You can change them to read:

Implementation Consultant, KPMG, New York, NY	1995–1999
Software Engineer, AMA, New York, NY	1992–1995

As you can see, the eight-month gap simply disappears.

Thom Lieb, MCSE   Thom.Lieb11@hotmail.com
231 Black Hills Road   310-655-4676
Los Angeles, CA 98765

Objective

Seeking a position where I can utilize my technical and leadership skills to manage a network engineering team.

Summary of Qualifications

- Five years experience as a network administrator with a solid foundation in network resource planning, capacity planning, disaster recovery planning, and network optimization.

- Demonstrated leadership and project management skills as the team lead for upgrading a 5-server, 1,000-user network from Windows NT Server to Windows 2000 with minimal business interruption and no data loss.

- Escalation support for junior support staff.

- Effective motivational and team building skills and serve as a mentor to junior network administrators.

- Manage procurement and leasing programs for all desktop, laptop, server, and networking equipment.

- Superior oral and written communication skills.

Technical Skills

Networking:	MS Windows 2000 Professional Server, MS NT 4.0, TCP/IP, Checkpoint, MS Exchange Server, Lotus Domino server, ArcServe, Cheyenne Antivirus, McAfee Antivirus
Software:	Windows 95/98/2000, MS Office, Acuity, MS Outlook, IE, Netscape
Hardware:	Compaq servers, Cisco routers, switches
Certifications:	MCSE NT 4.0, A+, Network+

Experience

Tier III Network Operations Center Analyst   2001–Present
Sylvan Learning, Baltimore, MD

- Primary person responsible for monitoring 300 Sun Solaris and NT servers' performance and reliability using HP Openview
- Managed network infrastructure upgrades
- Researched, documented, and recommended centralized administration and security products
- Responsible for diagnosing problems on the server and assigning the proper support personnel to solve any problems
- Evaluated new technologies for possible integration into the infrastructure
- Developed policies and procedures for crisis management

Server Team Lead   2000–2001
Sylvan Learning, Baltimore, MD

- Managed the server team consisting of four network engineers supporting ten

FIGURE 6-8   Manager résumé

Windows 2000 servers, two MS Exchange servers, and a Lotus Domino server

- Operated at a 99.8% SLA and interface with the LAN/WAN infrastructure and database teams to ensure 24/7 uptime
- Led the project team to upgrade five Windows NT servers to Windows 2000
- Developed the disaster recovery plan for the organization with the goal of restoring network connectivity within four hours
- Ensured that backups were completed on a regular basis and ensured the integrity of the backups
- Day-to-day operations include installing and upgrading software, security configuration, backups, network storage capacity planning, and performance tuning

Network Support Technician   1998–2000
Eduventures, Baltimore, MD

- Second level supported 70+ workstations and 10 servers running Windows NT Workstation/Server, Windows 95/98, and Office 97, supporting users via the phone and over email
- Trained end-users on the use of their desktop applications, including Windows, Outlook, and Internet Explorer
- Member of the team that physically converted the network from Token Ring to Ethernet
- Installed Ethernet cabling as part of the conversion
- Researched what it would take to upgrade workstations to Windows 2000, including testing Windows 2000 applications for backward compatibility with data
- Built the base images for upgrading laptops and desktops to Windows 2000
- Troubleshooting and resolving problems related to hardware/software installations and networking
- Designed, developed, and maintained IS intranet Web site using Microsoft FrontPage, Macromedia Dreamweaver and Flash

Helpdesk Analyst   1996–1998
T. Rowe Price, Baltimore, MD

- Supported 500 desktop environment distributed in three primary buildings
- Configured end-user workstations and laptops for network and remote access
- Installed and configured software on local machines
- Configured workstations for RAS and email access using MS Outlook and Netscape mail
- Internet Explorer and Netscape browser configuration and support
- Network administration for Win95 and WinNT, security permissions, scripting, and LAN management

Education

B.S. in Computer Science, University of Baltimore, Baltimore, MD   1996

FIGURE 6-8 *Continued*

Returning to School or Raising a Family

If you returned to school for a graduate degree or took time off to raise a family, you may have a gap of a year or more. A simple solution is to include the reason for such gaps within the job descriptions themselves. For example:

Implementation Consultant, KPMG, New York, NY   1992–1994

Left to pursue M.B.A., NYU, August 1994

or

Software Engineer, AMA, New York, NY   1995–1999

Left after birth of first child, July 1999

So often, hiring managers are simply looking to cover all the dates. Amazing as it may seem, they don't always actually care what's written there, as long as the dates make sense.

Too Many Jobs

Another potential problem area may be having too many jobs in a relatively short time. Job-hopping no longer carries the stigma that it once did. The average person is estimated to have seven to ten jobs in the course of a 40-year career. Having four different jobs in the course of five years is not a big deal. But there is a point at which "several" jobs become "a lot of" jobs, and prospective employers start questioning your commitment, discipline, and loyalty.

The Dream Job Turned Bad

We have all had these experiences—the dream job turned nightmare. The job that you probably should have researched a bit more and asked more questions during the interview process turns bad and you leave. So what do you do? Generally the rule of thumb is if you have held a job for less than three months, don't list it. Keep that one experience between you and the ex-employer rather than risk opening up questions that draw you in defensively trying to explain why it wasn't your fault. If no one has let you in on this secret yet, it might be time for us to do so. There is no employment "permanent record." Only you, the ex-employer, and the Social Security Administration will have any records of your previous employment.

If omitting a job leaves a gap in your employment history, you may want to consider camouflaging it using the method we described before of only referencing dates of employment by their years.

Several Jobs, Same Company

When you work for the same company for more than five years, you may end up having held five different positions within that timeframe. Though it demonstrates great mobility and recognition of your talents, it may be misconstrued by hiring managers as job-hopping as well. An easy way to paint this situation in a different light is how you group your positions within your résumé.

For example, here is an IT professional who spent six years working for a systems integration company. During those years, she held progressively higher positions.

Sr. Consultant, Methodologies and Best Practices	1996–1998
SBA Integration / Consulting Services Division	
Sr. Systems Engineer, Major Accounts	1994–1996
SBA Integration / Sales Division	
Sr. Technical Instructor	1992–1994
SBA Integration / Education Division	

One way to represent the same experience without listing each branch of the company separately would be to use the following format.

SBA Integration, Springfield, IL

▶ Sr. Consultant, Methodologies and Best Practices	1998–1996
▶ Sr. Systems Engineer, Major Accounts	1994–1996
▶ Sr. Technical Instructor	1992–1994

Too Few Jobs

While having too many jobs on your résumé is a bigger problem, sometimes having too few jobs can also been seen as a problem by hiring managers. Of course, there might be a perfectly good reason why you have held a small number of positions, especially if you are new to the workforce.

One Job Too Long

Too much job-hopping is bad, but sometimes staying in the same position for too long (more than three years) may not be a good thing either. Staying in the same position raises questions of ability to learn and take on new responsibilities, enthusiasm for one's job, and general issues of whether you are someone worth promoting.

New to the Workforce

If you are new to the workforce, you have an easy answer to why you have only held limited positions. Refer to earlier in this chapter to the section on recent college graduates for examples of how to address this situation using a qualifications section.

Lack of Formal Education

Another potential problem, depending on the position you are applying for, is the lack of formal education. Typically this means a two-year or four-year college degree. Even though IT certifications will get you into the entry-level positions, managerial positions including development manager and director positions will require a formal degree. CIO positions may even require an M.B.A. as well. The higher your ambitions, the more likely that a degree will be necessary.

In IT one way to compensate for the lack of a degree is through certifications and significant on-the-job experience. If you are applying for a job that lists a degree as a requirement, don't lose heart. By emphasizing your experience in a qualifications section at the beginning of your résumé, you can draw the hiring manager in with your skills and knowledge and divert him from the educational section. You can then downplay the educational section. The result of all this is that, upon reading the résumé, the reader may not even notice that you don't have a college degree.

See Figures 6-9 and 6-10 for a before and after look at how it's done. It is evident that Cameron only has a few years of networking experience, so the best thing to do is to highlight the acquired skills by bulleting the profile information, combining hardware and software experience to make it appear more substantial, eliminating the details of the retail experience, and summarizing college credit hours.

Layoffs and Firings

Two final scenarios may be red flags to hiring managers: layoffs and firings. Luckily, résumés don't have a "Layoffs and Firings" section, so it is neither necessary nor appropriate to bring these up on your résumé. Be assured, though, that these issues will come up when you actually go on an interview. For that reason, it's important that you prepare what you will say about them in advance of any such discussion. See Chapter 11 on acing the interview for more help planning your strategy.

Layoffs

If you have recently been laid off from your job, it is important for you to realize that layoffs are incredibly common these days. Mergers, downsizing, and reorganizations have made pink slips a way of life. The hiring manager himself may have been laid off from one of his previous positions. So instead of feeling like you did something wrong to bring about the layoff and will be branded for life, stop right now. There is no need to go into an interview with a defensive attitude about this situation.

Be open and honest, and don't blame your previous employer. "My entire department was eliminated when we lost second-round funding" is a perfectly acceptable description. If you can add something like, "Overall, it was worth the risk—it was exciting to work in such a cutting-edge field," so much the better. You come across as a big person.

Firings

It's not easy to be fired. Whether the firing is performance based or not, it hurts our confidence and self-esteem. But remember, even if you did lose your job for performance reasons, your life is not meaningless. The job may not have played to your strengths.

Instead of beating yourself up, consider this an opportunity to find a job or career that is better suited to your aptitudes and strengths. As with layoffs, it is best if you do not make reference to having been fired on your résumé.

CAMERON HOKANA
121 Lions Avenue
Garden Grove, CA 92843
Home: (555) 554-5554 Email: cameron.hokana1@hotmail.com

Summary

A results-oriented individual with the specialized training and dedication to successfully adapt to the ever-changing field of Information Technology. Skilled in assessing requirements, determining priorities, analyzing course of action, and making adjustments for peak efficiency to help reduce network downtime. Command strong interpersonal communication skills both verbally and written. Interface easily with all levels of management, co-workers, and clientele.

Hardware/Operating Systems

IBM PCs and compatibles, tape backup systems, Win NT, 9x, 3.1, MS DOS.

Software

MS Exchange Server, MS Internet Information Server, Veritas Backup Exec, MS Office 2000/97.

Work Experience

Computer Solutions Group, LLC   Los Angeles, CA   12/2000–Present
Consultant/In-House Tech Support
Provide on-site Microsoft Network Development Solutions to clientele, provide in-house technical support to clientele and on-site consultants, and interface with in-house MS Exchange Servers, MS Internet Information Servers, Veritas Backup Exec Server, and Windows NT Server.

Louden Security Inc.   Orange, CA   1999–2000
Network Administrator
Built small Windows NT network with remote dial-up capabilities. Maintained user accounts and network connectivity. Performed troubleshooting on hardware and software problems. Maintained Windows 9x workstations.

Ralphs Grocery Co.   Anaheim, CA   1994–1999
Grocery Clerk/Produce Clerk
Operated cash register, stocked shelves, maintained inventory records and ordered product, trained new employees on store and company policies and procedures. Handled customer service inquiries.

Education and Professional Certifications

InfoTech Commercial Systems   Santa Ana, CA
MCSE (Microsoft Certified Systems Engineer)   2000
MCP + Internet (Microsoft Certified Professional)   1999, 2000

Orange Coast College   Costa Mesa, CA
Courses taken in psychology, stress management, and information technology. No degree acquired at this time.

FIGURE 6-9 Lack of formal education example

CAMERON HOKANA
121 Lions Avenue
Garden Grove, CA 92843
Home: (555) 554-5554 E-mail: cameron.hokana1@hotmail.com

Summary of Qualifications

- Results-oriented individual with the specialized training and dedication to successfully adapt to the ever-changing field of Information Technology.
- Skilled in assessing requirements, determining priorities, analyzing course of action, and making adjustments for peak efficiency to help reduce network downtime.
- Commands strong interpersonal communication skills.
- Interfaces easily with all levels of management, co-workers, and clientele.

Technical Skills

- Windows NT, Windows 95/98
- MS Exchange Server, MS Internet Information Server, Veritas Backup Exec, MS Office 2000/97

Work Experience

Network Administrator, Computer Solutions Group, LLC   Los Angeles, CA   2000–Present

- Provide on-site Microsoft Network Development Solutions to clientele.
- Provide in-house technical support.
- Administer MS Exchange Servers, MS Internet Information Servers, Veritas Backup Exec server, and Windows NT Server.

Network Administrator, Louden Security Inc.   Orange, CA   1999–2000

- Built Windows NT network with remote dial-up capabilities.
- Maintained user accounts and network connectivity.
- Performed troubleshooting on hardware and software problems.
- Maintained Windows 9x workstations.

Ralphs Grocery Co.   Anaheim, CA   1994–1999

Education and Professional Certifications

- MCSE (Microsoft Certified Systems Engineer)   2000
- MCP + Internet (Microsoft Certified Professional)   1999

Orange Coast College   Costa Mesa, CA   1998–2000

- 60 credit hours in IT and general education studies

FIGURE 6-10 Downplaying the educational section

Swallow hard, shoulder some of the blame, and make a point of stressing what you learned from the situation, "Unfortunately, my manager and I disagreed on some of my job responsibilities. I've had to take a long look at my immediate and overall career goals. If I found myself in that situation again, here's how I'd handle it differently."

Again, Chapter 11 offers more examples on how to handle this situation in an interview.

Summary

Don't get hung up on one "bad" part of your résumé. You can still create a résumé that will catch a hiring manager's eye and land you the job you want. Never forget that presentation is everything—present yourself professionally and that's how you'll be treated.

Keep in mind your goal: to get a hiring manager to single out your résumé for attention. Bear this in mind as you address the problem areas of your résumé, and the solutions will come easily.

Chapter 7

Creative Ways to Get Hands-on Experience

How many times have you run into this situation? You open the paper to find ten ads for the system administrator position you have been seeking, but the ad calls for one to two years of experience. You have just earned your MCSE. It's the IT professional's "chicken and the egg" dilemma: how do you get that first job without having the hands-on experience it requires? In Chapter 6, we focused on how to address this issue creatively on your résumé. In this chapter, we'll take a sidestep and provide you with examples of creative ways to actually get that experience.

In this chapter, we'll cover:

▶ Using your training center as a resource

▶ Volunteer work

▶ Message boards

▶ Building your own lab

▶ Simulations and paid labs

▶ Differentiating yourself from the other applicants

Getting Experience at Your Training Center

Many career changers begin their IT careers at their local training center. Training centers offer a full suite of training options for you. The good ones will provide you with a career counselor who will work with you throughout your training and certification process. They will map out your course work, lab work, and possibly work with you on placement. Throughout the country niche training centers are popping up that specialize in providing intensive training programs that result in placement with local employers. In return for free or virtually free training, they will take a cut of your first year's salary to repay the training costs. This is a great alternative to financing your education on your own.

A more traditional alternative is an unpaid internship through your training center. Internships typically are one to three months of placement with a local company where you can get hands-on experience doing PC support, helpdesk duty, or general end-user support. It's a great way of setting your expectations and getting an idea of what areas you would like to work in once you are ready to join the full time workforce. And the experience is great on your résumé.

Another way to maximize your experience while you're still earning your certification is to get hands-on experience at your training center. Here are some ideas that will go a long way toward getting you the experience that you need and creating a network of professionals who might help you land a job after your training is finished:

▶ Volunteer to help set up your next class or lab.

▶ Stay after class to complete or redo labs that you didn't get to in class.

▶ Redo the labs by trying out other configuration options, especially manual configurations rather than using the product wizards.

▶ Ask to shadow a more experienced classmate on a typical workday to get an idea how his or her time and skills are utilized.

▶ Volunteer to help the instructor on one of his or her consulting projects to get real-world experience (and networking opportunities).

The instructor will be grateful for the assistance, and the training center will appreciate the extra free help.

On the (Unpaid) Job Training

It's not glamorous. It's unpaid and many times unappreciated. It's called volunteer work. In the end, it's hands-on experience that you can use on your résumé. Schools, churches, non-profit associations, friends, and family businesses all need extra help maintaining their PCs and managing their networks. That may mean upgrading their systems, installing new versions of software and operating systems, or customizing their environment so it's more streamlined and easy to use. Other times your help can be in the form of providing training services. There is no better way of testing what you know than having to teach someone else how to do it themselves. Skills transfer can help you make friends, get referrals for paying jobs, and secure excellent references.

To find these opportunities, let people know about your career change. Keep them up to date on where you are and what skills you have mastered. I still get phone calls from family members who want me to troubleshoot their systems, upgrade their hard drives or modems, and help them get connected to the Internet. Unfortunately, my technical skills are now limited to plugging my network cable in to the right jack, but I still get these calls every now and again.

Become a Sysop

Where do you turn when you have a technical question? One of the places you probably search first are online message boards. They provide the most timely information on incompatibilities and bugs. You probably have your own collection of your favorite message boards. If you don't, it's time to start making your list and checking in regularly. Visit the message boards or newsgroups of technical support sites and monitor the message forums for your particular area of training or certification. When someone posts a technical question, try to solve it yourself using your manuals, the vendor's support site, and genuine Internet research. Wait a few days for a support person to answer the question and compare the results to your findings. You will learn a lot doing this, including building your research skills and understanding real-world problems with the technologies you are learning about.

As you build confidence, you can also volunteer your services on these message boards. You can list your experience as a sysop on your résumé and possibly use the message board supervisors as your references.

Hands-on Experience at Home

No true IT professional is without their own home lab. Building your home lab is going to require hardware, software, and some creativity so that you don't break the bank. The benefits of having a home network are that it allows you to try out what you've learned, evaluate new software releases, try out new technologies, and become more productive.

Hardware

Whether it is two or ten PCs, you should invest in creating your own home network. It doesn't have to cost a fortune. Part of the fun of building your network is in literally building all the components from scratch. The typical hardware components you should include are:

▶ Multiple PCs, each configured with a different operating system, ranging from older models to high-end machines

▶ Hub

▶ Router

▶ Networkable printer

▶ Cable or DSL modem

▶ 56 Kbps modem

You can pick up used network components in a variety of places. You can start off with the major chains like Circuit City, Best Buy, and Good Guys. These stores perform lots of system upgrades and will have extra components that they will happily allow someone to take off their hands. Check your local yellow pages for the major stores in your area.

Major hardware vendors also sell their refurbished units at a considerable discount. Dell Computers and Gateway Computers offer great values on refurbished laptops and desktop systems. If a vendor doesn't advertise their refurbished equipment, give them a call anyway. Other good sources of returned or refurbished equipment are major distributors like Tech Data and Merisel.

Online auctions can sometimes yield good deals as well. Ubid.com, Egghead.com, and eBay.com are excellent places to look for the components to round out your network. PC fairs and swap meets are also opportunities to pick up low cost equipment.

Be creative in finding the equipment you seek out for your home network. You can use the experience you gain when you land your new job. You can even list this procurement experience on your résumé to help you get that first job.

Software

Getting the right software is also key for building your home lab and getting the right experience. The trouble here is affording to stay on top of the latest software. Vendors have made it easier, though, if you are tied in to the right places. Evaluation versions, beta versions, and certification versions can all be utilized to help you get on your way. In the following section you will see how to get your hands on these types of software.

What software should you be looking for to round out your network?

Major operating systems

▶ Microsoft Windows NT, Windows 2000 Server

▶ Novell NetWare

▶ Linux (Red Hat, SAIR, Caldera)

▶ Unix

Application packages

▶ Microsoft Office

▶ Corel Office

▶ Internet Explorer

Utilities

▶ VMWare

▶ Shareware utilities

Evaluation Versions

Most vendors now have 2-week to 90-day evaluation copies of their software available to preview before you buy. Most of the software is downloadable off the Web. If the vendor doesn't provide an eval off their web site, don't hesitate to call them directly. Let them know that you would like to evaluate their software product for possible implementation within your company. Most companies will happily send you an evaluation copy.

The downside of evaluation software is that you might have to give it back. Most evaluation copies time out. You might also have to deal with a limited feature set. If you need access to the full version, call the software manufacturer and ask for an unlimited version. It doesn't hurt to ask.

Beta Versions

It is always fun to try out beta versions of the latest operating systems and software packages. There's a certain cool factor associated with being in with software vendors and on their beta distribution lists. Your home lab is the ideal place to test these new products out, since you are not most likely playing with live mission-critical business data. It can be frustrating, however, when beta software messes up your existing installation. Remember that you're taking your system into your own hands when you install beta software on your system. Be sure to back up your system just in case those bugs haven't been worked out yet.

Certification Benefits

Are you maximizing your certification benefits from Microsoft and Novell? These software vendors offer tens of thousands of dollars worth of software for free or almost free as part of the benefits they provide to the professionals they have certified. Microsoft offers two software benefits to its certificants: TechNet and TechNet + Beta program. The TechNet program is a subscription service where you can receive convenient, timely access to technical information and resources for IT professionals. You get the latest technical information, service packs, resource kits, tools, utilities, Microsoft Knowledge Base articles, and much more. The TechNet + Beta program allows you to receive beta software of Microsoft's latest releases. A one-year subscription is provided free to MCSEs.

Novell offers its CNEs a Software Evaluation Library. The Software Evaluation Library (SEL) program is Novell's demo program, specifically designed for eligible channel partners worldwide. As a CNE you are eligible to receive this subscription library at a discount.

Other vendors may offer similar programs. Be sure to look into these.

Internet access is a requirement. You should allow for Internet access from all your machines. DSL or cable modems provide you with fast access at a reasonable cost. You'll want to invest in proxy software to enable multiple machines for Internet connectivity.

Magic Software: VMWare

Want to maximize your hardware investment? How do experienced IT professionals do it? They use a product called VMWare. This product allows you to split up your machine into virtual machines, each capable of running different operating systems. You can run Linux, Windows 2000, and even NetWare on the same machine! For more information on this magic product, visit the VMWare web site at http://www.vmware.com/.

Simulations

If you haven't built your home lab yet, other low cost alternatives are simulations and hands-on labs for hire.

Simulations have the advantage that you don't have to install any operating systems or applications. You can also take them with you. The disadvantage, of course, is that you're not working with the real product so your experience will be bound to how creative and flexible the simulation developers were.

You will typically find simulations in books from the vendors themselves. For instance, Microsoft Press offers simulations in their Microsoft Press books and in their official courseware. Another source for simulations is Wave Technologies. Their self-study materials include the NEXTSim product for Microsoft and Novell products. For the Cisco arena you can try out Routersim.com.

Hands-on Labs

Like simulations, hands-on labs on rented material (usually accessible over the Internet) allow you to work on high-end equipment without breaking your wallet. The way these labs typically run is that you rent time on the vendors' systems. Prices range from $60 on up depending on how much time you need to complete the lab.

The advantages of this method of getting hands-on experience is that you will work on real equipment, much like the equipment you will eventually work on at your job. Another advantage is that these labs are often structured with real work scenarios for you to try out. An added advantage is that they allow the flexibility to deviate from the prescribed lab, just in case you want to try out different configuration options. The disadvantage is the cost of the experience.

Some vendors who provide hands-on labs include:

▶ Fatkid.com (http://www.fatkid.com/)

▶ LabsOnline (http://labsonline.remote.net/)

▶ LearnITSoftware (http://www.mislab.com/)

▶ Mentor Technologies (http://www.mentortechnologies.com/)

▶ Network Learning (http://www.ccbootcamp.com/)

▶ RouterSim (http://www.routersim.com/)

▶ Router University (http://www.routeru.com/)

▶ SimRouter (http://www.simrouter.com/)

▶ SolutionLabs (http://www.solutionlabs.com/)

▶ Virtualrack.com (http://www.virtualrack.com/)

Beyond Hands-on Experience

No matter how much hands-on experience post-training you get, IT managers are always looking for professionals with the most extensive experience for the job. If you want top dollar, the truth is that you will have to work up to it by demonstrating your capabilities on the job. Most likely you will have to start in an entry-level position. Why not get that over with as quickly as possible? This means paying your dues early on and demonstrating your capabilities so that you can progress with your career. Here are some tips on getting the experience you need to build a successful IT career in an entry-level position:

▶ Become an expert in one particular application product. Access and Excel are excellent choices because they are more and more in demand within organizations. Most entry-level professionals settle on learning operating systems, but those who will be noticed most quickly are those who can work "magic" for executives using the applications they need to do their jobs.

▶ Take on difficult users and brush up your soft skills. Today's successful IT professional relies not only on technical skills but on people skills as well. Knowing how to survive in a corporate culture is a key part. The soft skills you should invest in developing include customer service and presentation skills.

▶ Continue your professional development by attending local conferences and users groups. Though users groups are decreasing in popularity, they are still critical for networking and discovering new opportunities for building your career.

IT Must-Visit Sites

The following sites host a plethora of information for IT professionals, offering everything from career tips and articles to industry and product news:

▶ Brainbuzz.com (http://www.brainbuzz.com)

▶ Deja Usenet Discussions (http://groups.google.com/googlegroups/deja_announcement.html)

▶ TechRepublic (http://www.techrepublic.com/)

▶ IT Career Network (http://www.brainbuzz.com/)

▶ Microsoft (http://www.microsoft.com/)

How to List this Experience

The experience you get from volunteer work contributes to your overall skills and qualifications. It allows you to list additional operating systems, software packages, and technologies in the qualifications section at the beginning of your résumé. Figure 7-1 shows how one entry-level candidate used the experience he got from helping friends and setting up his own home network as legitimate experience, and helped build a stronger résumé for himself.

HECTOR LOPEZ
121 Lions Avenue
Garden Grove, CA 92843
Home: (555) 554-5554 Email: hlopez@hotmail.com

Objective

Hard-working, recently certified IT professional seeking an entry-level position providing helpdesk support and network maintenance.

Summary of Qualifications

- Self-directed, results-oriented MCSE professional
- Highly motivated and eager to learn and apply new skills
- Strong interpersonal communication skills
- Work well independently and as part of a larger team

Technical Skills

- Windows NT, Windows 95/98
- MS Internet Information Server, MS Office 2000/97, QuickBooks, Outlook

Work Experience

Network Administrator, YMCA, Los Angeles, CA   2001 – Present

- Volunteer ten hours per week performing network administration and PC support services at the local YMCA
- Set up a 15-user Windows NT network with DSL Internet connectivity
- Configured MS Outlook email system and Internet Explorer
- Perform troubleshooting for hardware and software problems
- Install applications, upgrade PCs, and provide overall general maintenance of a Windows NT network

PC Support, Our Lady of the Nativity Church, Los Angeles, CA   2001 – Present

- Volunteer about five hours per month in general PC maintenance and provide technical support when needed
- Installed QuickBooks for managing church finances

Teacher Mentor, L.A. Public School System, Los Angeles, CA   2000 – Present

- Work one on one with four grade 8-12 teachers within the L.A. public school system providing mentoring and instruction on the use of Microsoft Office products
- Part of a city-wide program to increase teacher proficiency with office automation products and to help them increase the usage of IT technology in their classrooms

Ralphs Grocery Co., Anaheim, CA   1990 – 2000

Education and Professional Certifications

- MCSE (Microsoft Certified Systems Engineer)   2000

Figure 7-1   Pulling it all together

Just Use a Little Creativity

As you can see, where there's a will, there's a way to get that hands-on experience that you'll need to make you a better IT professional. Never underestimate the power of being resourceful. Determination and resourcefulness are qualities that will take you a long way. There are plenty of resources out there to help you get where you want.

Chapter 8

How to Network When You
Don't Know Anyone

Sure, it is easy to network in the IT industry...if you have been working in the field for ten years and
are well known in the local IT community or even around the country. Unfortunately, and realistically, most entry-level candidates do not have those years or connections under their belt. So how do you
network when you don't know anyone?

In this chapter, we'll cover:

▶ Telling everyone you're looking for a job

▶ The networking interview

▶ IT professional groups and associations

▶ Online networking

Tell Everyone: You're Looking for a Job

The first thing you have to do is get the word out that you are looking. Some people are too proud and don't want anyone to know they are looking for a job. If that is how you are going to be, you'll be looking even longer.

Of course, many people are not able to tell their employer, and maybe not even coworkers, but everyone else needs to know. Even if you *think* you don't know anyone who could help you out, you don't know who everyone else knows.

Alternatively, some employers will understand your leaving to advance your career, especially if you just received a new certification or are a career changer looking to move in the IT industry. Evaluate your personal situation and use your boss as a reference if possible. They may even be a great source for leads.

You've heard the phrase before, "It's not what you know, but who you know." Well, it didn't become a well-known saying for no reason—so get out there and meet people. Your best friend may have an uncle or a neighbor who is in a position to help.

So How Do You Bring It Up?

Whom you are talking to will determine how you approach them for help. With your friends, you can be blunt—just ask them if they know of anyone who is hiring or who can help you get a job. When you speak to someone you do not know as well, you will have to ask the right questions to get the assistance you need. The following are some key questions you can ask to uncover opportunities.

Talking to Your Friends

Your friends are your best place to start:

I am looking for a job in _____. Do you know anyone I could talk to about this?

Do you know anyone who is hiring?

Do you know anyone who works in IT? Can I have their phone number?

Talking to Acquaintances

If you are talking to an acquaintance, such as a neighbor or a friend of a friend, you will take a slightly different approach. Try to compliment them and see if they can help you out:

I really value your opinion and I was hoping to talk to you about my job search.

I know that you have worked in the _____ field for a while and I admire what you have done with your career. I was hoping to get some advice from you as I look for a new position.

I have seen what you have done at _____ and would love to get some advice from you as I enter the IT field.

The Networking Interview

Now that you have gotten the word out that you are looking, you will have hopefully come across someone in the IT industry. What is your next step?

Request a Meeting, Not an Interview

Request a time to meet. You are not requesting an *interview*. Do not use that word. You are not going to tell them that you want to meet to discuss a job opportunity—you are requesting time to get more information about what they do. Here are some examples of what you are requesting:

Hello, my name is _____. I was talking to _____ and he/she suggested that I call you to ask if we could get together for about fifteen minutes. I am entering the IT field and I was hoping to get your opinion on the industry and the workforce in our area. I also would like to find out what you did to become so successful in your field.

I am interested in getting into the industry. I know that you are very successful and I was hoping we could meet for a few minutes so you could tell me a little bit more about what you do.

I am preparing to begin my IT career and I wanted to get a better idea about what the industry is like. I know that you are doing very well for yourself and would like to get just a little bit of your time to find out more about what you do.

I am hoping I could get a few minutes to talk to you about the IT industry and find out how you got to be so successful in your field. Maybe you could provide me with a little insight into what I could do to get into IT.

What Do You Want to Get Out of this Interview?

Once you get the time to speak with someone in the industry, what are you going to say and what do you want to get out of the interview?

First of all, what do you want to accomplish?

To get a job   Even though you are not saying that you are there to find a job, this is your ultimate goal. This contact may have a position for you, either at their company or elsewhere.

Advice about what to do next   They can provide insight into companies that are hiring and what positions might best suit you.

References   People in the industry know other people in the industry. You want to leverage them to get to speak to others. Ask them for three to five other people you could speak to.

Tips for building experience   Find out what hiring managers in the industry are looking for and discuss ways to get that initial experience.

What Are You Going to Say?

When you are in the networking interview, begin by talking about the person you are interviewing. Do not waste this valuable time bragging about yourself. If you do, the interviewer will most likely cut the meeting short. Play off their ego.

Begin the conversation with the following topics:

Can you tell me a little bit more about what you do?

How did you become so successful in the industry?

What did you do to get into this position?

What steps did you take; where did you work?

Then explain your interests and what you would like to do:

If you were in my position what would you do?

What advice could you give me to accomplish my goals?

What steps can I take to achieve the success that you have?

It is imperative that you get *them* to talk about what you should do and that you solicit their advice. Because of this conversation, you will stand out in their mind later on. If they hear of an opening in their company or another company, they could recommend you as a good match for this position.

Ending the Interview and Getting More Names

You should not end the interview. Stay there as long as possible. If this person is taking the time to talk to you, take full advantage of their time and do not leave until they kick you out! Keep the interviewer engaged in conversation by asking as many questions about them as possible.

When you feel that they are ending the interview, ask for the names of three to five people in the industry that they think would be beneficial for you to meet. Do not feel uncomfortable asking for these references. They might have a friend who could use someone with your skill set and qualifications.

Now you have the names of some more industry contacts and you can contact them to set up networking interviews.

Think This Sounds Like Too Much Work?

Well, it does take work to network in the industry! But once you make this extra effort, who do you think will be the most likely to get a job? Someone who email-blasts their résumé, or you, who puts the time and creativity into your job hunt and makes contacts?

After you accept a position, contact and thank everyone who helped you out along the way—anyone who gave you a networking interview or a referral, or who took the time to give you some information. You want to keep these people as contacts as you are establishing yourself in the industry.

IT Professional Groups

There are IT professional groups in every metropolitan areas. Check out these organizations and associations when you are looking for a job, and then stay connected for future reference. If you live in a more remote location, the Internet has many groups or gatherings for IT professionals.

The following are some examples of professional IT associations and groups.

CompTIA: Computing Technology Industry Association

Web site: http://www.comptia.org/

Membership with CompTIA will provide you with the opportunity to network with top technology players at CompTIA's Breakaway Conferences throughout North America. You can participate in industry groups and committees that shape policies and standards. You'll also have unlimited availability to the membership database of more than 8,000 companies in the computing and communications markets.

ITAA: Information Technology Association of America

Web site: http://www.itaa.org/

The ITAA is a leading trade association of the information technology industry. They sponsor a wide range of services, meetings, and activities, and provide extensive opportunities for business development and networking. Reference the Web site for listings of upcoming events.

IEEE (Institute of Electrical and Electronics Engineers) Computer Society

Web site: http://www.computer.org/

With more than 100,000 members, the IEEE Computer Society is a leading organization of computer professionals. The society is dedicated to advancing the theory, practice, and application of computer and information processing technology. There are more than 140 chapters worldwide.

IWA: International Webmasters Association

Web site: http://www.iwanet.org/

IWA is the industry's recognized leader in providing educational and certification standards for Web professionals. IWA's initiatives now support more than 100 official chapters representing more than 22,000 individual members in 106 countries. Benefits of membership include access to the international member database, employment opportunities, a wide range of professional contacts, and leadership roles at the chapter, regional, and international levels.

ACM: Association for Computing Machinery

Web site: http://www.acm.org/

This was the first educational and scientific computing society. There are 80,000 professionals who hold conferences several times a year. There are 160 professional chapters and 600 student chapters, currently in 27 different states and 39 countries. Career opportunities, special interest groups, and an online membership directory are some of the benefits of membership.

Many More Local Organizations

These are just a few examples of computer professional organizations. The local chapters of these organizations host meetings and social gatherings that will enable you to network with other local IT professionals. There are also groups organized by the specific profession within IT.

Career fairs are an excellent way for entry-level professionals to network with hiring employers and other IT professionals attending. Find out about career fairs happening in your area, arrive early, talk to everyone, and make as many contacts as possible. You can find out about online career fairs in Chapter 10.

Online Networking

Look on the Internet for more information about local groups in your area and online networking opportunities. Go make some contacts and maybe even some friends. And remember, not everyone in IT is a computer geek—you aren't, right?

Chapter 9

Résumé Faux Pas: Why You Are Not Getting Any Phone Calls

You wrote your résumé and sent it out to countless employers, but you are not getting any calls. So what's the problem?

You might think your résumé is great, but you may be surprised to find out how many rules you are breaking. Analyze your résumé against some of the most common résumé faux pas and change that lack of response. Keep in mind, a simple faux pas can cost you an interview, even if you have outstanding information on your résumé. In this chapter we will analyze your résumé by using the Résumé Faux Pas Checklist, which includes:

▶ Generic objective statements

▶ Burying top qualifications

▶ Sending the same résumé to all employers

▶ Unrelated experience or job titles

▶ Missing keywords

▶ Unfriendly formatting of electronic résumés

And many more!

The Résumé Faux Pas Checklist

Get out your résumé and a pen, and see if your résumé contains any of these blunders.

Generic Objective Statements

Out with the traditional objective statement, including the generic, comments about the type of position you are pursuing. Instead, use this opening space to write something powerful about yourself, highlighting your strong points and key qualifications. Avoid statements such as:

> I want to work in an environment where I not only learn from the company, but the company learns from me as well.

> Position as a computer technician in a challenging and growing company with possibility for promotion.

> I am looking for a position in IT where I can apply my skills and knowledge while working in a fast-paced environment.

> I plan on furthering my technology education as needed.

Now that you know what *not* to include in your objective statement, get some tips on how to write a winner in Chapter 2.

Burying Your Top Qualifications

Lead with your strong points as they relate to that job. We have seen many examples where people stuck to the traditional résumé format of listing an objective statement followed by education, experience, achievements, and additional information. This layout does not work best for everyone. Here is a scenario where that is evident:

> A branch manager working in retail is changing careers. In his experience section, he lists all of the daily responsibilities of his current position first, such as increasing sales, hiring employees, managing finances, and scheduling. His last point is that he set up a network in the store. This is a prime example of burying his top qualifications.

If he were applying for another retail management position, this résumé would be fine. But since he is trying to get into IT, he should leverage his networking experience.

Here is another example of hiding key qualifications:

> A candidate has a technical background, but in his experience section he only listed his daily duties. He waited to quantify his accomplishments in his final section of "Additional Information," which included: "Decreased CPU downtime by 80%, achieved 15% reduction in CPU maintenance costs, and increased stability in classroom CPU production by reducing downtime, enabling students and staff to produce efficiently and on time."

These points are key and should be at the beginning of his résumé, not buried at the end on the second page.

Sending the Same Résumé to All Employers

You need to customize your résumé for each job or you will miss your opportunity to show an employer exactly how you can help them. You need to utilize the details of each job description when creating a résumé, as well as adding in some points about the company that you discovered through research. Do not just blast a generic résumé to every job opening you find. Take the additional time and it will pay off.

Unrelated Experience or Education

Those things not related to IT should be left off your résumé or at least de-emphasized. For example:

▶ Courses taken in psychology, stress management, and physical education

▶ Degree in Ministry of Spirituality or Cellular Biology

▶ Designer of Class of 2000 yearbook from cover to cover

▶ Internship as a middle school English tutor

Job Titles Not Related to IT

You may need to camouflage some of your experience by leaving out titles and descriptions of unrelated jobs, especially if you are a career changer. Instead, just list the company and the years of employment. We have received actual résumés that included job descriptions of a press operator, Burger King cashier, and sanitation dispatcher. If you have anything like this on your résumé, get rid of it. Find out more about common résumé dilemmas, including those for career changers and recent graduates, in Chapter 6.

Weak Job Titles

If your job title does not accurately depict what you actually did, get creative. If you have multiple job roles, do not try to represent them all through your title, such as Computer Technologist/Helpdesk/Telecommunications. Think of a more powerful title rather than listing all three. For some insider tips about powerful job titles, refer to Chapter 1. There you will also find a chart of interchangeable job titles you can use to project a stronger image.

Missing Keywords

Use keywords to get your résumé noticed. Be sure to include all of the buzzwords for qualifications you possess, as related to the position. Also, utilize what the employer wants and include those key phrases in your résumé. If you are unsure of what keywords relate to the position you are seeking, analyze several job descriptions and try to incorporate the keywords used. Refer to Chapter 3 for more specifics about the use of keywords.

Mismatched with the Job Description

Be sure that what you are saying in your résumé and your cover letter is appropriate to the position you are applying for. Use the key points of the job description to match yourself to it.

For example, a candidate was applying for director of IT. She stated that she wants a position that is project oriented. This put her out of the running right away since a management position is not appropriate for someone with those wants.

Similarly, if you are applying for a management position, do not highlight all of your project experience. You need to demonstrate your management abilities, not your ability to handle tasks.

Excluding Studies in Progress

If you don't have a formal degree or certification, but have studies in progress, include them in your résumé. For example:

▶ If you are attending college, but haven't graduated, list the number of credit hours you have toward your degree (if you have at least one year under your belt), such as "Orange Coast College, 24 credit hours toward Computer Science degree."

▶ If you have taken relevant courses, list those. Include a section entitled "Related Courses" and include the course titles, such as Data Communications, Network Administration, or Network Administration and Installation. It is not necessary to include descriptions of each class. Remember to exclude irrelevant courses.

▶ If you are currently taking a class or studying for a certification exam, include that certification with the expected date of achievement.

Emphasizing Your Age

If your age could hurt your odds of being considered for the position—either too young or too old—de-emphasize whenever possible. As a career changer, you do not want to highlight that you have 24 years in the workforce. If you were seeking a position in the same industry where those years were accrued, it would be valuable. Conversely, this is the same as announcing that you are over 40 with no experience in the industry.

Unfriendly Formatting of Electronic Résumés

When sending your résumé electronically, you need to format it differently than you would for paper. You can find out more about formatting your résumé for the eWorld in Chapter 3. The following are some key points:

▶ Use carriage returns or hard breaks to guarantee consistency and easier reading. If your text all runs together, nothing will catch the reader's eye.

▶ Highlight areas of your résumé by using capitalization and special characters such as asterisks, hyphens, and lines.

▶ Remember that formatting you do in word processing, such as bold and italics, will often be lost through email. Create your electronic résumé in a text editor such as Notepad and make sure it is easy to identify the key points of your résumé.

▶ Use a descriptive subject line (not just "Résumé"), because that will get lost in the sea of résumés in the Human Resource manager's inbox. Instead, include the position you're responding about and something about your skill set. For example, "Job #142, Network Engineer, Certified MCSE, Available Immediately" will get noticed.

Using the Wrong Layout for You

Make sure that you put your best foot forward. If you don't have experience in the industry, begin your résumé with your skill set and your education. On the other hand, if your experience is your strong point, lead with it.

Don't think you have to stick to the traditional résumé layout. Modify it to whatever best serves you. Review the Resume Encyclopedia in Chapter 12 for examples of different ways to present your experience and background.

Simply Listing Your Job Responsibilities

Do more than just list your daily tasks under each job title. Quantify your accomplishments whenever possible. Demonstrate how you solved problems and what the results were. Chapter 4 walks you through the process of uncovering your hidden talents and tailoring your résumé for any job posting.

Highlighting Trivial Skills

You need to highlight your top computer skills, especially as a recent graduate or someone without experience in the industry. Even if you do not have the highest level of experience or strongest skill set, do not highlight outdated or basic skills, such as:

▶ Passed Microsoft Networking Essentials exam

▶ Proficient in Windows 3.1

▶ Extensive experience with Web surfing using Internet Explorer 4.0

You can also build your skill set even if you don't have any professional work experience. Find out about creative ways to get hands-on experience in Chapter 7.

Including Why You Left Each Position

It is not necessary to include why you left each position. Save it for the interview, especially if it was for negative reasons. Phrases such as "company-wide layoffs," "my boss doesn't know what he is doing," and "wanted to make more money" do not belong on your résumé.

Exaggerations that Backfire

Be careful to present yourself honestly. If you try to exaggerate your qualifications, you may be setting yourself up for failure. Here is an example of a candidate who got caught in a tall tale before even making it to the interview:

> Becky made an opening statement about her "20 years of professional experience." Most would think that is referring to post-college experience. But when you drill down into her experience, her total work history only added up to about six years. She must have been including her lawn mowing jobs starting at age ten and her part-time college positions. This exaggeration cost her credibility and threw her out of the running.

Typos or Spelling Mistakes

Proofread, proofread, proofread. And then have at least five other people proofread for you. Even a small spelling or grammatical error can cost you. Here are some classic examples:

> Certifications: CompuTIA, Aplus, Cisco Networking 1
>
> Disposed of $15 million in assets.
>
> Temporary labtop computer support technician
>
> Director of IT from 1896 – 2000
>
> Explicit attention to to detail
>
> Ability to meet deadlines while maintaining composer
>
> Competed 14 years of college (and only received a B.S.!)
>
> Accomplishments: Oversight entire IT department

Too Long or Too Wordy

Be concise in the words you use and don't be long-winded. You want the employer to be able to read your résumé quickly and catch all of the key points. Readers should have a summary of your experience and skills, with just enough detail to show them the depth of your abilities. Save the rest for the interview. Remember to keep your résumé to one or two pages unless truly warranted. Find out more about the technical requirements for a winning résumé in Chapter 2.

Unprofessional Appearance

Remember that appearance counts, so don't try to save money by using cheap paper. Use high quality paper with a matching cover letter. When mailing your résumé, use a large envelope so you don't have to fold it. This will keep your résumé crisp, which is important if it needs to be scanned or faxed.

Salary History

Do not include your salary history or salary requirements anywhere on your résumé. If your request is too high, you could eliminate yourself from the running before an employer even meets you. Once they want to hire you, you can negotiate the salary, as an employer is more flexible after they have made up their mind that they want you. By revealing this information too soon, you may not even be considered.

You may also be selling yourself short if you state salary requirements that are lower than the position usually pays. You may need to disclose your salary requirements in the interview or in a cover letter, but do not place it anywhere on your actual résumé.

Outdated Extracurricular Activities

First, extracurricular activities are only appropriate if related to the position you are applying for. Second, realize when they are outdated and need to be removed. Here are some prime examples of what not to include (note how outdated or irrelevant these activities are):

Secretary of the debate team, 1991

Graduated 1983, GPA 3.4, Dean's List

Math Club member, 1998

Use of Personal Pronouns

Your résumé is a business communication, so it needs to be professional and concise. Do not use any personal pronouns, such as "I" or "me." Here is an example of how you can get rid of personal pronouns:

I implemented a tracking system for the technical helpdesk, and when I did this, productivity was increased and reporting was enabled.

This statement should be changed to:

Implemented a tracking system for the technical helpdesk, which increased productivity and enabled reporting.

Personal Interests or Information

There is no place in your résumé for personal interests. Even if you are using a résumé tool that prompts you to include such information, disregard it. Far too many résumés we have received include hobbies such as reading books, surfing the Web, or water skiing. No hiring manager wants to hear any of this.

Along those same lines, do not include personal information such as your age, sex, religion, race, and marital status.

High School Graduation Date

There is never a time when you would want to include that you graduated from high school in 1978. Even if you are in college and have not yet graduated, it is more impressive to state that you have studies in progress than to default to your high school diploma.

Unprofessional Email Addresses

This should go without saying, but make sure the email address you are listing on your résumé is professional. You do not want an employer to try to contact you at gobaltimoreravens@beer.com.

Sending Additional Materials with Your Résumé

Do not enclose letters of recommendation or other papers with your résumé unless they are specifically requested. You can bring these items to your interview and present them if appropriate.

Including References on Your Résumé

References do not belong on your résumé. Since you are sending your résumé to many people and you do not know where it may end up, you don't want just anyone calling your references. This information should be shared during the interview process, separate from your résumé.

Likewise, the statement "References available upon request" should be removed. It is obvious that you will have references when required, and this only wastes space. To view a sample reference sheet, refer to Chapter 2.

Humor

Your résumé is not the place to demonstrate your cheesy sense of humor. Do not try to be cute, clever, or funny when preparing your résumé. Here are some examples of humor gone bad:

You have seen the rest, now meet the best.

You will only need to keep this résumé and can use the rest to heat your house.

Let's meet so I can astound you with my excellence.

Also known as…Mr. Right, Mr. Perfect-for-this-Job, or Mr. Productive.

I am enclosing a few bucks to guarantee my interview.

How Did You Do?

This was not like one of those quizzes in *Maxim* or *Cosmopolitan*, where a less-than-perfect score means you're still in the game. After analyzing your résumé against these classic résumé faux pas, if you scored less than 100 percent, you need help. It is time to reevaluate and rewrite.

The earlier chapters can offer you solid advice on how to improve all aspects of your résumé. After pinpointing those areas that need improvement, find the chapter or chapters that outline your weaknesses. Make some enhancements and hit this checklist again to see how much you have improved.

Chapter 10

. . . .

Finding IT Jobs Online

There are many avenues for finding job openings, but as an IT professional your best method will be online. You will find that most companies today utilize the Web in one way or another to find candidates.

In this chapter, we'll cover:

▶ Job-hunting Web sites

▶ Job sites that don't waste your time

▶ Tips for posting your résumé

▶ Bonus resources on job-seeker Web sites

▶ Making online connections

▶ Online career fairs

Job-Hunting Web Sites

Many companies use the Internet exclusively for their recruiting needs. Going online can give you an advantage over those who stick to the traditional classified ads as their only form of job searching. This is because job openings can get to the Web faster. For example, a company may list a position on the Web on Tuesday and then put it in print when the next Sunday paper comes out. Job-hunters who use the Web are able to apply for the job almost a week earlier.

Job Sites that Don't Waste Your Time

When you start your job search online, you will find that there are many sites out there. You could waste hours or even days searching through the thousands of listings and hundreds of pages. How can you best utilize your time when looking online?

Using the top job sites will make your job hunt less of a monster. Make sure you are using reliable Web sites, where information is kept current and there are plenty of employers available. The last thing you want to discover is that the job you applied for was filled three months ago, especially after you've taken the time to find the openings relevant to you.

Here are some sites that won't waste your time:

- ▶ Career Builder (http://www.careerbuilder.com/)

- ▶ ComputerJobs.com (http://www.computerjobs.com/)

- ▶ DICE (http://www.dice.com/)

- ▶ Headhunter.net (http://www.headhunter.net/)

- ▶ Hot Jobs (http://www.hotjobs.com/)

- ▶ Monster.com (http://www.monster.com/)

While on these sites you can search for job listings, post your résumé, and even apply for a position directly.

Tips for Posting Your Résumé

When posting your résumé, keep in mind the formatting issues that are related to electronic résumés. (For specifics, refer to Chapter 3.) These guidelines will help make your résumé stand out from those who simply cut and paste their paper résumé and hit the submit button.

Unfortunately, on some of these sites, you will be prompted to add information that is not appropriate for a résumé, such as personal information and your description of the perfect job. Be sure to exclude those items when submitting your résumé.

And don't limit yourself to just one site. Post your résumé to as many sites as you can to increase the likelihood of getting it viewed. Although this will take extra time, be patient when searching for jobs online. It is time consuming to sort through the many job listings and to post on multiple sites, but you need to cover all bases to make sure you are doing an effective job.

Do More than Just Post Your Résumé

After you post your résumé, the phone calls will start pouring in, right? Don't bet on it. With the millions of résumés posted online, you can't just count on a leap of faith. You need to do more than just post. Utilize the option to electronically submit your résumé directly to employers, and follow up just as you would with a paper résumé submission.

Remember to keep it professional. Just because you are responding online, don't think you can use more casual language. You still need to include a cover letter and customize your résumé for different jobs.

In addition, sign up with job search agents, who will notify you of new job postings and help you search for those positions that meet the criteria you denote. You can receive email as new jobs become available, saving you valuable time.

Bonus Resources on Job-Seeker Web Sites

You can also utilize the many resources available through job sites, such as:

▶ Salary surveys to make sure you are getting offered what you are worth

▶ Listings of technical organizations and associations, especially those that provide regional listings

▶ Publications, white papers, and articles about your area of expertise and the job market

▶ Information about companies to help you research those places you are applying to

▶ Relocation information if you are looking for a job in another region

▶ IT events happening in your area

▶ Career information and articles about job searching

Company Web Sites Provide Unpublished Listings

If there is a specific company that you are interested in applying to, check their Web site. This is where most of their job openings will be posted. Since this method is free for the company, it saves them the expense of posting on a job site or listing in a newspaper, so they are likely to post here first. If they are able to find applicants this way, they will not have to advertise elsewhere.

Send out your résumé to companies even if jobs aren't posted—call it a preemptive strike. With some sites you can apply through the Web site electronically. If not, you will be able to find the contact information you need to submit your résumé to Human Resources or the hiring manager directly.

Search Engines Are a No-No

Using a search engine like Yahoo! or Google to find job openings will *definitely* waste your time. If you were planning on searching for a job this way, it is time for a new plan.

For starters, your search will most likely produce page after page of irrelevant information. You will bring up everything from personal home pages to message board posts. If you do actually find job openings that you are interested in, it is highly likely that they are outdated. Plus, it will be even more difficult to produce successful searches of jobs in your region, so you will waste time just trying to find out where a job is located.

These are probably enough reasons for you to agree that using a search engine is not the way to go.

Making Online Connections

Several job and career Web sites host chats that you can participate in to make online connections. You can also meet people in your field by attending industry chats and joining user groups. Then localize your online job hunt by checking out local associations and local user groups. These are all great ways to network in the industry. You can find many more suggestions in Chapter 8.

Online Career Fairs

An excellent way to make connections online is to attend an online career fair. You can find details about upcoming fairs on many of the job sites. Unlike traditional career fairs, online career fairs are almost always targeted at specific industries. Through a career fair you will be able to learn about the companies with openings, submit your résumé, and even meet employers. The fairs allow companies to promote themselves, search for candidates matching their criteria, post their jobs, and use the interactive features of the fair to efficiently and effectively recruit top candidates.

Some online job fairs have real-time chat rooms, giving you the opportunity to make a connection with an employer or recruiter by meeting them online. This is far more effective than simply submitting your resume, so attend an online job fair whenever possible.

Other job fairs consist of resume postings. The employer is notified of every new post as it happens and then responds. The online career fair usually lasts for about a month, instead of just a few hours like a traditional fair. This gives the employer much more time to review and interview candidates.

Online career fairs have several advantages over face-to-face career fairs. If you are looking for a job in another state or country, you can attend an online career fair without the expense of time and travel. Plus, you might not be able to attend a local career fair because the fair hours conflict with your schedule. These obstacles are overcome through virtual career fairs.

Use All Methods of Job Hunting

Utilize all of these methods for job-hunting to be most effective in your online search. Also, don't forget to still utilize other forms of job searching, such as the newspaper and networking. You shouldn't rely on any one way to find your perfect job.

Chapter 11

. . . .

The Interview

Remember, the real purpose of your résumé is to get you the interview. Once you've landed the all-important interview, you're halfway to a new job. At this point, whether you get the offer or not is mostly up to you and how you handle the interview Your role at the interview is that of a salesperson—you're selling yourself. Your goal is simple: to walk away with a job offer. In this chapter, we'll cover how to handle the interview. Here's what's in store:

► What really happens in the interview process

► Skills to demonstrate

► How to prepare

► Common questions for different areas of IT

► Questions to ask the interviewer

► Following up after the interview

What Really Happens in the Interview Process

Interviews intimidate many professionals in all fields. In the IT world, where so much is done by email, phone, and fax, an in-person meeting can be especially difficult. But getting past your fear and fine-tuning your interviewing skills can give your career a real boost.

A crucial first step is to understand that, at an interview, you play a specific role. With practice, you can play your role to perfection. To give a command performance, it's important to think of the interviewer as an ally, not as the enemy. Avoid a smug and overconfident attitude; rather, approach the interview as a chance to help solve a problem. The interviewer wants to be able to hire you. You can help her make that decision by showing her why you're right for the job—and the company.

Along these same lines, avoid appearing too eager to land the job. Over-eagerness hurts your credibility and may be a turn-off to the interviewer, who may question your reasons for wanting the position so badly.

At a typical interview, you'll first meet the hiring manager, whose job it is to make sure you're not a homicidal maniac. Once he has established that you are indeed a normal, functioning member of society, you'll be handed off to a more technical person, most likely the person who will be your immediate supervisor when you start work. Other members of the technical team may also be present.

Your interviewer will want to get a sense of who you are, certainly, but she'll also want to gauge your technical ability. Expect to be asked fairly specific questions (we'll cover these in detail later in this chapter) that will test your technical knowledge, your ability to think on your feet, and your response to common crisis situations in your particular field. Don't be surprised if you're asked many of the same questions the hiring manager previously asked you.

If you've been sitting with one person answering questions for some time and she suggests meeting the rest of the team, take it as a good sign, but don't start pouring the champagne just yet. Never assume that the second, third, or even seventh interview is "just a formality," even if the person who first interviewed you says it is. Smile and shake hands with everyone you're introduced to. Always be your best, keep track of everyone you meet, and never get irritated at answering the same questions again.

So just how do you put your best foot forward? Read on.

 TIP *If possible, arrange your interview for a Tuesday, Wednesday, or Thursday morning. You want your interviewer to be fresh, not pressed to get her week started or daydreaming about the weekend. Avoid after-lunch interviews when your interviewer is likely to be sleepy. Most people are at their least productive in the early afternoon.*

Skills to Demonstrate

One of the first things your interviewer will notice is your communications skills. Do you speak clearly and coherently? How's your grammar? What kind of an impression will you make on the company's clients? Make an audio or video recording of yourself speaking and analyze it. Brush up on your writing skills if they're an important part of the job you want.

TIP *Ahead of time, listen carefully to yourself speaking. Is your speech peppered with "like," "you know," "stuff," and other unprofessional filler words? Instead of these words, pause. Take a breath. Try to eliminate these words completely—or at least, you know, get rid of most of them.*

Of course, an interview isn't only about the questions posed and the answers given. There's a lot of reading between the lines that goes on. By anticipating what hidden clues the interviewer is looking for, you can make them easy for her to spot.

Here's a rundown of some of the most crucial skills you should make an effort to display.

TIP *Be specific. It's great if you're good at a lot of different things, but don't talk about them in general terms. Be ready to share examples of how you used specific tools to solve problems and get results.*

Technical Capability

Your interviewer needs to know that you possess the necessary skills to do the job, especially if you don't have extensive hands-on experience in the specific technology you'll be working in.

What to say: My [class projects/internships/previous work] gave me a chance to put theory into practice. I don't have years of hands-on experience, but I'm confident that I can handle the work here. I was trained for this position; I'm ready for the responsibility.

Flexibility and Passion for Technology

Can you keep up with the rapid pace of change in the IT world? Technology quickly becomes obsolete—if you're not interested in learning, your job will, too.

What to say: I love being in a field that requires me to stay on top of cutting-edge developments. It's exciting to watch technology evolve and work with the latest tools.

Team Orientation and Enthusiasm

The ability to work well with others is an important skill in any organization. In IT, it's often necessary for architects, developers, and sales engineers to work together to satisfy clients.

What to say: I'd like to have the chance to work with people from different parts of the company and to be involved in the whole life cycle of a project from conception through completion. It's a great way to gain a better understanding of the company's role in the industry, and it's always rewarding to be part of a team that brings an idea to fruition.

Responsibility

Do you pass the buck? If you say you'll finish a job, do you? A potential employer needs to know you're responsible, and that you'll set goals for yourself and for the good of the company.

> **What to say:** I'm realistic and honest about what I can and can't do in a given period of time. I want to constantly improve my skills as a developer and the company's position in the industry. I won't promise a rush job just to make you happy, but if I tell you you'll have something by deadline, you'll have it.

How to Prepare

Invest a little extra time at the beginning of the interview process, and it will pay off richly in the end. If you're offered a last-minute chance to interview for the job of your dreams, you'll be able to accept without hesitation. Also, by properly preparing yourself, you'll exude confidence, appear more organized, and be better able to concentrate on the task at hand: getting that job offer.

Make sure you have a stack of printed copies of your résumé, as well as matching paper and envelopes for printing cover letters, thank you notes, and other important correspondence. Keep the templates for your letters in an easily accessible folder on your computer. Stamp the envelopes ahead of time and put your return address on them. Set up a form to keep track of when and where you sent your résumé and when you need to follow up. Include a column for notes you can enter after the interview.

You should have a neat briefcase to take on your interviews. Keep an interview folder in your briefcase. Include several clean copies of your résumé, pen and paper for notes, and copies of written references you might have. You should also have a comb and small mirror, tissues, and breath mints or a travel toothbrush and paste. Check the contents of your bag regularly, and replenish when necessary.

TIP *Don't let your bag or briefcase become a catch-all for clutter. Clean it out every night. You don't want to wade through wadded-up tissues, leftover lunch remains, and 27 receipts from the gas station while you tell a potential employer about your organizational skills.*

Research the Company

As soon as you're offered an interview with a particular company, spend some time at their Web site. (If a recruiter arranged the interview, he should be able to provide you with some basic information, but always double-check it.) Read the company's mission statement. How do they present themselves? Use your favorite search engine to find any recent press coverage of the company. If you have time, call the corporate office and request a copy of their last annual report. Take notes. If you have questions about a large, public company, call their corporate communications department and pretend you're interested in buying some of their stock. They should answer your inquiries. Also check out http://www.vault.com/ for "insider information" posted anonymously by actual employees. Of course, be sure to verify all information. If you can't verify it, don't even think about bringing it up at your interview.

The day before the interview, make sure you know where you're going and how to get there, the name and phone number of the person you'll meet, and what time your meeting is. Always allow at least 20 minutes extra travel time. You should arrive about 10 minutes early.

Psych Yourself Up

Convince yourself first. Read over the accomplishments you list on your résumé. Read them out loud—hearing them spoken is a powerful ego-booster. Envision yourself on the job, solving problems, participating in staff meetings, accepting an award from the company president. If you believe you're the best person for the job, it'll be that much easier to convince the interviewer.

TIP *Carry a small index card with some of your greatest life achievements recorded on it. Review it immediately before an interview for an instant kick in the seat of the pants.*

Dress Up

Ask the interviewer what the company's dress code is, but always err on the side of caution. Choose clothes that are a bit conservative. Never show up at an interview in jeans, even if they tell you that the company is casual. Business casual means nice slacks and a pressed, button-down shirt at the very least. You can't go wrong in a suit and tie (or a nice dress)—they may tease you a little, but it's better than being underdressed.

Choose two or three outfits that will work for interviews—clothes that look professional and make you feel good about yourself. Make sure they are clean, pressed, and in good shape. Shine your shoes. Trim your nails, get a haircut, and make sure your mother wouldn't be embarrassed to see you.

TIP *Call ahead to verify the correct spelling and pronunciation of the interviewer's name. See if you can get any other information about the interviewer from her assistant, but don't be pushy. Honesty is much more effective. A simple, "I'd really like to get this job. Any 'inside information' you can give me?" asked in a lighthearted way could yield gold.*

Common Questions for Different Areas of IT

Your interviewer has five major concerns. Every question she asks you helps her answer one or more of those concerns. Yes, the questions—and your answers—are important at face value, but it's critical to understand the underlying concerns, as they're the ones that determine whether you get the offer or the boot. During an interview, the interviewer has to determine:

▶ If you can do the job

▶ If you will do the job

▶ If you get along with others

▶ If you're manageable

▶ If the company can afford you

As you go over the questions and answers provided in the following sections, bear in mind that your answers should serve both the asked and unasked questions.

TIP *If you don't understand a question, don't try to answer it. Instead, be honest. Say, "I'm not sure I understand what you're asking." The interviewer will rephrase the question. Once you know what they're asking, you can give a clear answer.*

Common Questions

The questions that follow are sure to pop up in just about every interview you have. Make sure you can answer each one. Write out your answers, if need be, and practice saying them until they sound natural.

TIP *If you're being interviewed by more than one person at once, try to position your chair somewhere that allows you to keep all the interviewers in your line of sight. This is generally more effective than swiveling back and forth frantically while you speak.*

Tell me a little bit about yourself.   Keep your answer short and professional. A 20-minute description of the yoga class you teach is not going to win you any points. Review your résumé ahead of time and come up with a one-minute capsule description of who you are. Try a catchy introduction, along the lines of: "I'm a California native, and I've been interested in technology ever since I took my Speak 'n' Spell apart." Give your pitch, which should touch briefly on your strongest skills, and then stop talking.

What do you know about our company?   Use the research you did earlier to your advantage. Talk about what you learned, and invite the interviewer to share more information. "I've read about the self-driving cars you're developing. It must be fascinating to work with that kind of cutting-edge technology. How long do you think it will be before they're on the road?"

TIP *Look at the language the company uses in the job ad and in other company literature. Try to use their words when describing yourself and your work. It's a subtle way to make yourself fit in to their culture.*

Why do you want to work here? Why do you want this position?   The key here is to focus on the company's needs, rather than what you want. "I understand from my reading that the problem you're trying to solve now is keeping your cars from crashing into walls.

I've solved similar problems in my current job, and I can help you, too." Give specific examples of how your skills can help.

What is your greatest weakness?   This is a classic interview question. The typical advice is to make your "weakness" perfectionism, one of the oldest tricks in the book. Try for a slightly more original response, but never share your personal weaknesses. Aim for an industry-specific response: "I get frustrated when technology doesn't keep pace with what I want to do. I'm constantly trying to develop new solutions." Or "I have a hard time working on just a single part of the development process. I prefer to be involved in the whole life cycle of a project."

TIP *Say what you need to say and then stop. Don't fear silence. "Um..." at the end of a strong answer weakens it. If you've said your piece, sit back, and wait for the next question.*

Where do you see yourself five years from now?   The interviewer wants to know if you have ambition. Do you see this position as a stepping-stone? Do you plan to leave the company after they invest time and money in training you? Try to tailor your answer to the company's products and services, and aim at a position one or two levels above where you currently are: "In five years, I'd like to be managing your wireless device team—but I'd still like to be involved in the hands-on technical work from time to time."

Why are you leaving your job?   The interviewer needs to know if you had problems with your previous employer, and what those problems might mean for you now. If your reason for leaving is simple and clear, say so. "I'm moving and the commute will be too difficult" or "There's no more room for me to grow" are perfectly acceptable reasons. If you've been fired, see the next section.

TIP *If you're offered a drink during the interview, take one. Most interviewees are quick to decline when offered coffee, juice, or water. Accepting indicates a certain amount of confidence. You can take sips to buy a few seconds while you think about your answers.*

The Tough Questions

These questions aren't designed to trip you up. The interviewer really needs the answers. Remember, the unasked questions are at the heart of the interview. Can you get the job done? Can the company afford you? Remind yourself that they want to hire you or they wouldn't have invited you to interview. Your job is to show the interviewer that she can, in fact, bring you on board.

TIP *If the interview isn't going the way you want it to, don't be afraid to stop and start over. If you've fumbled an answer, simply stop speaking, take a deep breath, and say, "I'm sorry. I really want this job, and I'm a bit nervous. Let me try that again." What's the interviewer going to do, stab you with a letter opener? On the contrary, admitting that you're human goes a long way toward establishing rapport.*

Salary History

There's often that awkward moment when the interviewer asks what you're currently making. Whether you're grossly underpaid (and therefore looking for a new job) or just ready to make the jump to the next level, you probably don't want to toss those numbers around lightly. You can't just ignore the question, and it's not always easy (or wise) to turn it around, à la "Well, how much are you offering?" So what can you do?

First, give the big picture answer. "Most people at my level earn in the mid-50s. I chose to work at my last job for less than my market value because I needed the experience. But now that I have it, I need to be sure that I'm compensated adequately for my skills."

If the interviewer persists, "But how much are they paying you?" try to avoid a specific number. "The high 40s" should suffice. But you must know exactly how much you want to be making, so that if they ask, you're ready to answer. Give a $3,000 to $5,000 range, because the company will undoubtedly come back with something lower than what you said. By giving yourself some wiggle room, you improve your chances of getting what you want.

Salary Negotiations

If the interviewer puts a figure on the table and it's less than you want, you'll have to negotiate. Believe it or not, you're in the best position now, before you have the job. The company wants to hire you, and you can convince them that you're worth the extra money.

If you've researched salary information ahead of time (and you wouldn't be negotiating unless you had, right?), you know what your range is. So when the interviewer says, "We're prepared to offer you $50,000 a year," you can respond with confidence, "The typical range for people at my level is $65,000 to $70,000 a year." Then shut up. Do not speak. As the silence stretches out, repeat silently, "This is not their final offer." Be careful not to move your lips. Let the interviewer fill the awkward silence with explanations.

 TIP *Make sure you really know what the market will bear for someone with your experience. Never underestimate your worth—it's very hard to make a significant salary jump after you've started working. But don't delude yourself into thinking you'll make $100,000 a year in an entry-level position, either.*

If the company can't afford you, decide how badly you need this particular job. The oldest rule of negotiating is he who cares least wins. If you're absolutely not willing to work for what they're offering, walk away. They may surprise you and come back with a new offer.

If, on the other hand, the electricity was shut off last week, your rent is due, and there's nothing else on the horizon, you may have a problem. Try for a compromise: can you take extra vacation days or pick up your commuting costs in lieu of more money? Will the company give you a salary review after three months? Or can you work a four-day work week and pick up some extra money on the side by doing freelance projects?

Getting Laid Off or Fired

Getting laid off no longer has the stigma it once carried. Especially in the IT world, job turnover has suffered with the economy's downturn. If your company went bankrupt, lost an important round of funding, or had to downsize to stay afloat, that's not your fault. Give a straightforward answer: "Unfortunately, the company was forced to cut costs and many people were let go."

If you're really not sure why you were let go, find out. Talk to your old employer, and really listen to the reason. Figure out what you need to do better this time. Try to put a positive spin on your firing. Use it to show that you can accept responsibility and that you've learned from your past mistakes. "My boss and I weren't able to see eye to eye on many issues. But I've had some time to think, and here's how I would have handled the situation differently." In other words, explain any problems you had (or still have) with an employer, but don't describe that employer in negative terms.

TIP *Here's a phrase that works like magic to put an interviewer on your side: "I agree." If you can find a way to use this phrase once or twice—any more than that and you'll sound like a yes-man—you'll score big points. People like to hear that they're right. Tell them that they are, and they'll like you. Simple, but true.*

Leaves of Absence

Be prepared to explain your leave of absence in matter-of-fact terms: "I had two children and took time off to be with them. Now that they're in day care, I'm eager to get back to work." Or "I had the opportunity to travel around the world for several months. It was a chance to broaden my world perspective."

If your "leave of absence" was simply the result of not finding a job quickly, explain that you are being selective. Try something like, "I'm more interested in finding the right fit than in taking a quick fix. It's easy to find a job. Finding the right position is more difficult."

Changing Careers

If you are new to the IT world, you may have to explain why you've chosen to change careers. Turn your past experience into benefits for your potential employer. Don't be afraid to get a bit passionate—in fact, that's a good thing. For example, you might say, "I worked in customer relations for many years, but I became fascinated by technology when I first discovered the Internet. I've taken several programming courses, and now I'm ready to make the switch to full-time developer. My CR background is a real plus for this position because I'm very familiar with client needs and the usability of the databases you develop here."

TIP *Never say, "I can't." If the interviewer asks, "Can you use this technology?" the correct answer is always yes or a variation of it. Try, "My exposure to X is limited, but I'm happy to put in the time necessary to become more familiar with it."*

Questions to Ask the Interviewer

At the end of the interview, you'll have a chance to ask the interviewer your own questions. Always take advantage of this opportunity. First of all, you should be genuinely interested in some of the company specifics. Merely asking the questions displays that interest to the interviewer as well as gets you answers you'll need to make your final decision. These are just a few of the possible questions you can ask:

▶ What's a typical working day like?

▶ How much contact is there with management?

▶ Are there opportunities to take seminars or attend conferences?

▶ Is this position more analytical or people-oriented?

▶ How much travel is normally expected?

▶ What is the best thing about working here? The worst thing?

▶ Why did you choose to work here?

▶ Do you have any reservations about hiring me that I can address?

For your final question, bolster your confidence and ask for the job. Say something like, "I'm very interested in this position. What's the next step?" Granted, not every company will make an offer on the spot. But you'd be surprised at how many will be willing to do so if you "ask for the sale" at the end of the interview.

 TIP *If your interviewer is frequently interrupted by office goings-on, acknowledge it. Say something like, "I really appreciate your taking the time to speak with me. I can see people depend on you a lot here— your time must really be at a premium."*

Other Situations

While you can't prepare for every single possibility at a job interview, a bit of research will cover most eventualities. Take some time to review these special situations.

Getting Past the Gatekeeper (Recruiter) Interview

A gatekeeper is anyone who stands between you and the hiring manager you want to approach. In the past, secretaries and administrative assistants were the first line of defense. Today, you may have to get past two assistants just to get to the recruiter, who can still decide not to send your résumé on to the company. How can you improve your chances?

▶ Always be professional and courteous in your correspondence and phone calls. Don't regard the gatekeeper as an obstacle, but rather as a partner. Recognize their importance to your career. Be genuinely interested in what they have to say. Always start off with, "Hi, my name is... and I'm calling about... Can you tell me the best person to speak with?" When you have the person's ear, your first question should be, "Do you have a few minutes to speak with me now?"

▶ Get a bit personal. A simple, "You must really be swamped" can work wonders.

▶ Make every contact count. Even if you're not speaking to the decision-maker, get at least one piece of useful information. "What's the best time of day to speak to him?" Or "Does he prefer to be addressed as Mr. Smith or John?"

▶ Be honest, and try to get the recruiter on your side. "From the description I read, this job sounds perfect for me. How can I get an interview with that company?"

TIP *If you get an answering machine when you call, don't be afraid to leave a message. State your name, ask for confirmation that information you sent was received or for a callback with more information about an advertised position, and leave your number.*

Phone Interviews

A phone interview can be intimidating for many people. You don't have the opportunity to make eye contact or size up the person you're speaking with. But a phone interview can be a great way to make a first impression if you know what you're doing.

Ahead of time, type up and print out the major points you want to make, such as your strengths and how you've put them to use for your current employer. Be sure to include some questions for the interviewer in your notes, too. As long as the person isn't sitting opposite you, you can refer to your written sheet. Just make sure you don't read long, prepared statements verbatim.

Use a phone that works well and that is comfortable for you. Don't do a phone interview on a cell phone! The connection is too unreliable. And try not to use a cordless phone, either. Sit in one place—preferably, a quiet, closed room—for the duration of the interview. Have a glass of water nearby.

It goes without saying that you should disable your call waiting feature while you're on the interview. If the connection is terrible and you're afraid you won't be able to hear everything, ask to call back. Do a trial run with a friend the day before. Test your equipment, presentation, and preparation. Then relax and wait for the call!

TIP *Smile when you speak on the phone. People can hear it in your voice. A genuine smile tells the interviewer that you're friendly, easygoing, and relaxed.*

Dining Interviews

The dining interview can be awkward for many people. But if you make a good impression at this one, it goes a long way. If you must face the dining interview, follow these simple rules for success:

▶ Place your napkin in your lap as early as possible.

► Wait for your host to open his menu before you open yours. Ask your host if he has any recommendations. Don't choose the most expensive item, but don't go for the cheapest, either.

► Eat to the left, drink to the right. The bread plate to your left is yours, as is the glass on your right. Utensils go from the outside in. Skip a course, skip a fork.

► Unless you are very adventurous, do not order something you've never heard of. Stick with what you know—and do not order spaghetti.

► Don't order alcohol, even if your host does.

► Don't speak with your mouth full. If your host asks you a question just as you take a bite, chew, swallow, then speak. He'll understand, and you can use the extra time to form your response.

TIP *Take small bites. They're a lot easier to swallow in a hurry.*

► Eat at a normal pace. Don't rush or drag it out.

► At the end of the meal, fold your napkin up and place it on the table.

► Don't offer to pay.

► Send a thank you note after the interview and specifically thank your host for the meal.

Illegal Questions to Watch Out For

It's illegal for a prospective employer to ask you certain questions, but some will do it anyway. This puts you in an awkward position. Do you answer the question and possibly risk the job? Or do you refuse to answer and mark yourself as uncooperative?

There's a third option: look at what the employer really wants to know, and answer that question. If the interviewer asks if you have children, you can say, "If you're worried about my availability, you don't need to be. When I commit to a job, I give it everything I have." Always smile and speak confidently when you give your answer. The interviewer should be well aware of what she can and cannot legally ask. Here are several other examples of illegal questions and answers you can offer.

Question	Answer
Are you a U.S. citizen?	The interviewer needs to know if you are authorized to work in the United States.
Where were you born?	
What's your first language?	**What to say:** I'm authorized to work in the United States.
How old are you?	The interviewer needs to know if you are over 18 or how close you are to retirement.
When did you graduate?	
When were you born?	**What to say:** I have been in IT for more than *xx* years.

Question	Answer
Are you married? Do you plan to have children? How many children do you have? What kind of child care arrangements do you have?	The interviewer is allowed to ask you about your willingness and ability to relocate, travel, and/or work overtime—if every applicant is asked the same questions. **What to say:** I can travel and work overtime as necessary for the job. I'm willing to relocate if needed.
Do you have any disabilities? How is your health? Have you had any recent or past illnesses or operations?	The interviewer needs to determine whether you can perform the essential functions of this job with or without reasonable accommodations. **What to say:** I am physically able to perform this job without any problem.

TIP *Not every question is asked to try to elicit illegal information. The interviewer may actually be intrigued by your accent. Use your best judgment—if a question doesn't offend you and you don't think your position is in jeopardy, go ahead and answer.*

Following Up After the Interview

So few people bother to send a written note of thanks after an interview. Set yourself apart from the crowd. A simple handwritten or typed note thanking the interviewer for her time and consideration is a great way to get your name in front of her again, plus it's truly a nice thing to do. To make a stellar impression, send an actual piece of mail. In the age of electronic communications, people really do appreciate letters.

Your note doesn't have to be fancy. Try something like this:

Thank you for taking the time to meet with me today. I was delighted to share with you my vision for how I would fit into your team, and I enjoyed very much your explanation of [insert specific technical detail answered by the interviewer here].

Please don't hesitate to call me if you have any more questions about my qualifications. As we agreed, I'll follow up with you at the end of next week. I look forward to speaking with you then.

Summary

Dozens of candidates apply for IT positions every day. Only a few are chosen to interview. If you've made it to that level, the company wants to hire you. Whether they choose you depends almost entirely on the interview. Set yourself apart from the crowd by following these steps:

▶ Research the company and prepare answers to common questions ahead of time.

▶ Arrive at your interview a few minutes early.

▶ Dress the part, and err on the side of conservatism.

▶ Take your time when answering questions. Don't let tough questions trip you up.

▶ Ask the interviewer intelligent questions that indicate your interest in the company and the position.

▶ Determine your worth and hold your ground in salary negotiations.

▶ Send a thank you note immediately after the interview. Mention specific information you were grateful to receive.

Careful preparation on your part indicates to the company that you care about the job. Companies need reliable people who are passionate about their work. If you can't put a little effort into your appearance or aren't interested enough in what the company does to ask questions, why should they hire you? Go the extra mile now to take your career to new heights.

In our next and final chapter, you will find all the examples you need to create a winning résumé for any position in IT.

Part II

Résumé Encyclopedia

In This Part

Chapter 12

. . . .

Résumé Encyclopedia

Getting started is the hardest part of any writing task. The Résumé Encyclopedia is just what you need to turn your experience, or lack thereof, into a masterpiece that will get noticed and get you the job.

This chapter provides you with examples of résumés for the top jobs in the industry today, along with job descriptions, outlines of the qualifications, and related certifications. Be sure to include the qualifications that hiring managers are looking for when you write your résumé. Additionally, the Résumé Encyclopedia can help you in planning your career path.

The templates used to create these résumés are available for download at http://www.acetheitresume.com.

Database Administrator/Data Analyst

Job Description

DATABASE ADMINISTRATOR (DBA) Administers, maintains, develops, and implements policies and procedures for ensuring the security and integrity of the company database. Implements data models and database designs, data access and table maintenance codes. Resolves database performance issues, database capacity issues, replication, and other distributed data issues. Guarantees the performance integrity and quality of databases. Controls system capacity for existing requirements and plans for future needs. Sometimes will supervise or mentor data analysts.

DATA ANALYST Responsible for the inventory and associations/relationships of data within an organization. Designs, implements, and maintains moderately complex databases, including maintaining database dictionaries and ensuring system integration. Writes codes for database access, modifications, and constructions including stored procedures. May work with database administrators on complex projects. May be assigned one application area or have responsibility for all of an organization's databases depending on the size of the company. Usually responsible for all data modeling and heavily involved in data reporting.

Qualifications

DATABASE ADMINISTRATOR Typically two to four years experience in database design and data analysis. Start off as programmers and data analysts. May require a bachelor's degree in a related area and two to four years of experience in the field or in a related area. Typically reports to the director of IT or the software engineering manager.

DATA ANALYST Usually requires an IS degree with a heavy focus on database systems. Usually requires one to two years of intensive database experience, which is primarily attained by working in other fields and focusing on programming, querying, and report writing.

Related Certifications

▶ Microsoft Certified Database Administrator (MCDBA)

▶ Oracle Certified Professional (OCP) – Application Developer, Database Operator (DBO), Database Administrator (DBA), Solution Developer – Jdeveloper, Java Enterprise Developer, Internet Application Developer, Oracle Forms Developer

▶ Sybase Certified Professional – Database Administrator, Performance and Tuning Specialist (CSP-PTS), SQL Developer

▶ Authorized Crystal Engineer (ACE)

Figures 12-1 through 12-3 are examples of résumés in the area of database administration.

Shantanu Braza   shantanub@yahoo.com
65 Avenue C   405-555-3434
Toronto, Ontario CANADA

OBJECTIVE

Accomplished IT professional with a proven track record in applying technology to engineering and decision support systems seeking a position in data warehouse analysis and data mining.

SUMMARY OF QUALIFICATIONS

- Graduate degree in MIS with a concentration in data warehousing
- Four years experience in designing and implementing Oracle 8i and DB2 databases
- Experienced in systems analysis and design, and conceptual and physical modeling using ERD and UML
- Performed data mining tasks in Weaka, DBMiner and IBM's Intelligent Miner
- Designed and implemented software in Matlab for data mining tasks (clustering and classification)
- Information retrieval on commercial databases, DialogWeb, ProQuest, and major search engines
- Experienced in creating XML schemas and transferring XML schemas into relational schemas using XML Authority, IBM XML extenders, and Oracle XML
- Expertise in statistical data analysis, using Matlab, Statistica, SPSS, and WizRule

RELEVANT WORK HISTORY

Faculty of Information Studies, University of Toronto, Ontario   8/2000 – 3/2001
Inforum Systems Advisor

Troubleshooting and maintaining member profiles, supporting students and faculty in the use of Visual Age for Java, DB2, M/A Access, Visual Basic, HTML authoring (HTMLed32, FrontPage, Dreamweaver), and XML authoring (X-Metal). Maintained computing facilities including performing upgrades and administration of a Windows NT server.

IBM Canada and University Health Network, Toronto, Ontario   4/2000 – 8/2000
DBA/Data Warehouse Analyst

Designed the database infrastructure for analyzing the extract principles of the crystallization process. As a part of this work, improved representation and quality of Biological Macromolecule Crystallization Database (BMCD) by creating appropriate relational schema, improving data consistency, and implementing integrity constraints. Data was cleaned using both manual as well as automated techniques. Tables in Oracle 8 DBMS were populated using the loader utility. A Java applet was created to query the database using JDBC (AIX on IBM SP-2).

FIGURE 12-1   Sample résumé for a data architect/analyst

Asian Center for Engineering Computations, Singapore   6/1998 – 5/1999
Application Developer

Part of the engineering team to develop, debug, and test the engineering software. Authored and developed software for interaction-surface diagrams for columns subjected to biaxial loading. Projects include structural analysis and design software SDL and ROBOT. Most of the work was done in Basic with some extensions in Java.

TechnoPhix Computer Applications, Saudi Arabia   1/1993 – 5/1996
Programmer/Structural Engineering

Worked as a team member of SDL (Structural Designers Library), a comprehensive software for analysis and design of concrete structures. Currently SDL is being updated and marketed by ACECOMS, Asian Institute of Technology Thailand. Developed engineering utilities, and performed debugging and crash control of the software. Wrote manual for the software. Projects include SDL and engineering utilities.

ADDITIONAL RELEVANT ACADEMIC PROJECTS

XML Documents Warehouse: *Complementary requirement of Advanced Topics in Data Warehousing.* In this project I used inlining techniques to transform DTDs into a relational model. I transformed XML queries (in this case XML-QL and path queries) into SQL queries using IBM's fixpoint operator. XML documents were loaded into relational schema (Oracle 8) using a parser written in Perl. Finally, the SQL results were transformed to XML documents. The data used was from a biomedical domain (genome database).

Data Cleaning for Data Mining: *Complementary requirement of Advanced Topics in Data Mining.* Surveyed automated data cleaning techniques and presented a new model for semi-automated data cleaning for data mining, including a partial implementation of the concept.

EDUCATION

University of Toronto, Ontario, Canada   5/2000
Master of Information Systems
   Selected course list:
   Database Management Systems
   Advanced Topics in Data Mining
   Advanced Topics in Data Warehousing
   Computations in Neural Networks
   Parallel Computing
   Analysis and Design of Information Systems
   Knowledge Management
   Text Information Retrieval Systems

FIGURE 12-1 Continued

Jacques Montand
Ave. de Paris, 5
Paris 3456 France

Jacques@telecom.fr
+31 2345 45565

OBJECTIVE

Seasoned Oracle DBA seeking a position with a large organization to employ his database design and architect skills to realize strategic business objectives.

SUMMARY OF QUALIFICATIONS

- Ten years of experience working for international companies in a variety of industries, including financial, telecommunications, publishing, and energy
- Proven database design and architecture skills on high profile projects
- Excellent project management and supervisory skills
- Skilled in Oracle 6 to 9i, Unix Solaris, HP/UX, Tru64, AIX, n-tier design and architecture
- Willing to relocate to any English-speaking country

TECHNICAL COMPETENCIES

Operating Systems
Unix (AIX, Compaq Tru64, Sun Solaris, HP-UX, Linux), Windows (from 3.1x to 2000), VMS, OS/2, Mac OS, MS/DOS

Network/System Administration
TNG, Patrol, OpenView, Legato

Languages
C, C++, Fortran, Ada, Smalltalk, Lisp, Prolog, SQL, PL/SQL, Pro*C, O2C, OQL, NCL, Shell, DCL, Sed, Awk, Perl, HTML

DBMS
Oracle 7/8/8i (Developer, Designer, DBA)
MS SQL Server, MS Access
AIRS (Multimedia Retrieval System)
O2 (Object DBMS)

Design/Development Tools
NSDK, NSDK/2, NatStar, PowerBuilder, Visual C++, Visual Basic, Hypercard, OAS, SQL Forms, SQL*Plus, Toad, PL/SQL Developer, Tuxedo, Visual Source Safe, ClearCase, PowerDesigner, Objecteering, UML, RUP

RELEVANT EXPERIENCE

Global One, Telecom and Internet Provider,   June 2000–Present
Oracle 8i DBA, technical architect, project leader

- Supported the IS Operations Europe team, based in London. Environment: Unix (HP-UX, Sun Solaris, Red Hat Linux), Windows NT 4.0, Windows 2000, Oracle 8i, PowerDesigner 7, PL/SQL Developer, Netscape Communicator, Netscape Web Server, Livelink, Oracle Application Server, HP OpenView, NetWorker Legato.
- Migrated Oracle databases from Windows NT to Unix and optimized access and storage.
- Applications monitoring and KPIs: designed and developed a set of generic Perl scripts, connected on one side to HP OpenView, and on the other side to a KPI's Oracle database, aimed at improving reaction time in cases of software failure and preventing failure.
- Project leader and technical architect of an in-house groupware application for the U.K. unit, with responsibility for defining requirements (interviews and meetings with the end-users), overall general design, evaluating and selecting project management, design, development, and versioning tools.
- Performed internal consultancy and support including evaluating outsourced applications, providing recommendations about database and software upgrade procedures, and providing level 2 support with local groupware software.

FIGURE 12-2 Sample résumé for an Oracle database DBA

Société Générale, Leading French Bank　　　　　November 1998–April 2000
Oracle 8 DBA

- Database lead for the largest strategic project for SG in the last 10 years. Replaced branch information system, a project that involved migrating 35,000 MS Exchange end-users and 2,500 web servers. The project involved 150 IS personnel over a three-year period. Environment: Unix clusters (Digital Unix, Sun Solaris, IBM AIX), NT 4, Oracle 8, MS SQL Server, MS Exchange, IIS, Tuxedo, BMC Patrol, TNG, Unicenter, SSO.
- Installed and upgraded Oracle servers on several Unix systems.
- Created, configured, backed up, and tuned database instances.
- Helped analysts design Oracle/SQL Server databases and centralized conceptual and physical model changes.
- Defined a common logical architecture for Oracle databases and developed low-level technical PL/SQL packages.

Adways, Advertising Market Software Editor　　　September 1996–October 1998
Oracle 7 functional designer and administrator

- Managed the server team.
- Designed and implemented a multimedia database merging different company data (TV, radio, press), accessed by ad agencies, helping them choose best available marketing offers.
- Developed server-side data conversion and integration tools.
- Environment: Unix (HP UX), Windows 95 and NT, Oracle 7, Exceed, Desktop DBA, S*Designer, Access, Visual C++, Visual Basic, Visual Source Safe.

EDF GDF Services, French Utility Company　　　　May 1996–August 1996
Technical project manager of a telecom and data management system

- Oversaw the technical architecture of an automated billing system that interfaced directly with electricity meters for professional customers
- Object analysis and design, three-tier client/server, TP monitor, real-time processing.
- Environment: Unix (DPX/20 and ESCALA) and Windows NT, Windows, Objecteering, AMC*Designer, Sybase SQL Server, PowerBuilder, Tuxedo, Access Master, PVCS.

Caisses d'Epargne, Savings Bank　　　　　　　　January 1995–April 1996
Systems analyst, technical project manager

- Designed several user-friendly tools around an electronic documents database to present banking products in comparison to competitors' offers using a client/server information retrieval system.
- Managed a team of two developers.
- Environment: Unix (DPX/20 and ESCALA), OS/2 PM, Windows NT, Windows for Workgroup, Windows, OS/2, AIRS DBMS, AMC*Designer, Visual C++, Visual Basic, Access, Microsoft Word 6.

Bull, Computer Manufacturer　　　　　　　　　　January 1993–December 1994
Development engineer

- Designed, developed, installed, and presented a multilingual customer care database intended for banking and insurance companies.
- Object Database Management System, Unix (DPX/20), X Terminals, Object DBMS (O2), X11/Motif.

EDUCATION

Bachelor of Science, Math and Sciences, University of Paris　　1992
Oracle Certified Database Administrator (DBA) – Oracle 9i　　2000

FIGURE 12-2 Continued

Tony Storm
20454 Stirdown Run
Newark, Delaware 19711
555-234-7546
tstorm@compuserve.com

SUMMARY

- Certified Sybase Professional (CSPDBA) bringing over ten years of Sybase experience.
- Vast experience in client/server assignments covering all the major roles from DBA to performance and tuning specialist to key Sybase mentor/developer.
- Combination of Sybase/SQL Server experience with complimentary front-end development experience (PowerBuilder, Visual Basic, Access, 4D, APT, SmartStream) on a multitude of platforms (Unix, Microsoft 95/98/NT, VAX/VMS).
- Dedicated to performing tasks enthusiastically.

Databases: Sybase 11.02, MS SQL Server 6.5, Oracle 8i.

Tool Sets: Embarcadero's DB-Artisan (Sybase, MS SQL Server, Oracle components), Rapid SQL, Schema Manager, ER-Studio, Erwin, Platinum's Desktop DBA, BMC's Datatools, Cyrano Developer Workbench, Cyrano Production Workbench, Sybase's Unix utilities (BCP, ISQL, defncopy), Open Client (DB-Lib/CT-Lib) custom developed utilities (Bcpxfer, transfers data between servers without using intermediary files), Open Server applications (Open Switch, gateway redirecting client connections between primary and warm standby servers, Cyrano Developer), Oracle's Unix utilities (SQLDR, SQLplus), Tuxedo client, services and servers, C.

Hardware: Windows NT, HP9000, Sun.

PROFESSIONAL HIGHLIGHTS

PHH Fleet Management Services
Database Administrator   Sept. 1997 to Aug. 2001

- Senior Sybase DBA with one of America's leading vehicle fleet management companies.
- As a project DBA, performed logical and physical data modeling supporting several components of an asset management system.
- Integrated more than ten web-based information system products into one compact portable NT ASE server for demonstration purposes. Took a flexible table-driven approach to allow the business to define what was to be included and how the underlying data was to be transformed.
- Shared day and night production support for more than 20 data servers, 10 rep servers, 1 IQ server, 1 historical server, and for more than 10 web and OLTP products.
- Wrote a generic, reusable DBA shell tool that allows for easy development of scripts that a DBA commonly requires. Applied this tool to create a data warehouse of meta data about the enterprise. Especially useful in troubleshooting, predicting, and forecasting growth for the enterprise.

First USA
Lead Developer   Oct. 1996 to Sept. 1997

- Designed and developed n-Tier Leads Management System with America's second largest bank. The mission-critical project resulted in a leads management system so flexible and reusable that common modules were shared by all business units.

FIGURE 12-3   Sample résumé for a SQL Server DBA

- Iterated, prototyped, and coordinated the efforts of various business groups to ensure a perfect fit for each business, with a common code base.
- Designed the logical and physical data model to support a table-driven approach for the front-end application.
- Designed and developed reusable presentation layer objects in PowerBuilder. This allowed the PowerBuilder application to behave according to instructions read from tables where the business unit was part of the key.
- Designed and developed several Tuxedo services using Sybase C – Open client.
- Designed, developed, and tuned back-end batch processes in SQL to perform lead loading, list searching, and list creation functions with optimal performance. This resulted in the first proven business-dependent application implemented with Tuxedo middleware, providing high availability, responsive, flexible system critical to the success of each business unit.

First USA
System Architect   Sept. 1996 to Nov. 1996

- Demonstrated ability to contribute in a fast-paced team environment by designing and developing a set of automated tools to quantify and pinpoint year 2000 problems. This tool suite identified potential problems from 7 million lines of code of many different front-end applications, middleware layers, and the leading back-end platforms (Oracle, Sybase, Informix, Tuxedo).

Siemens Information Technology Group
Database Analyst   Jan. 1996 to Aug. 1996

- Primary Database Analyst on the SATRN (Service And Tools Responding to Needs) project.
- Played a key role in the successful implementation of several DBS (Dunn & Bradstreet, SmartStream) financial products.
- Installed, maintained, and tuned nine SQL servers supporting DBS applications on a Sun Solaris platform.
- Specialized in optimizing DBS applications to conform to resource constraints.

Trans Canada Pipelines
Systems Analyst/Sybase Developer   Apr. 1994 to Dec. 1995

- Key Sybase resource for the Accounting FST (Functional Systems Team) by providing the expertise and advice for evaluating several Sybase tools, utilities, and products.

Trust Company of the West
Systems Analyst/Sybase Developer/Project Leader   Oct. 1991 to Jan. 1994

- Responsible for the design and implementation of an automated "Data Warehouse" named TED (The Enterprise Database).
- Performed the analysis of financial data requirements needed to support an executive information system.
- Supervised a four-man development team; wrote the communication scripts to allow data stored in legacy systems to interface with a Sybase client server architecture.

EDUCATION

Certified Sybase Professional Database Administrator   1996
Bachelor of Commerce/MIS Concentration, University of Manitoba 1991

FIGURE 12-3 Continued

Desktop Support Technician

Job Description

Similar to a helpdesk position, supporting end-users within an organization. Generally less specialized in one area, but have a wide range of knowledge and the ability to troubleshoot and solve a variety of computer-related issues. Attends to problems around the office or even in other buildings, while helpdesk analysts spend most of their time at a desk on the phone, chat, or email.

Qualifications

Can gain qualification through degree programs that include PC support training, but many technicians enter the field through certifications. Specific skills required may include building and repairing computer systems, installing and configuring software, assisting users, and strong communication and documentation skills. Strong knowledge of operating systems and office software applications is needed. Knowledge of the following usually required: hardware, software, configuration, device drivers, networking concepts, Internet skills for research, troubleshooting techniques and shortcuts, peripherals, DOS, and computer maintenance.

Related Certifications

▶ CompTIA A+, Server+, and Network+

▶ Microsoft Certified Professional (MCP)

▶ Novell Certified Network Administrator (CNA)

Figure 12-4 is an example of a résumé in the area of support.

Documentation Specialist/Technical Writer

Job Description

Develops, writes, and edits computer-related technical and administrative documentation and publications including technical specifications, requests for information (RFI), requests for proposals (RFP), application help screens, user manuals, policies and procedures, and emergency recovery plans.

Qualifications

Must really enjoy writing. Second passion must be technology. Must have a knack for translating difficult concepts into English, especially with user documentation. Should have at least an associate's degree in either English or IS. Should also be familiar with basic networking, programming, or application functionality and processes.

Related Certifications

May choose to become members of the Society for Technical Communication (STC), the largest professional society in the world dedicated to the advancement of the theory and practice of technical communication. Often possess technical certifications as well that increase their subject matter expertise. Recommended entry-level certifications include:

▶ CompTIA A+, Server+, and Network+

▶ Microsoft Certified Professional (MCP)

▶ Certified Novell Administrator (CNA)

Figure 12-5 is an example of a résumé in the area of technical writing.

Director of IT/IT Manager

Job Description

Manages IS operations, including computer operations, technical support, systems analysis, and programming. May also direct database management, telecommunications, IS training, and microcomputer technology. Establishes technical priorities, standards, and procedures and ensures sufficient systems capacity for organizational needs. Typically reports to the chief information officer.

Qualifications

Requires an MIS degree and five or more years of experience.

Related Certifications

May have achieved technical certifications in previous positions, but may not have these current at this time. These certifications may have included:

▶ Cisco Certified Design Associate (CCDA), Design Professional (CCDP), Internetwork Expert (CCIE), Internet Solutions Specialist

▶ Project Management Professional (PMP)

▶ CheckPoint Certified Security Engineer (CCSE)

▶ Certified Help Desk Director (CHDD)

▶ Novell Certified Directory Engineer (CDE)

Figures 12-6 and 12-7 are examples of résumés in the area of IT management.

Leon Melkonian

1502 Battery Ave., Laguna Hills, CA 90211, (714) 841-9931
drmelkonian@computer.com

KEY QUALIFICATIONS

- **Desktop Support Technician** with expertise in computer maintenance and technical support, including building, repairing, diagnosing, and upgrading PC hardware.
- Additional understanding of hardware components, such as bus architecture, CPU, motherboards, RAM, and hard drives.
- Strong communication and interpersonal skills with excellent troubleshooting and problem solving abilities.

TECHNICAL SKILLS

Operating Systems

Installation and repair of Windows 95/98/NT/2000 and Novell.

Applications

Microsoft Office 97/00, Norton Antivirus 5.0 and Corporate Edition, pcAnywhere, Lotus Notes, Visio, Symantec Ghost, phone system software, and modem software.

Technical Knowledge

Partitioning and formatting hard drives. Assembling and disassembling desktops. Installing, configuration, and upgrading of applications. Demonstrated diagnosing and troubleshooting skills.

CERTIFICATIONS

CompTIA A+ Certification
MOUS Access Master Certification
MOUS Excel Master Certification
MOUS Word Master Certification

EDUCATION

Computer Certification Training Institute, 2/01
B.S., Mass Communication, Towson University, 5/00

EXPERIENCE

Computer Technician Consultant

- Set up a local network consisting of two PCs running Windows NT and one running Mac OS 9, all connected to a Windows 2000 file server.
- Installed and configured the router on the network to increase network performance and download speeds.
- Installed a network printer to minimize costs and decrease need for multiple printing systems.
- Installed and maintained virus software, and automated downloads of the latest DAT files to ensure maximum security on the network.
- Upgraded all machines from Office 97 to Office 2000 to utilize the latest software.

FIGURE 12-4 Sample résumé for a desktop support technician

Julie Smith
47 Clement Street
Baltimore, MD 21298

jsmith@yahoo.com
410-555-1212

OBJECTIVE

A position as a technical publications manager supporting the development of core communication materials, including technical specifications, proposals, product documentation, and marketing communications.

EXPERIENCE

New Horizons Computer Learning Centers, Baltimore, MD   4/2000 – Present
Technical Writer, Marketing and Sales

- Prepared professional proposals in response to Requests for Information (RFI) and Requests for Proposal (RFP) for enterprise customers.
- Developed product marketing literature for corporate customers, including product brochures and white papers.
- Wrote competitive analysis white papers on positioning the company and its product lines.
- Web content management in support of product offerings and promotions.
- Wrote contributing articles for IT training industry magazines.

ILearning, Inc., Baltimore, MD   6/1999 – 4/2000
Technical Publications Manager

- Worked with product managers and development teams to develop product documentation for company's product line of e-learning solutions, ensuring that corporate quality standards were adhered to for documentation and training materials.
- Managed the documentation available in the CVS repository, an email server (using Outlook Public Folders), and the corporate intranet.
- Managed outsourced copywriters for IT-related issues for the company's web site.
- Developed online help for the company's learning management system.
- Edited all documentation and training materials produced. Also reviewed marketing materials, development specifications, technical support advisories, and other written communications.

LANSource, Glen Burnie, MD   3/1996 – 3/1997
Documentation Manager

- Wrote all documentation for three products including five user guides, one API guide, and eleven online help files.
- Reviewed all marketing material.

FIGURE 12-5 Sample résumé for a documentation specialist/technical writer

- Trained and managed 11 translators, many of whom had no formal computer or documentation experience.

Delphi Computers, Newark, DE   7/1995 – 3/1996
Technical Writer

- Developed HTML technical notes, peer reviews, and WinFax for Networks documentation.

Santoc, Newark, DE   9/1992 – 7/1995
Technical Writer

- Wrote 11 manuals for an AS/400 enterprise software program.
- Analyzed online help and computer-based training packages.
- Created training materials, including instructor-led slides and computer-based training tutorials.

Communications & Training, Philadelphia, PA   9/1991 – 9/1992
Technical Writer

- Wrote Technical Writing course book.
- Edited and revised project material.

EDUCATION

Loyola College, Baltimore, MD   1992
  Certification in Technical Writing

University of Maryland, Baltimore, MD   1991
  Bachelor's Degree in English, Minor in Psychology

AFFILIATIONS

Society of Technical Communicators member   1999

FIGURE 12-5   Continued

Jon Duffy
11 Cardinal Place
Reading, PA 19610

jon@yahoo.com

SUMMARY

- Six years experience managing IT projects and systems, development teams, and customer service centers using in-house and outsourced resources
- Experienced network infrastructure and capacity planner
- Internet technology skills, including TCP/IP, VPN, and firewall setup and administration
- Excellent communication and interpersonal skills, including helpdesk skills
- Detail oriented, with very strong organizational and planning skills

TECHNOLOGIES

Windows 2000/NT 3.1–4.0 Server Administration

Internet Information Server 3.0+ Administration

Microsoft Project

Microsoft Office 97, 2000 and XP

IBM Netfinity Manager

Visual Studio 6.0

Networking/IP Technologies

Internet Technologies (DNS, FTP, POP3, SMTP, WWW)

Windows 3.1, 3.11WFW, 95, 98, ME

EXPERIENCE

Blue Streak Utility Services Inc., Concord, Ontario
Manager, Technology Division   1/2000 – 7/2001

Managed outsourced development team, created new team and brought development services in-house. Outsourced web design and e-branding. Assisted in logical application development and systems architecture of online energy management and profiling service. Managed all Internet-based systems and equipment, including web, email, ftp, application, SQL ColdFusion, site minder servers, and all routers, switches, and redundant connectivity. Designed and implemented corporate network/intranet and satellite office connectivity and integration of technologies across companies that were acquired.

YourHome.com Inc., Toronto, Ontario
IT Manager   9/1998 – 1/2000

Project and technical management of a large home-based web portal. Included logical design and systems/network architecture. Managed development staff of six (DBA, two programmers, web developer, web designer, HTML coder). Acted as technical liaison representing the organization to investors and clients.

Interlog Internet Services Inc., Toronto, Ontario
Manager, On-Site Support   10/1996 – 9/1998

Helpdesk/call center management covering telephone and on-site support with a staff of 20 employees.

EDUCATION

Humber College, Rexdale, Ontario, Canada   1996
    Certified Electronics Engineering Technician, Two-Year Program

FIGURE 12-6   Sample résumé for an IT manager

Joseph Mathews
675 Highlands Avenue
Kansas City, Kansas 56445

jmathews@yahoo.com
(876)555-1212

QUALIFICATIONS

- 6 years of proven technical team leadership
- Results-driven manager and coach of junior technicians
- Skilled at providing superior customer service
- Trained in cultural diversity
- Effective communicator

EXPERIENCE

GE Capital ITS, Kansas City, Kansas   4/2000 – Present
Helpdesk Support Team Leader

- Managed 18 agents supporting 120,000 employees. Responsible for ensuring that the team provided first-level support for Nortel Networks' employees worldwide. Created a graduated perk system for rewarding helpdesk staff for outstanding performance as monitored by spot checks and silent monitoring, creating plans to help poor performing agents achieve their objectives, and if needed, recommending them for termination.
- Prepared, analyzed, and acted upon the team's daily performance in relation to customers' SLAs (service level agreements). Improved average calls per hour 22% to the highest in the organization.
- Conducted coaching/training for the team to achieve team goals and organized team building events and methods of motivating the team.
- Managed escalation issues in PC and customer service environment.
- Prepared reports and presentations for upper management.
- Decreased talk time through effective use of call handling techniques.
- Created a project tracking system to ensure all projects started were successfully completed.

GE Capital ITS, Kansas City, Kansas   8/1999 – 4/2000
Helpdesk Analyst

- Provided first-level PC support for Nortel employees worldwide, maintaining 80% first-level resolution. Coordinated with second- and third-level support groups to ensure that the appropriate support group was informed of the issue, and then monitored it to ensure the issue was resolved to the customer's satisfaction.
- Skilled in diagnosing and repairing server/workstation network connectivity issues (Win9x, WinNT, Win2000, OS/2).
- Supported Office 2000, Palm, Netscape, IE, RAS, cable modems, DSL modems, VPDN, Exchange and Notes environment.

FIGURE 12-7 Sample résumé for a technical team lead

- Worked as a field technician troubleshooting PC, laptop, and hardware issues.
- Used Remedy support tool.

ABC Computer Group, Kansas City, Kansas   9/1995 – 2/1999
Senior Desktop Support Technician

- Supervised four junior technicians.
- Created a database for tracking repairs and replacements.
- Developed new processes for handling incoming stock for tracking.
- Set up and directed trade shows.
- Trained customer employees in several PC-related topics.
- Tracked stock and maintained records of inventory.
- Handled escalations and irate customers.

EDUCATION

DeVRY Institute of Technology, Kansas City, Kansas   6/1999
B.S., Computer Science

AFFILIATIONS

IEEE Member

FIGURE 12-7   Continued

E-commerce Manager/Director of E-business

Job Description

A relatively new position that came into being with the dot-com craze of the last few years. Directs, establishes, plans, and implements overall policies and goals for an organization's marketing strategy on the Web. Works with the marketing department to come up with email marketing campaigns, opt-in marketing strategies, monetization strategies, and customer demographic collection. Also works with the IT department in creating a secure environment for conducting transactions on a company Web site, build-out of the IT infrastructure, and development of Web site functionality. A very strategic position within an organization.

Qualifications

Requires a bachelor's degree, preferred slant toward business and management information systems. M.B.A. with a concentration in marketing or e-commerce highly desirable. Should have at least seven years of overall experience, preferably with lots of experience in a variety of different disciplines, including marketing, operations, IS, and sales. Experience in managing outside vendors also a plus.

Related Certifications

May have achieved technical certifications in previous positions, but may not have these current at this time. These certifications may have included:

▶ Certified Internet Webmaster (CIW) Professional, Master Administrator, Master Designer, Enterprise Developer, Web Site Manager

▶ Brainbench Certified Internet Professional (BCIP) – Web Administrator, Web Designer, Web Developer

Figure 12-8 is an example of a résumé in the area of e-commerce management.

Enterprise Resource Planning (ERP) Consultant

Job Description

Provides project management, software configuration planning, conference room pilots, and building/implementing systems for large-scale enterprise system projects. Can include enterprise asset management, collaboration and integration, customer relationship management, financial management, fulfillment management, implementation and systems management, knowledge management, marketplace and exchange management, procurement management, and workforce management.

Qualifications

Extensive business experience and seven to ten years development and project management experience. Bachelor's degree required and M.B.A. preferred. Typically focus on supporting particular industries, such as financial, medical, or manufacturing.

Related Certifications

▶ Baan ERP Certification, IV Certification, Supply Chains Solutions (SCS) Certification

▶ SAP Certified Application Consultant, Technical Consultant

▶ J.D. Edwards Certification Program

Figure 12-9 is an example of a résumé for an ERP consultant position.

Pete Orologas
1234 Hardin Ave.
Toronto, Ontario DFR 567
(619) 555-2222 · peteo@yahoo.com

SUMMARY OF QUALIFICATIONS

- E-Business Director with programming, business, and client/affiliate services background with a passion for new media, technology, and e-business/services development
- Consulted on, developed, and provided solutions for 100+ internet initiatives
- Cross-functional IT experience in areas of corporate Web administration, MIS/systems analysis, technical support, and computer training
- Skilled in project management, needs analysis, and technical writing
- Works well on interdepartmental teams
- Manages change and effectively solves problems
- Team player with excellent communication and problem-solving skills

TECHNICAL QUALIFICATIONS

Web project management, Web development, technical writing, data analysis, market research, Internet research/search engine optimization, marketing communications, business analysis, Web communications, Web content management, e-commerce/e-business industry, Internet sales, Internet security, Internet technologies, EDI, XML, extranets, intranets, VPN (virtual private network), CRM

EXPERIENCE

Director of E-Business
Teleconnix, Toronto, Ontario   5/2001 – Present

Reporting directly to the VP of Sales and Operations and EVP of World Wide Sales. Responsibilities encompass online advertising and marketing (B2B, B2C and B2G), focusing on business development, strategic planning, revenue generation, project management, corporate Web site development, partner affiliation and acquisitions, sales/technical support presentations, affiliate services. Additional responsibilities include:
- Strategic Web site relationship management
- Product engineering support and development
- Sales management for email and sponsorship opportunities
- Rich media and new technology development and support
- Creative development and in-house marketing and sales collateral
- In-house Internet/advertising training seminars

Principal, E-Business Consultant
FUSE Interactive, Toronto, Ontario   1/2001 – 5/2001

Worked with over 100 customers specializing in corporate Web site development, design and consulting, e-commerce/e-business development, marketing, and corporate Internet

FIGURE 12-8 Sample résumé for an e-commerce manager

research training, including search engine methodologies to improve overall sales and business effectiveness.

Director of Internet Programming
Sparrow Communications Ltd., Montreal, Quebec   11/1998 – 1/2001

As director, supervised and implemented the complete development cycle for 20 client Web sites. This included initial consultation with prospective clients, storyboarding, application programming, testing and debugging, optimization and deployment, service/maintenance support.

Other responsibilities included organizational and account management liaison with account representatives and graphic designers, internal computer maintenance for company PC systems, and all aspects of company purchasing of new technology equipment and software.

This position required a high degree of initiative, flexibility, programming knowledge, and patience for the successful completion of several high-profile Web-based projects.

Software Engineer
Telecommunix, Toronto, Ontario   2/1997 – 11/1998

With high exposure to Internet technologies and to e-commerce, working in this company enhanced experience of working in teams, on project coordination, and knowledge in practical applications of Internet technologies.

By working on the programming and the designing sides, acquired a deep knowledge of how e-commerce works. Responsibilities included application and database design, programming, and working with other areas to deliver high-quality solutions. Multiple Web projects using ColdFusion Server and Studio, JavaScript, HTML, and interacting with Oracle databases. Research and adaptation of video/audio encoding using Windows and Real Media Technologies for efficient broadcasting of live and archived events over the Internet.

EDUCATION

McGill University, Quebec, Montreal, Canada   6/2002
Graduate Diploma in Management with a concentration in E-Commerce
McGill University, Quebec, Montreal, Canada   6/2000
Bachelor's Degree in Computer Science

Additional Courses

Time Management, Effective Supervision, MS Project 1 and 2, Effective Internal Consulting, Project Management

Rogen International – Consultative Selling, Toronto, Ontario, Canada 3/2001 Certification, three-day, highly intensive consultative sales training program

AFFILIATIONS

Canadian Marketing Association Planning Committee
International Society for Professionals in E-Commerce

FIGURE 12-8   Continued

Thomas Hoit
4503-B Avenue C
New Brunswick, NJ 07200

thoit@yahoo.com
201-678-0087

OBJECTIVE

To lead CRM implementation teams, including process design, requirements gathering, testing, and training.

QUALIFICATIONS

- Experienced CRM and SAP professional with more than 10 years experience in JAD analysis and building large-scale deployment solutions
- Consultant for the top big firm names in CRM and SAP deployment in Fortune 500 companies worldwide

EXPERIENCE

PricewaterhouseCoopers, East Brunswick, NJ
eCRM Consultant   11/2000 – Present

As a CRM subject matter expert (SME), develop and design CRM solutions for a variety of clients. Assist clients in defining requirements by conducting joint application development (JAD) sessions with all levels of personnel, from executive management to operations staff. Manage testing and training projects, develop project documentation (end vision, discovery, use cases, test scripts, training materials, user documents).

PricewaterhouseCoopers, Arlington, VA
Senior CRM Management Consultant   6/1999 – 11/2000

Managed Siebel and Clarify training and testing projects for clients in a variety of industries including Internet technology, telecom, energy, sport apparel, and entertainment.

KPMG, Mountain View, CA
Y2K Consultant   10/1998 – 2/1999

As a Year 2000 Consultant, worked with America West Airlines, Wells Fargo Bank, and MicroAge in their preparations for the new millennium. Conducted reviews of the software remediation efforts undertaken by the companies, worked with their vendors to estimate the state of the vendor software products employed by the companies, and assisted in preparing these companies for Y2K litigation that might arise in the future. Worked with executive management to assist in the deployment of their Y2K strategies and communications, and helped them assess their readiness and understanding of the diverse range of Y2K issues they might encounter.

FIGURE 12-9 Sample résumé for an enterprise resource planning consultant

Catholic Healthcare, West Phoenix, AZ
SAP Configuration/Interface Design   6/1998 – 10/1998

Responsible for configuring the procurement portion of the MM module, designing the procurement processes, and writing business activity scripts that were later used to 1) configure the SAP system, 2) develop training materials, 3) develop user documentation, and 4) develop technical and user procedures. This was an ASAP implementation involving the centralized shared business services for 48 hospitals in three Western states. Responsible for designing the EDI and other interfaces to SAP, and instructing the development teams responsible for coding the interfaces when the designs required changes to either SAP, EDI, or other client or vendor systems.

Lucent Technologies, Dallas, TX
SAP-Siebel Consultant   4/1997 – 6/1998

Siebel data construction and verification. In this implementation, Siebel was used as a sales force automation tool in conjunction with SAP. Assisted the SAP development team in verifying that the Lucent product information was correctly recorded and presented in Siebel, and assisted in developing strategies to perfect the data collection and transmission processes.

IBM Corporation, Poughkeepsie, NY
SAP Consultant   11/1996 – 4/1997

Designed, developed, and tested the MM training materials. Assisted in rolling out SAP R/3 to 2,800 users worldwide. In this phased implementation, the materials were designed as instructor-led, and later to be used as both self-study and reference material. Assisted in the design of the Lotus Notes database that contained the materials and were used to deploy them globally.

Qube, New York, NY
QA Consultant   12/1994 – 11/1996

Assisted three companies in obtaining their ISO 9000 certification, setting up their quality systems, conducting internal audits, and managing the registration process.

EDUCATION

University of Arizona, Tucson, Arizona   1986
Master's Degree in Corporate Policy
University of Arizona, Tucson, Arizona   1981
Bachelor's Degree in Business Administration

FIGURE 12-9   Continued

Helpdesk Analyst

Job Description

Provides support to end-users on a variety of issues. First line of support for a company or a product, usually through phone, email, or chat communication. Identifies, researches, and resolves technical problems, either software or hardware related. Tracks and monitors the problem to ensure a timely resolution. Issues that cannot be solved are escalated to other staff or support personnel. In these situations the analyst is the liaison between non-technical users and highly technical IS professionals. Depending on the size of the company, may have dual roles as the PC technician and/or the telecommunications specialist. Hours may vary as many helpdesks provide service beyond the 9 to 5 workday (even 24 hours a day).

Qualifications

Generally include a working knowledge of commonly used applications, operating systems, and hardware configurations. May also require specialized knowledge of specific hardware or software packages. Personal skills, such as communication and customer service skills, necessary to work directly with people consistently throughout the day. May require an associate's degree in a related area and up to two years of experience in the field or in a related area. Often the starting point for IT professionals.

Related Certifications

- ▶ CompTIA A+, Network+, and iNet+
- ▶ Oracle8 Database Operator (DBO)
- ▶ Microsoft Certified Professional (MCP), Microsoft Office User Specialist (MOUS)
- ▶ Certified Novell Administrator (CNA)

  Figure 12-10 is an example of a résumé for a helpdesk analyst position.

Helpdesk Manager

Job Description

Oversees the operations of the helpdesk and is held accountable for the performance and productivity of the helpdesk, including timely issue resolution and customer satisfaction. Effectively manages and trains staff, creates schedules, hires new employees, and tracks and reports on helpdesk activity. Analyzes issues reported, determines escalation procedures, routes issues appropriately and recommends improvements. Participates in management roles through attending and scheduling meetings, and creating budgets. Since many helpdesks are staffed 24 hours a day, may be expected to have a flexible schedule and be on call to react to issues.

Qualifications

Requires excellent communication, presentation, and management skills, as well as attention to detail, respect for customer service, and ability to work in a high-stress environment. Must be able to manage people, projects, and technical resources. Knowledge and proficiency in the company's toolset required, which may include specific networks, servers, operating systems, and applications. Previous experience as a helpdesk analyst often required, along with knowledge of call tracking software. May require a bachelor's degree in a related area, such as computer science or management of information systems, and at least two or more years experience in the field or related area. Certifications and related experience can substitute for degree in the field.

Related Certifications

▶ CompTIA A+, Network+, and iNet+

▶ Oracle8 Database Operator (DBO)

▶ Microsoft Certified Professional (MCP)

▶ Microsoft Office User Specialist (MOUS)

▶ Other certifications depending on type of support and company's unique requirements.

Figure 12-11 is an example of a résumé for a helpdesk management position.

Independent Consultant

Job Description

One of the most highly paid employment options. Typically is an expert in a particular field. Has worked in this area of technology for at least five to seven years and chooses to concentrate on expertise by working with a number of clients. The most popular consultant fields are:

▶ E-commerce

▶ Enterprise Resource Planning (SAP, PeopleSoft, BAAN)

▶ Development (in a specific industry)

▶ Security

▶ Directory services planning

▶ Needs analysis

Qualifications

Must be highly disciplined. Must be a self-directed worker and must also motivate the customer and drive their projects to completion. Should be highly skilled in assessing political situations and recognizing true needs of an organization. Must be a great self-promoter since that's the only way projects will continue to stream in. Must possess good business acumen to ensure a profitable business. Certifications are important and credentials should be outstanding. If possible, should include work experience at a major software/hardware vendor or integration company.

Related Certifications

Certifications build credibility. Exactly which certification depends on area of specialty. Aim to have the highest-level certification available. PMI's Project Management Professional (PMP) always a plus.

Figure 12-12 is an example of a résumé for an independent consultant.

IT Management: CIO/CTO

Job Description

CIO (CHIEF INFORMATION OFFICER)   Executive officer in charge of an organization's information processing and information systems. Responsible for aligning an organization's technology deployment strategy with its business strategy. Contributes to general business planning regarding technology and systems required to maintain company operations and competitiveness. Recognizes new developments in information systems technology and anticipates organizational modifications. Establishes long-term needs for information systems, and plans strategy for developing systems and acquiring hardware to meet application needs. Ensures confidentiality and reliability of corporate data, proprietary information, and intellectual property. Generally manages middle managers and directors. May report to the chief operating officer in large corporations and the chief executive officer in medium-sized organizations.

CTO (CHIEF TECHNOLOGY OFFICER)   Responsible for the technology underpinning the company's business. More often aligned with the consumer or customer of the company's services and products. Focused outward to solve challenges and create value to the company. The primary officer looking for solutions and opportunities outside the company; compared to the CIO, the primary officer handling the internal technology needs for the company.

Qualifications

CIO AND CTO   Important to have sharp business acumen, to interpret business requirements as well as information systems requirements. Both positions rely on seasoned IT veterans with solid management experience. Must have experience and judgment to plan and accomplish goals. Typically require an MIS degree and ten or more years of experience. Master's degree highly desirable, especially M.B.A.

Related Certifications

Typically, candidates for these positions are not required to have up-to-date certifications.

Figure 12-13 is an example of a résumé in the area of IT management.

Brian McMahon

156 Centennial Park Way, La Jolla, NM 09882, (555) 226-4977

bjmcmahon@email.com

KEY QUALIFICATIONS

- Qualified **Helpdesk Analyst** with extensive knowledge of Windows 95/98/NT/2000, multiple software applications, and hardware repair.
- Proven troubleshooting and research skills for developing successful solutions to users' problems, as well as ability to write effective documentation of technical procedures.
- Excellent customer service skills with proven effectiveness in organization and communication. Interpersonal skills, self-motivation, and quick adaptation to new applications and technologies.

TECHNICAL SKILLS

Operating Systems: Windows 95/98/NT/2000, Mac OS 8/OS 9.

Applications: MS Office 97/00, Microsoft Project, Visio, Norton and McAfee virus software, pcAnywhere, Internet Explorer, and Netscape Navigator.

Technical Knowledge: Command Line Prompt, Windows 9x, and Windows 2000 for installing, configuring, upgrading, troubleshooting, and repairing microcomputer systems; partitioning and formatting hard drives; and hardware maintenance relating to PC terminals, printers, modems, and other components.

Additional: Project management expertise and demonstrated troubleshooting abilities.

CERTIFICATION

CompTIA A+ Certification

RELATED COURSES

A+ Certification – Core Hardware

A+ Certification – Operating Systems

EXPERIENCE

Office Specialist, OfficeMax, Jan. 1998 – present

- Set up a network to connect three PCs and a central printer to facilitate communication and reduce hardware expenses.
- Established a computerized inventory tracking system to ensure accurate account of items and reduce expenditure of unnecessary overhead.
- Technical writing of detailed instructions for using the new digital inventory tracking system to increase user adaptability and train employees.
- Provide exceptional customer service to hundreds of clients daily, assisting with solving problems and providing expedient solutions to meet their needs.

EDUCATION

B.A., Graphic Design, Coastal College, 1998

FIGURE 12-10 Sample résumé for a helpdesk analyst

Elizabeth Carroll

2121 12th St. SE, Wilmington, DE 44201, (555) 416-7362
ecarroll@computer.com

KEY QUALIFICATIONS

- 2+ years experience in helpdesk support, providing exceptional customer service to more than 100,000 users across the country.
- Management experience as Technical Lead for the helpdesk team, conducting training and support to improve productivity, quality and performance of the company.
- Additional experience with networking, configuring LAN/WAN environments and workstations. Intricate knowledge of Windows, Macintosh and Unix/Linux operating systems.
- Effective communicator with strong leadership abilities and demonstrated troubleshooting skills with demand for expedient and high quality customer service.

TECHNICAL SKILLS

Operating Systems
Windows 95/98/NT/2000, Macintosh OS 9/OS 10, Unix, Linux.

Applications
Heat call-tracking software, Visio, Crystal Reports, Terminal Server, Visual Intercept, Norton Antivirus, pcAnywhere, Lotus Notes, Microsoft Office 97/2000, Microsoft Project.

Databases
SQL Server 2000, Oracle 8, Access 97/2000.

Technical Knowledge
Networking skills, such as LAN/WAN and TCP/IP. Expertise in computer workstation setups, including installing applications, modems, and printers, troubleshooting client configurations and hardware maintenance.

EXPERIENCE

Helpdesk Technical Lead, EarthLinx, June 1999 – present

- Manage and train a team of eight helpdesk analysts to provide first and second level support to more than 100,000 end-users, explaining complex technical concepts and striving for first call resolution on every incident.
- Troubleshoot, analyze, research, and diagnose Internet connectivity problems and cable modem/DSL line difficulties for clients, to produce quick response time to user issues.
- Implemented and configured Heat call-tracking tool to increase productivity of staff and provide validated solutions in a shorter amount of time, reducing call time by more than 50 percent.
- Document incoming calls to create procedural information as a best-practice troubleshooting guide for first level support, which is used in ongoing training.

EDUCATION

B.S., Computer Information Systems, Rhode Island State, 1998

FIGURE 12-11 Sample résumé for a helpdesk manager

Peter Sholms
Security Consultant
1999 Ocean Blvd.
Corona del Mar, CA 92625

949-555-1212
peter@sholms.com

Peter has 12 years experience working as an independent consultant to Fortune 500 organizations and big house consulting firms. His experience ranges from building best practice methodologies for large scale application deployment to performing security audits to ensure network integrity. Peter backs his consulting experience with an MBA from Wharton Business School and an undergraduate degree from Brown College.

Capabilities

- Overseeing and coordinating efforts across companies to identify key corporate security initiatives and standards regarding virus protection, security monitoring, intrusion detection, access control to facilities, and remote access policies.
- Identifying protection goals and objectives consistent with corporate strategic plan.
- Identifying key security program elements.
- Managing development and implementation of global security policy, standards, guidelines, and procedures to ensure ongoing maintenance of security.
- Assisting with the investigation of security breaches and assist with disciplinary and legal matters associated with such breaches as necessary.
- Coordinating implementation plans, security product purchase proposals, and project schedules.
- Overseeing the establishment, implementation and adherence to policies and procedures that guide and support the provision of information security services.
- Conducting risk assessments and risk analysis to help the organization develop security standards and procedures that support strategic, tactical, and operational objectives on a cost-effective basis.
- Recommending appropriate personnel, physical, and technical security controls.
- Developing and delivering information security seminars and training classes.
- Coordinating the communication of information security awareness to all members of the organization.
- Certifying IT systems meet predetermined security requirements.
- Working with vendors, IT associates, and user departments to enhance information security.

References

- Accenture Consulting (Previously Arthur Anderson)
- KPMG
- Exodus Communications

FIGURE 12-12 Sample résumé for an independent consultant

Thomas Banks
2343 High Road
Catonsville, MD 23433

(410) 455-5678
tbanks@aol.com

Summary of Qualifications

- Innovative and dynamic Director of IS with 13 years of diversified IT experience including applications development, network architecture and operations, security, voice/data communications, and EDI processes.
- Responsible for an IS operations team of 20 with a $10 million operating budget.
- Direct oversight of computer operations, technical services, and development departments to support a 24 x 7 business environment.
- Responsible for proper capacity and disaster recovery planning as well as all data and network security.
- Proven success in solution providing, project management, systems analysis, designing, development, pre-sales technical support, implementation and post-implementation support and maintenance.
- Customer focused, with excellent communication and interpersonal skills.

Experience

Director of IS   11/1998–Present
Data Processing Institute, Baltimore, MD

- Outsourcing systems consulting company supporting client network infrastructure, voice communications, security management, email, VPNs, and web sites. Serviced 50 clients with typical installations of 200–500 distributed users. Services provided included:
  - Hosting and maintenance of global web sites
  - Intranet and VPN installations to support partners and remote users
  - MS Exchange email services supporting corporate and remote users
  - Network security (Checkpoint firewall/VPN)
  - Ecommerce transactional capabilities
- Managed procurement and lease programs for all desktops, laptops, servers, and networking equipment (Dell, GE Capital, Cisco) on behalf of all clients in order and leveraged aggregate buying power for deeper discounts.
- Managed 18 full-time staff members, an outsourced helpdesk, in-house and consultant development groups to support a 24 x 7 operations environment.
- Responsible for business recovery and capacity planning for internal and client systems and networks.

IT Manager, Development Services   8/1997–10/1998
Blue Streak Utility Services Inc., Baltimore, MD

- Managed outsourced development team, created new team, and brought development services in-house for overall cost savings and increased productivity.
- Assisted in logical application development and systems architecture of online energy management and profiling service.
- Managed all Internet-based systems and equipment including web, email, ftp, application, SQL, ColdFusion, SMS servers, and all routers, switches, and redundant connectivity.
- Designed and implemented corporate network/intranet and satellite office connectivity and integration of technologies across companies that were acquired.

FIGURE 12-13 Sample résumé for an IT manager, specifically CIO/CTO

QA Consultant   1/1997–7/1997
JetStream Technologies Inc., Jersey City, NJ

- Developed the test plan and test script to allow the QA department to validate a new market data interface (DEC Alpha, HP Unix).

Director of Development   6/1990–12/1996
Dow Jones Markets, New York, NY

- Member of a cross-functional team (12 people) set up to assist a strategic partner (JetStream Technologies Inc.) develop and deploy a new automated order match and trading system.
- Responsible for development, operations, and networking interfaces between JetStream and Dow Jones' systems (ActiveX, Java, CORBA, TCP/IP, NT 4.0, Web Server, Lotus Notes).

Education

B.S., Computer Science, University of Maryland, Baltimore, MD   1988
Minors: Math and Business

FIGURE 12-13 Continued

LAN Support Technician

Job Description

Supports, monitors, tests, and troubleshoots hardware and software problems pertaining to LAN. Provides end-user support for all LAN-based applications, recommends and schedules repairs, and installs and configures workstations. May install file servers, backup systems, maintain LAN security, manage user accounts, document problems and resolutions, and provide assistance to first level support. Depending on the size of the company, may also maintain vendor contact for maintenance and new products, as well as evaluate and recommend hardware/software products and services.

Qualifications

Must have knowledge of the network, workstations, operating systems, software, hardware, and servers unique to the organization. Additionally, must understand browsers, email systems, virus software and Internet connectivity. Knowledge of workflow tracking software and TCP/IP a plus. Must possess ability to research and analyze problems independently, and have excellent communication and customer service skills. May require an associate's or bachelor's degree in a related area and up to three years of experience in the field or in a related area.

Related Certifications

- ▶ CompTIA A+, Network+, and iNet+
- ▶ Microsoft Certified Professional (MCP)
- ▶ Microsoft Certified Systems Engineer (MCSE)

Figure 12-14 is an example of a résumé in the area of LAN support.

Network Administrator

Job Description

Installs, configures, and maintains the network for an organization. Performs general system maintenance, applies software updates and fixes, attends to network-related PC support issues, and performs backups. Troubleshoots network problems to develop solutions, documents the systems, and evaluates new solutions. May work independently and jointly with other staff members through meetings and second-level support for desktop personnel and helpdesk analysts.

Qualifications

Depending on the type of network used by the organization, may be required to have knowledge of Microsoft, Novell, or Unix/Linux systems. Requirements may include a bachelor's degree in a related area or appropriate certifications, and up to two years of experience in the field or in a related area.

Related Certifications

- ▶ Microsoft Certified Systems Engineer (MCSE), Certified Professional (MCP)
- ▶ Cisco Certified Network Associate (CCNA)
- ▶ CompTIA Network+, iNet+, Linux+
- ▶ Certified Novell Administrator (CNA), Engineer (CNE), Master Engineer (MCNE)
- ▶ Linux Certified Administrator (LCA), Engineer (LCE), Master Engineer (MLCE)
- ▶ Red Hat Certified Engineer (RHCE)
- ▶ Sun Certified System Administrator/Network Administrator

Figures 12-15 through 12-18 are examples of résumés for jobs in the area of network administration.

Blaine Voightman
CCNA, MCSE, Network+
17 Cedar Place, Apt. 2B ~ Santa Monica, CA 90210 ~ (310) 555-4141
blainev@computer.com

KEY QUALIFICATIONS

- **LAN Administrator** with experience in large-scale enterprise network design, deployment, security, and administration fields.
- Extensive troubleshooting and administration skills on IP networks, routers, and switches. In-depth knowledge of TCP/IP, IPX/SPX, and AppleTalk protocol suites and common WAN/LAN (leased line, FR, ATM) technology.
- Proven diagnosing abilities with attention to detail and ability to work effectively in a fast-paced environment.
- Bachelor's degree in computer science and CCNA, MCSE, and Network+ certified.

EXPERIENCE

LAN Administrator, *OneScape Inc.*, Jan. 2000 – present
Troubleshooting and resolving operational issues of LAN/WAN Internet/intranet remote access; enabling system backup and recovery while maintaining system security.

- Assisted telecommunication project manager in designing the WAN/LAN network and phone system structure, comprised of two Cisco 7507 core routers, two Cisco 6509 core switches and 20+ Cisco 5509 site switches, and a Nortel Opt 81c PABX with 2000 phone lines installed.
- Contract implementation and administration, management, and support of servers, networks, and workstations at the operating system level.
- Monitoring network and server activity for performance and reliability, and working with the networking team to develop viable solutions and long-term resolutions.
- Managing the installation, configuration, and networking of system devices, operating systems software and applications throughout the network.
- Migrated PCs from Windows 95 to Windows NT 4.0, including organizing and implementing staff training to increase user adaptability.

Helpdesk Technician, *OneScape Inc.*, April 1998 – Jan. 2000

- Maintaining enterprise Exchange mail server, providing reliable email service to more than 2,000 employees.
- Provide first-level hardware, software, and network support to more than 2,000 end-users, providing expedient resolutions with total customer satisfaction in mind.
- Assisted LAN technician with shifting users information stored from one server to another when transitions occurred.

COMPUTER SKILLS

LAN/WAN, Linux/Unix, Sun Solaris, Cisco router/switch/access server, Internet, intranet service, Windows 95/98/NT/2000, SAS, MS Exchange Admin, RACF, TCP/IP, IPX/SPX and AppleTalk protocol, ATM, Microsoft Office Suite 97/2000.

CERTIFICATIONS

CCNA, MCSE, Network+.

EDUCATION

B.S., Computer Information Systems, University of Missouri, 1998.

FIGURE 12-14 Sample résumé for a LAN support technician

Shelly Cooper
MCSE/ MCP/A+/MOUS
3829 Beach Ave. ~ Huntington Beach, CA 92707 ~ (714) 715-2014
cooper@xemail.com

KEY QUALIFICATIONS

- 3+ years networking experience with advanced technical support experience with Windows 95/98, NT Workstation and Server, and Unix. Expert in cable modem and xDSL technologies.
- Effective network troubleshooting and software fault isolation skills.
- In-depth knowledge of product rollout and implementation strategy of proprietary software, delivered to more than 200 franchise locations.
- Strong interpersonal, communication, and project management skills while working in a fast-paced environment, with an assertive, productive, and self-starter attitude.

EXPERIENCE

Desktop Support Technician, Weiss Technologies, Jan. 2000 – present

- Configuration, installation, and maintenance of more than 100 end-user workstations, IBM-based PC clients and servers, including new hardware and software components, rebuilds, and design.
- Monitoring and maintenance of hardware (including servers, UPS, A/C unit), as well as strategizing the enterprise type backup solutions.
- Extensive knowledge and experience in local and wide area networking, communications and related hardware/software (bridges, routers, hubs).
- Review and monitor security policies, approve external WAN connections, oversee Internet protocols (TCP/IP), firewall management, intrusion detection, new routing requests, and conduct audits.
- Provide second-level support for ARCServe, antivirus, firewall, SQL, Unix, HBOC software, term servers, routers, cabling, hardware installation and configuration, and end-user support and training.

Helpdesk Analyst, *Tri-Cities Corporation*, Nov. 1998 – Jan. 2000

- Implemented ticket tracking system through Remedy to improve quality of customer service for customers and employees.
- Worked with a team of developers to modify proprietary software to increase productivity, time efficiency, and technological advancement for the users.
- Supported end-users in more than 200 locations worldwide through phone and email correspondence with primary focus on customer service.
- Quality assurance testing of web-based applications for development department to assist with conversions and guarantee successful transitions.

TECHNICAL SKILLS

Windows NT Server/Workstation and 2000 Professional/Server, Novell 4.11/5.0, Exchange Server 5.x, IIS Proxy Server 2.0, TCP/IP, MS-DOS, RIP, FTP, DNS, HTTP, ATM Fast Ethernet Frame Relay, SONET, firewall configuration/administration, LAN/WAN, Red Hat Linux 6.0, Mandrake Linux 7.x, 3Com network hardware, Office 9x, Office 2000.

CERTIFICATIONS	MCSE, MCP, A+, and MOUS
EDUCATION	**B.S.**, Mathematics, University of Washington, 1996

FIGURE 12-15 Sample résumé for a network administrator with expertise in Microsoft

Megan Welsh, CNA

905 Lilac Ave. ~ Marina Del Rey, CA 90210 ~ (443) 226-4977
Megan_Welsh@emails.com

KEY QUALIFICATIONS

- **Novell Network Administrator** with extensive experience and education in networking, specifically Novell 4.11/5.0 and Windows 95/98/NT/2000.
- Expertise in troubleshooting and implementing solutions specific to the users' needs.
- Additional skills in business communications, time management, and strategic project management.

COMPUTER SKILLS

Networking Skills

Novell 4.11/5.0, Windows NT 4.0 Server/Workstation, Windows 2000 Server/Professional. Planning, installation and configuration, perform system upgrades, improve network printing performance. Manage network databases, LAN administration, DHCP, DNS, subnets. TCP/IP protocol family and network security, administration and setup of WWW, FTP, e-mail, DNS, DHCP, SNMP, remote access, and virtual services hosting.

Operating Systems

Expertise in installing, troubleshooting, configuring, and updating: Novell 4.11/5.0, Windows 95/98/NT/2000, Linux, MS DOS.

Applications

Microsoft Office 97/00, Lotus Notes, Crystal Reports, Microsoft Project, Norton Antivirus.

EDUCATION

Bachelor of Science, *Computer Science*, May 2001, Cum Laude.

RELATED COURSES

- Novell NetWare: User and Group Account Management, Login Scripts, File and Folder Management, Installation.
- Windows NT 4.0 Server: Workgroup and Domain Management, User and Group Accounts, Installation.
- Windows 2000: Active Directory Services, NTFS Permissions.

EXPERIENCE

Network Administration Intern, *TransMatics Systems Inc.*, 2/2001 – Present

- Network cabling, testing of subnets, IP addressing, configuring HP printers, hardware testing, and building systems specific to users' needs.
- Knowledgeable of several OS: Novell NetWare, Windows 95/98/NT and 2000.
- Software and hardware upgrades and troubleshooting, including Outlook 2000, Windows 2000, and Microsoft Office Suite.
- Assisting in monitoring system availability, batch production, system backups, system hardware maintenance and report distribution.

CERTIFICATIONS

Certified Novell Administrator (CNA) Certification in progress.

FIGURE 12-16   Sample résumé for a network administrator with expertise in Novell

Scott Clausson
Linux+/CCNA/Network+/Sun Certified
1915 Battery Ave. ~ Baltimore, MD 21404 ~ (701) 383-5471
Scott_Clausson@baltimore.com

KEY QUALIFICATIONS

- 2+ years experience in Unix (Solaris, Linux, OpenBSD, FreeBSD) administration, setup, and securing.
- Extensive knowledge of firewall setup and administration, NAT, VPN, bandwidth management, and quality of service.
- Expertise in networking concepts, TCP/IP protocol family and network security, as well as PC and Sun hardware.

EXPERIENCE

Assistant Unix Administrator, *University of New Hampshire*, 12/2000 – present

- Administration of Digital Alpha 4100 clustered servers, including backup administration on Unix and Windows NT using Seagate backup exec at DLT and IBM tapes.
- Configuration and troubleshooting problems with 3600 routers, Xylan switches, including upgrade of IOS; running debugs to troubleshoot connectivity problems.
- Assist in defining and implementing campus-wide ATM data network backbone.
- Maintenance of the campus network cable infrastructure, including single, multi-mode fiber and category 5 copper cabling (22 campus buildings with approximately 2,000 Category 5 drops).
- Assist in ISP migration project, including campus-wide IP numbering scheme redesign and conversion.
- Expansion of existing network, including establishing security on network, creating users and granting security rights, establishing interdepartmental and lab-specific file and printer sharing.
- Provide support to user community, including hardware and software installation and troubleshooting, network troubleshooting and analysis using Sniffer and SNMP alarm manager. Implementation and installation of Windows 95/NT Workstation project.

COMPUTER SKILLS

- **Operating Systems:** Unix, Linux 6.0 (Red Hat), Windows 95/98/2000, NT Server and Workstation, Novell 4x/5x, Solaris.
- **Software:** Symark Power Broker 2.5, Veritas NetBackup, Exceed, Citrix, Visio2000, MS Office 97/2000, Norton Utilities, ARC Serve IT, Seagate Backup Exec.
- **Hardware:** Sun Hardware, Ultra stations, AS5000, Cisco routers, Xylan switches, 3Com and HP Ethernet hubs, APC UPS, Intel and 3Com network adapters, HP DeskJet printers, Digital Alpha 41xx servers, IBM PC servers, HP PC servers, IBM PC-Compatibles.
- **Other Technical Skills:** C, C++, Basic, TCP/IP, VPN, NAT, QOS, WAN, WWW, FTP, e-mail, DNS, DHCP, SNMP, Web server (Apache 1.2.*/1.3.*), LAN/WAN planning, installation and upgrading, CheckPoint Firewall-1.

CERTIFICATIONS

Linux+, Sun Certified Systems Administrator, CCNA, Network+

ADDITIONAL TRAINING

- Checkpoint VPN-1/Firewall-1 Management I & II
- Completed a ten-week intensive program in advanced system Unix administrator Sun Solaris 2.7, including topics such as administration, NFS, NIS, DNS, installation, and troubleshooting

FIGURE 12-17 Sample résumé for a network administrator with expertise in Unix/Linux

Scott German, MCSE

119 N. 12th St. ~ Guelph, MI 58447 ~ (701) 522-8591
sgerman@dtel.com

Network Engineer with experience in design, implementation, and support for Ethernet and AppleTalk local and wide area networks. Additional experience includes purchasing, planning, and cost control. Background includes administration of Unix, PC, and Macintosh operating systems and software. Interpersonal skills with excellent problem solving skills.

TECHNICAL SKILLS

Operating Systems
Windows NT Server 4.0, Windows NT Workstation 4.0, Windows 95/98, DOS, Novell 3.12/4.11, SCO Unix 5.0.5, Novell 4.11.

Applications
SQL Server 7.0, GoldMine 4.0, MS Office 97/00, Unidata, Richter, Support Magic 3.31, Lotus Notes 4.6, Norton Antivirus.

Technical Knowledge
DHCP, routers, switches, PBX, POP3, TCP/IP, NetBIOS, NetBEUI, SNMP, and other networking protocols, HTML.

EXPERIENCE

Systems Administrator, Rufael Enterprise Inc., May 99 – present

- SCO Unix Administrator for 47 remote servers.
- Performed regular maintenance via modem and dedicated lines: created users, reset passwords, reset ports, tape backups, and restores.
- Installed and configured hardware, including hard drives (SCSI and EIDE), tape drives, digi boards, muxes, printers, and network adapters.
- Identified LAN/WAN problems covering 60 leased lines (56K frame relay), CSU/DSU, modems (async and sync), Multimux, and dial-up servers.
- Built many servers, including IBM and Compaq. Installed and configured software and operating systems; SCO Unix 5.0.0, Unidata.
- Purchased all PCs and equipment, reducing the cost allocated for equipment by 40 percent.
- Wrote backup scripts to save the company $15,000 in backup software.
- Database administrator for Support Magic, a SQL database used to log support calls and generate reports. Ran daily, monthly, and yearly statistical and graphical reports for the support desk, management, and budgeting, respectively.
- Resolved application conflicts through experience and a high level understanding of memory usage, DLL files, operating system deficiencies, and application limitations.

EDUCATION

Bachelor of Arts in Economics, Lafayette College of Detroit, 1996

Certification

MCSE (Microsoft Certified Systems Engineer)

FIGURE 12-18   Sample résumé for an experienced Microsoft network administrator

Network Engineer

Job Description

Installs, configures, and maintains organization's network, as well as builds networks, maintains external and internal Web presence, and administers networks. Performs system backups on internal and external Web network servers, designs and supports the server system(s), and supports software. Also performs regular network checkups and tests, and is called in when networks are slow or need professional care.

Qualifications

May need a bachelor's degree in a related area and two to four years of experience in the field or in a related area. Must be familiar with standard concepts, practices, and procedures within a particular field, depending on the network used within the organization. Will often manage a team of network administrators or engineers. If so, requires management skills, such as communication and project management.

Related Certifications

Depending on the type of network used within the organization, desired certifications can vary from Microsoft, Novell, Unix/Linux, Cisco, and others.

Figure 12-19 is an example of a résumé for a network engineer.

Programmer/Developer

Job Description

PROGRAMMER OR DEVELOPER Actually codes the software applications that run businesses. The complexity of the software piece a programmer gets to work on is dependent on knowledge level and experience. Typically, a programmer plans, develops, tests, and documents assignments. Performs routine assignments, which normally require following detailed specifications. Mid-sized to large organizations typically have their own internal development team to meet the demands of maintaining business software. Small organizations tend to outsource development projects to IT development companies that employ large staffs of developers and project managers. Programmers typically report to a software engineering manager.

Qualifications

PROGRAMMERS Typically have a bachelor's degree in computer science, math, or logic, for a solid foundation in programming, logic and flow diagrams, and testing and debugging. Should be proficient in at least two modern programming languages (Visual Basic, C++, Java, SQL). Should also have a solid foundation in database structures and SQL. Type of job hired for is directly related to amount of experience.

SENIOR-LEVEL DEVELOPER   Requires advanced technical knowledge in all areas of applications programming, system design, and update, storage, and retrieval methods. Usually requires at least two to four years programming experience.

Related Certifications

▶ Microsoft Certified Solution Developer (MCSD)

▶ Oracle Certified Professional (OCP) – Application Developer, Solution Developer

▶ IBM Certified Advanced Technical Expert – DB2 Universal Database

▶ Configuration Management II (CMII)

▶ Sybase Certified PowerBuilder Developer (CPD), SQL Developer

Figures 12-20 and 12-21 are examples of résumés in the area of programming.

Quality Assurance Specialist

Job Description

Performs testing to ensure proper functioning of software, programs, Web sites, or other technologies. Develops, publishes, and implements test plans, writes and maintains test automation, and develops quality assurance standards. Defines and tracks quality assurance metrics such as defect densities and open defect counts, and must monitor and troubleshoot area of responsibility, including researching technical issues and communicating potential risks. Accountable for final approval before launch or release. May work independently or with a QA team depending on the scope of the project.

Qualifications

Depending on the company, required to have specific knowledge of the applicable software, programs, or technologies being analyzed, developed, or supported. Working knowledge of quality assurance methodologies and excellent attention to detail necessary, along with skills and abilities in the areas of problem solving, communication (both written and oral), and project management. Often requires a bachelor's degree in a related area and/or two or more years experience in the field or related area. Certifications and related experience can substitute for degree in the field.

Related Certifications

▶ Dependant on the technology tested

▶ Project Management Professional (PMP)

▶ Certified Software Quality Analyst (CSQA), Software Test Engineer (CSTE), and SPICE Assessor (CSA) from the Quality Assurance Institute

Figure 12-22 is an example of a résumé for a quality assurance specialist.

Tigist Gebreye

1231 Black Hills Place ~ Raleigh, NC 98765 ~ (222) 650-1132
tigist_gebreye2@hotmail.com

SUMMARY OF QUALIFICATIONS

- Five years experience as a **Network Administrator** with a solid foundation in network resource planning, capacity planning, disaster recovery planning, and network optimization.
- Demonstrated leadership and project management skills as the team lead for upgrading a five-server, 1,000-user network from Windows NT Server to Windows 2000 with minimal business interruption and no data loss.
- Effective motivational and team building skills, serving as a mentor to junior network administrators. Escalation support for junior support staff.
- Manage procurement and leasing programs for all desktop, laptops, servers, and networking equipment. Superior oral and written communication skills.

TECHNICAL SKILLS

Networking: MS Windows 2000 Professional Server, MS NT 4.0, TCP/IP, Checkpoint, MS Exchange Server, Lotus Domino Server, ArcServe, Cheyenne and McAfee Antivirus

Software: Windows 95/98/NT/2000, MS Office, Acuity, MS Outlook, IE, Netscape

Hardware: Compaq servers, Cisco routers and switches

Certifications: MCSE NT 4.0, A+, Network+

EXPERIENCE

Tier III Network Operations Center Analyst, Crowd Pleaser, Inc.   2001–Present

- Primary person responsible for monitoring 300 Sun Solaris and NT servers' performance and reliability using HP OpenView.
- Managed network infrastructure upgrades.
- Researched, documented, and recommended centralized administration and security products.
- Ensured backup integrity using Omniback.
- Responsible for diagnosing problems on the server and assigning the proper support personnel to solve any problems.
- Evaluated new technologies for possible integration into the infrastructure.
- Developed policies and procedures for crisis management.

Server Team Lead, Sylvan Learn Corporation   2000–2001

- Managed the server team consisting of four network engineers supporting ten Windows 2000 servers, two MS Exchange servers, and a Lotus Domino server.
- Operated at a 99.8% SLA and interfaced with the LAN/WAN infrastructure and database teams to ensure 24 x 7 uptime.
- Led the project team to upgrade five Windows NT servers to Windows 2000.
- Developed the disaster recovery plan for the organization with the goal of restoring network connectivity within a four-hour time period.
- Ensured that backups were completed on a regular basis and ensured the integrity of the backups.
- Day-to-day operations included installing and upgrading software, security configuration, backups, network storage capacity planning, and performance tuning.
- Recognized for excellent customer service, Service Excellence Award, 2001

EDUCATION

B.S., Computer Science, University of Baltimore, Maryland, 1996

FIGURE 12-19 Sample résumé of a network engineer

Jan Blok
24 Gandhi Street
Newark, Delaware 55690
908-876-0990

jblok@hotmail.com

TECHNICAL SKILLS

10+ years development experience specializing in ASP, VB, Visual Interdev, COM+, SQL Server, ActiveX, XML, VBScript, Jscript, and IIS.

EXPERIENCE

NYInternet.net, Syracuse, NY   7/2000 – Present
Sr. Developer/Team Lead – VB/SQL Server

- Developed a CRM ASP application deployed in a server farm/cluster environment servicing 24,000 online concurrent users. Application was written in VB 6.0 and .NET platform and included over 600 ASP and XML style sheets, 400 COM+ and ActiveX components supporting search engines, client/server reporting engine, e-commerce and role-based security modules in SQL Server 2000.
- Engineered and implemented the SQL Server 2000 database, which consisted of 40 tables, 700 stored procedures, 200 views and triggers.
- Improved overall application performance by 40%, reducing the memory footprint by 33% over original specifications by applying object-oriented methodologies in the ASP and XML style sheets.

NC State Department of Children and Family, Charlotte, NC   10/1999 – 6/2000
Sr. Software Developer – Internet/Intranet

- Mentored a team of three programmers and two QA testers building a purchasing/requisition application built in ASP 3.0, ADO 2.5, XML, VBScript, JavaScript, and FrontPage 2000. Application was deployed on a web server farm supporting 31,000 concurrent users in the state of North Carolina. The environment used Visual SourceSafe as source control.
- Solved firewall deployment issues by developing a solution that used remote scripting over port 80 for page refreshing and user authentication.
- Built more than 30 ASP pages that encapsulated business logic in MTS package, resulting in faster transactions and an environment that was easier to debug and enhance.
- Wrote detailed business and technical use cases for stored procedures connecting business logic layer (BAL) to data access layer (DAL) using ADO and COM objects. Results included a significant improvement gain when working with sessions, error handlers, cookies, and caching within ASP, XML techniques, and coding.
- Utilized object-oriented design principles in more than 70 ASPs, which resulted in higher performance, improvements in speed, and easier code maintenance.

FIGURE 12-20   Sample résumé of a programmer specializing in client/server

Great Falls Hydro, Reno, Nevada   2/1998 – 10/1999
Senior Developer

- Led the redevelopment of an antiquated finance OO-application. Increased the team's productivity by utilizing proven implementation strategies and developing in VB 5.0, VBScript, ASP, Visual Interdev HTML, XML, and CSS.
- Wrote the technical specifications for data access layer and business logic layer.
- Successfully improved the performance of transactions by fine tuning ATL and ADO components by up to 800% and significantly reduced the load time by using load balancing techniques.

Bank of America, San Francisco, CA   2/1996 – 2/1998
Senior Developer

- Designed and built complete object-oriented, two-tier intelligent database system for DBRS in VB 5.0 and MS Access 97, utilizing Rational Rose and Visual Modeling. Migrated the company's historical database to advanced Crystal Reports.
- Part of a 12-member team that remodeled several financial applications including a life insurance app, a life/auto insurance app, and a bond rating app using a three-tier client/server architecture deployed on SQL Server and Oracle 7.3. Used VB 5.0, MTS Transaction Server, ADO, ODBC, VBScript, Win32 API, COM/DCOM, ODBC data extraction, and DAO.
- Provided centralized data warehousing on NT SQL Server using stored procedures to increase application's performance.

EDUCATION

Seton Hall University, NJ   12/1991
   B.S., Computer Science

FIGURE 12-20 Continued

Peter Bussjeager
7677 Highlandtown Road
San Clemente, CA 45676
756-989-0087
pbussjeager@yahoo.com

TECHNICAL SKILLS

VB 6.0, ActiveX, COM, COM+, MTS, Java, C, C++, Perl, SQL Server 7.0, SourceSafe, and Windows NT

EXPERIENCE

Fast Track Enterprises, Santa Ana, CA
Technical Programmer/Technical Lead   1/2000 – 5/2001

- Technical Lead role in the continued development and enhancement of the company product, Vantax. Design and development of code to enhance and support new and evolving functional and architectural specifications. Software development using Microsoft Visual Basic 6.0, COM, COM+, ActiveX, Microsoft Transaction Server, and SQL Server 7.0.

- Mentored and supervised new employees and co-op students. Provided leadership, facilitation, and performance evaluations. Delivered presentations and conducted business meetings regularly.

- Database administration supporting in-house, multi-phased development pipeline using Microsoft Transaction Server and Microsoft SQL Server 7.0 supporting ten software developers and business analysts.

- Management, administration, and maintenance of four LANs running Windows NT Server and Windows 2000 Professional.

High Top Systems Consultants Inc., Los Angeles, CA
Software Developer/Helpdesk Technician   7/1998 – 10/1999

- Software Developer for large government finance project. Coded business and interface objects using Microsoft Visual Basic 6.0, ActiveX, COM, SQL Server 7.0, and Oracle. Member of the technical architecture team and the data conversion team.

- Operated a helpdesk in support of 80 employees. Responsibilities included NT Server administration and maintenance, PC troubleshooting and maintenance, telephone and on-site user support, and troubleshooting PC software problems.

EDUCATION

Golden West College, Los Angeles, CA   2000
B.S., Computer Science

FIGURE 12-21   Sample résumé of a programmer specializing in Microsoft technologies

Ryan Thorpe

9778 106th Ave. SE, Oakes, ND 58474, (701) 783-4382
ryan_thorpe@abccompany.com

KEY QUALIFICATIONS

- **Quality Assurance Specialist** with solid academic and experienced background in information systems and the application of IT to business solutions.
- Additional experience includes data warehousing and disaster recovery, as well as thorough knowledge of hardware, including PC assembly.
- Special interests in manual or automated software testing, client/server applications, testing Web-based applications and security testing.
- Possess exceptional leadership, analytical, interpersonal, and communication skills.

EXPERIENCE

Quality Assurance Specialist, *ABC Company*, June 1999 – present

- Write test scripts and conduct QA to diagnose logical work of servers, databases, and network, studying behavior of bandwidth. Developed test plans and test cases for analytical investigations of problems, using special and traditional software and hardware diagnostic tools.
- Test embedded web page objects such as COM objects (Active X, OCX), Java applets on client side, and Java scripts, VBScripts, and Active Server Pages on server side.
- Full testing of many features, including GUI, billing system, work orders, attachments, address book, 3CX mail accounts (signing up, password security, sending and receiving mail/video mail, reply, and so on).
- Use business requirement, system requirement, process, and data flow in test plan formulation to determine expected results and test cases.
- Analyze trends and holes in the usage of new products and services using MS Excel, MS Access, and SQL.
- Recover missing CDRs/holes using Unix (HP/SRV4). Impact analysis of changes that may affect production applications.
- Understand technical issues and the implications on the business and communicate them with other operating departments within the business.

TECHNICAL SKILLS

- **Programming:** Java, C/C++, Perl, Visual Basic, HTML, XML, ASP, JSP.
- **Operating Systems:** Windows 95/98/ME/NT/2000, Linux/Unix, Mac OS, MS DOS.
- **Networks:** Windows NT Server/Workstation, Windows 2000 Professional/Server. Maintain Ethernet network and computers at a small business and at home.
- **Applications:** Microsoft Office 97/2000, Visual C++ 6.0, Symantec Visual Café, Adobe Photoshop.

EDUCATION

Bachelor of Science, Computer Science, Ohio State University, 1998

RELATED COURSES

- D1-9000 Quality System
- Data and Computer Communications
- UML (Unified Modeling Language)
- Advanced C/C++ and Java Programming

FIGURE 12-22 Sample résumé of a quality assurance specialist

Sales: Technical Sales Representative

Job Description

TECHNICAL SALES REPRESENTATIVE (CHANNEL SALES, OEM SALES, DIRECT SALES, INSIDE SALES, FIELD SALES, ACCOUNT EXECUTIVE)   Responsible for selling IT solutions to customers. IT solutions range from single software packages the customer can install themselves to integrated - solutions that require considerable planning, development, and deployment resources. Positions readily available because of the number of software/hardware vendors and solutions providers.

Inside Sales   Cold-calls potential customers from purchased databases. Should have exceptional phone skills to build an easy rapport with customers without having to personally meet them. Often makes the initial customer contact and qualifies the prospect to turn the lead over to the field sales person.

Field Sales   Located throughout a region and meets with customers in person. Provides customer presentations and demonstrations and works with the customer in performing a needs analysis. Relies on inside sales personnel to help support a customer or potential customer.

Qualifications

TECHNICAL SALES REPRESENTATIVE   Though not a requirement, should have some experience with technology. Should be comfortable operating a PC, including working with remote software since office will most likely be at home. Should understand sales cycles, performing needs analysis, follow-up techniques, and the basics of solution selling. Should be personable and genuinely enjoy working with people.

Related Certifications

TECHNICAL SALES REPRESENTATIVE   Certifications may not be needed or even expected. Product understanding and familiarity more important.

▶ Microsoft Certified Sales Person

Figure 12-23 is an example of a résumé in the area of technical sales.

Stephanie Remos
23 Elm Street
San Diego, CA 92020

sremos@yahoo.com
765-908-8877

Profile

- 25 years sales and marketing experience in IT, real estate, life insurance, and mutual funds
- 18+ year veteran of IT training in sales, marketing, management, strategic business development
- Client prospecting, qualification, closing and account planning in mid to large companies
- Call center management, conference and networking events planning and production
- Implementation, design and launching of new products and programs
- Communication and rapport building with clients and co-workers

Work History

Program Director   **2/2001–6/2001**
Strategies for Success 2001 Conference, ITTA

Responsible for securing the sponsors for this event, designing the program, securing the speakers and achieving the participant quota for the conference.

Call Center Consultant   **5/2000–1/2001**
Productivity Point International, San Francisco, CA

Provided fast, time-effective outbound call center solutions and management for the San Francisco regions. Delivered certification seminars in California resulting in increased revenue for technical training passports.

Marketing Consultant   **3/1999–4/2000**
New Horizons Computer Learning Centers, Santa Ana, CA

Responsible for the design, implementation, and launch of the New Horizons "Certified Training Program." Facilitated training for the 200 franchises as well as developed the marketing kits that included direct mail programs, media and press releases, and sales.

Regional Channel Manager, Western Region   **7/1998–2/1999**
Sylvan Prometric, Baltimore, MD

Drove IT computer-based testing delivery through 30 Authorized Prometric Testing Centers in the western region. Worked with partners on innovative ways of driving testing revenues, negotiated renewal agreements, and strategic relationships to grow their overall training businesses by partnering with Prometric's vendor clients. Rolled out 25 regional partner events through the western U.S.

FIGURE 12-23 Sample résumé of a technical sales representative

Area Education Sales Manager, Western Region   **2/1997–4/1998**
Novell Inc., Santa Monica, CA

Responsible for a quarterly revenue quota of $5M from the Novell Education centers in
nine states. Designed and implemented advertising programs, organized lead-generating
educational seminars, and increased revenue numbers. Region exceeded revenue targets
three out of five consecutive quarters.

Vice President, Sales and Marketing, Western Canada   **2/1996–1/1997**
Excelnet, Edmonton, Alberta

Developed and implemented certification programs for both Microsoft and Novell.
Responsible for revenue, budgeting, telemarketing and incentive programs, advertising,
media, and sales training. Managed a six-person sales team.

Branch Sales Manager   **1983–1993**
PBSC Training, PC Etcetera Training, Network Learning Masters

Proven leadership managing both sales and marketing teams for the top training centers
throughout Canada.

FIGURE 12-23   Continued

Security Administrator

Job Description

May include managing and analyzing systems and network security and authorization environment. Specifically, security involved with network, operating system, database, interface, Web
site, and data privacy. Defines network security issues, develops plans and procedures, and
ensures safety and privacy of Internet, intranet, email services, and/or extranet sites. May perform risk assessments, identify potential security risks, maintain and configure firewall systems, and monitor network for unexpected behavior. Provides consultation on new technology
and products, and conducts security education and training.

Qualifications

Depending on the infrastructure of the company, may include information security and practical
experience with firewall implementation and administration. In-depth knowledge of the specific platform the company operates on, such as Windows, Novell, or Unix. Familiarity with
virus/security software. Often requires a bachelor's degree in a related area and two to four
years of experience in the field or in a related area.

Related Certifications

▶ Certified Information Systems Security Professional (CISSP) from ISC

▶ CheckPoint Certified Security Administrator (CCSA), Engineer (CCSE), Addressing Engineer (CCAE), Quality of Service Engineer (CCQE)

▶ SANS GIAC Security Engineer (GSE), Unix Security Administrator (GCUX), Windows Security Administrator (GCNT), Firewall Analyst (GCFW)

▶ Depending on the type of network used within the organization, desired certifications can vary from Microsoft, Novell, Unix/Linux, Cisco, and others.

Figure 12-24 is an example of a résumé in the area of security.

Software Engineer/Systems Analyst

Job Description

SOFTWARE ENGINEER   Turns business requirements into software programming applications. Designs, modifies, develops, writes, and implements software applications. Researches, designs, and develops computer software in conjunction with other development teams, including hardware, networking engineers, and database architects. Applies principles of computer science, engineering, and mathematical analysis to build a solution that meets the business objectives. Develops systems specifications documents based on user requirements and may partake in the coding of the actual software.

SOFTWARE ENGINEERING MANAGER   Leads a team of software engineers to design enterprise software products. Ensures that product requirement documents are written and properly reflect business requirements. Implements track development timelines, negotiates feature sets with the development leads and business users. Generally manages a group of software developers/engineers. Relies on business experience and judgment to plan and accomplish goals. Typically reports to the director of IT.

Qualifications

SOFTWARE ENGINEER   Typically has worked as a software programmer/developer for at least two years before progressing to software engineer. Should have a bachelor's degree in computer science and general knowledge of Internet systems, e-commerce, database processes, and overall infrastructure optimization.

SOFTWARE ENGINEERING MANAGER   Requires a bachelor's degree and at least five to seven years of experience with software development in Java and C++, strong relational database knowledge, knowledge of e-commerce infrastructure, customer relationship management, data warehousing, and general business acumen.

Related Certifications

▶ Microsoft Certified Solution Developer (MCSD)

▶ Oracle Certified Professional (OCP) – Application Developer, Solution Developer

▶ IBM Certified Advanced Technical Expert – DB2 Universal Database

▶ Sybase Certified PowerBuilder Developer (CPD), SQL Developer

▶ Certified Quality Analyst (CQA), Software Test Engineer (CSTE)

▶ Project Management Professional (PMP)

▶ Configuration Management II (CMII)

Figure 12-25 is an example of a résumé for a software engineer or systems analyst.

Technical Trainer

Job Description

Instructs at a training center or college, or within an organization to train employees. May instruct an audience ranging from nontechnical users to highly technical individuals. Translates technical topics into methods that can be comprehended by the audience. May train on standard software, hardware, or systems, such as Microsoft Office, PC repair or Cisco networking, or on proprietary software specific to an organization. Provides training that will enable the end-user to proficiently perform the tasks at hand. Increases productivity and understanding of the technology being used.

Qualifications

One area of IT where personality may be more important than skill set. Good presentation, speaking, and teaching skills required. Background or skill set relevant to the organization recommended. Training is often possible if all details of the software or product are not known. Ability to learn new technologies quickly is extremely valuable. Other qualifications include organization, listening skills, and project management. Bachelor's degree may be required, but certifications and experience can often substitute.

Related Certifications

▶ Microsoft Certified Trainer (MCT)

▶ Certified Novell Instructor (CNI)

▶ Certified Lotus Instructor (CLI)

▶ CompTIA Certified Technical Trainer (CTT+)

▶ Certifications related to the topic being taught, such as MCSE, CIW, MCSD, Cisco, A+, and so forth

Figure 12-26 is an example of a résumé for a technical trainer.

Shawna Kvislen

MCSE/CNE/Network+/A+

1632 Prairie Pot Hole Drive, Apt. 301 ~ Sioux City, IA 58474 ~ (443) 782-5512

shawna_kvislen21@yahoo.com

KEY QUALIFICATIONS

- **Security Administrator** with 2+ years of experience with managing systems and network security, specifically operating systems, databases, interfacing, and data privacy.
- Excellent ability to identify system vulnerabilities and possible threats and then apply prerequisite safeguards (technical and administrative) to defend against potential attacks.
- Detailed experience performing risk assessments, maintaining, and configuring firewall systems, and monitoring network for unexpected behavior.
- Professional knowledge and hands-on experience with Windows, Novell, and Unix.
- Function well in a team environment while being self-motivated to work effectively without supervision. Excellent organizational, interpersonal, and communication skills with the flexibility to adjust to changing work priorities.

TECHNICAL SKILLS

Operation Systems: Windows 2000 Advanced Server, Windows 2000 Server, Windows 2000 Positional, Window NT 4.0 Server/Workstation, Windows 95/98/Me, Sun Solaris Unix, Novell 4.2.

Hardware: PC hardware, HP printers, 3COM switches, Nortel switches, Cate5, Cabletron SSR2000 router, Cabletron SS2200, Tigris, ATM switches, Ethernet, fiber optic.

Applications and Software: Exchange 5.5, IIS Server, TCP/IP, HTML, MS Office 98 Professional, MS Project Manager, MS Office 2000, Visio 2000, Terminal Server, MS FrontPage 98, Adobe Photoshop.

EXPERIENCE

Network Administrator Assistant, Team Leader, Shaw College, 10/1999 – present

- Manage and perform the statistical and tactical aspects of disaster recovery, auditing, and security policies, procedures, and guidelines.
- Perform security administration functions (such as maintaining users, groups, IDs, and passwords) for HP, Unix, and FileNet systems at corporate and field office locations.
- Implement and oversee the installation and configuration of 25+ computers with Windows (95, 98, NT Workstation, NT Server), Novell (4.x, 5), and Unix (SCO UnixWare 7) operation systems.
- Assisted the network administrator in administrating, troubleshooting, and maintaining the network with over 200 client computers while ensuring top security.

CERTIFICATIONS

MCSE, CNE, Network+, A+

EDUCATION

Bachelor of Science, Computer Science, Cal Tech University, 1997

FIGURE 12-24 Sample résumé for a security administrator

Kirk Watkins
435 Aspen Drive
Kirkland, WA 87654

kwatkins@pacbell.net
809-765-5678

Summary of Qualifications

Java, C/C++, HTML/XML/CSS, JavaScript, Perl/CGI Perl, SQL, MS Windows, Linux/Unix

Professional Experience

Kirkland Air Force Base, Kirkland, WA
Software Engineer   10/2000 – Present

> Develop n-tier client/server software applications that enable the delivery of information to wireless devices using Java and Java Servlet in Linux/Unix environment. Use SpatialFX developer suite to design and create a geographic services module that provides mapping, routing, and geocoding capabilities. Build web interface using Java Servlet, HTML, and JavaScript. Prepare design documentation, installation, and configuration guides.

Lockheed Martin Space Operations, Houston, TX
Applications Software Engineer   6/2000 – 10/2000

> As a member of the Integrated Planning Systems software engineering team for the International Space Station, was involved in redesign of a Battery/Solar Array Model (BSAM) using Java. Developed BSAM GUI using Java Swing. Participated in software design and prepared design documentation. Interacted with end-users to identify and refine application requirements and functionality. Modified existing code using C/C++ and Fortran.

Navigation Technologies, Houston, TX
Field Analyst/Researcher   1/1998 – 5/2000

> Used GIS applications to maintain and update a digital database for in-vehicle satellite navigation systems. Verified database positional and informational accuracy throughout the Houston/Galveston metropolitan area using GPS tools and field research. Performed systems tests to ensure superior performance prior to product release.

G.A.S. Unlimited, Inc., Houston, TX
Engineering Technician   10/1997 – 1/1998

> Contract position for Houston Lighting and Power GIS department. Created and updated electrical distribution maps for the Houston area using ArcInfo software. Maintained customer and equipment databases. Provided GIS support for various departments within the company.

FIGURE 12-25   Sample résumé for a software engineer/systems analyst

Navigation Technologies, Sunnyvale, CA
Special Project Geographer   5/1997 – 8/1997

Supported specially targeted production efforts, including database coding, specification upgrades, quality assurance, and employee training. Also involved in software and process development and testing, and database customization.

Navigation Technologies, Sunnyvale, CA
Aerial Editor   10/1996 – 4/1997

Responsible for adding and updating positionally accurate geometry information, including transportation network and cartographic features in digital framework using ArcInfo software, aerial photographs, and other sources.

Navigation Technologies, Sunnyvale, CA
Geographer I/Geographer II   6/1995 – 10/1996

Created and updated a navigable digital database using both custom and commercial mapping applications to manage GIS data from aerial photos, maps, and field research. Performed quality assurance tasks and new employee training within production team.

Education

University of Houston, Houston, TX, 1999
B.S., Computer Information Systems
Cum Laude, Phi Kappa Phi Honor Society member

Moscow Institute of Geodesy and Cartography Russian Federation, 1986
Bachelor's Degree, Applied Geodesy
Completed three-and-one-half years of study in a five-year program.

Figure 12-25 Continued

Anne Gourde

MCT/MOUS

8343 Cherry Lane, Chicago, IL 12554, (334) 883-9090

anne.goude@chicago.com

KEY QUALIFICATIONS

- **Microsoft Certified Instructor** with expertise in teaching beginner-to-expert levels in multiple applications, including Microsoft Access, Word, Excel, PowerPoint, and Outlook.
- Exceptional presentation, communication, and organizational skills with natural ability to break down and explain complex technical topics for maximum comprehension to even beginning students.
- High-energy, confident professional with enthusiasm for technology.
- Working toward MCSE to instruct technical courses in addition to application courses.

CERTIFICATIONS

Microsoft Certified Instructor (MCT)

Microsoft Office User Specialist (MOUS) Master Certification, Office 97

Microsoft Office User Specialist (MOUS) Master Certification, Office 2000

Microsoft Certified Systems Engineer (MCSE) in progress

MICROSOFT INSTRUCTOR COURSE TRANSCRIPT

Microsoft Word 97/2000 Advanced

Microsoft Excel 97/2000 Advanced

Microsoft Outlook 97/2000 Advanced

Microsoft Access 97/2000 Advanced

Microsoft PowerPoint 97/2000 Advanced

Microsoft 2000 Project Beginner

Windows 95/98/NT/2000 Advanced

ADDITIONAL TECHNICAL SKILLS

Operating Systems: Windows 95/98/NT/2000 and Mac OS 8/OS 9

Networking: Installation and configuration of Windows 2000 Server/Professional, TCP/IP

Additional Applications: Adobe Photoshop, Dreamweaver, QuarkXPress, Microsoft FrontPage, FTP

EXPERIENCE

Computer Lab Technician/Instructor, Bayview Community College

- Instruct students for proficient use in Microsoft Office and Windows 98 through private and group training sessions.
- Troubleshooting client system problems; installed and configured workstations, network printers, and network interface cards.
- Effectively communicate technical information to non-technical audiences, improvising curricula and style to meet diverse audience needs.

FIGURE 12-26 Sample résumé for a technical trainer

Web Content Editor

Job Description

Writes, edits, proofreads, and copyedits a variety of documents, and plans and prepares articles for online dissemination. Coordinates with writers, producers, and other contributors to the Web site to ensure consistency in style, tone, and quality of the organization's site. Responsible for accuracy of all information pubiished to the Web site. Must analyze the effectiveness of the content and the site, and ensure timely and accurate delivery of content to keep the site up to date. Additionally, may be responsible for email marketing campaigns and newsletters, including the layout, design, and messaging schedule. Works in a fast-paced, deadline-oriented environment, striving to keep competitive through marketing strategies and ongoing research.

Qualifications

Must possess strong writing, organizational, and project management skills, in addition to a thorough understanding of Internet technologies. Requires a strong technical skill set, which may include graphics and multimedia software, an understanding of Web design, and basic HTML and/or JavaScript knowledge. Degree of technical skills varies depending on the position. Usually requires a bachelor's degree in a related area, such as communications, journalism, English, or marketing, and two to four years of experience in the field or in a related area. Knowledge of commonly used concepts, practices, and procedures within a particular field. Proven ability to write and edit marketing-related content for the Web while summarizing technical information clearly and concisely. Writing samples and example of previous Web work usually required.

Related Certifications

▶ CompTIA iNet+

▶ Microsoft Office User Specialist (MOUS)

▶ Prosoft Certified Internet Webmaster (CIW) Foundations, Site Designer

▶ Project Management Professional (PMP)

Figure 12-27 is an example of a résumé for a Web content editor.

Web Designer (Site Designer)

Job Description

Generally designs, implements, and maintains hypertext-based publishing site using authoring and scripting languages, content creation and management tools, as well as digital media tools. Typically well versed in all areas of Web development and graphical user interface (GUI) design with the primary role as an interface between the client or company management and the development team. Project management of site creation, promos and ad banners, and content creation. Interacts with the client (or management and other departments depending on the type of company) more than a Web programmer.

Qualifications

Skill set required varies depending on the role of other members of the Web development team. May include experience with HTML, JavaScript, ASP, Photoshop, Microsoft FrontPage, Microsoft Visual InterDev, and perhaps Macromedia Flash. Knowledge of Internet security, project planning, testing, and research. Additionally, familiarity with Java, Visual Basic, C++, and SQL may be required. Strong communication and project management skills required to interface with various individuals involved with the production and maintenance of the site. Understanding of the business needs associated with the functionality of the site, and possibly e-commerce. May require a bachelor's degree in a related area and at least two years experience in the field or related area. Certifications and related experience can substitute for degree in the field.

Related Certifications

▶ CompTIA i-Net+

▶ Prosoft Certified Internet Webmaster (CIW) Foundations, Site Designer, Master Site Designer

   Figure 12-28 is an example of a résumé for a Web designer.

Webmaster

Job Description

WEBMASTER (WEB ADMINISTRATOR)   Various job functions depending on the company. In a small company, may be responsible for all design, programming, and upkeep of the site. In a larger company, typically develops and maintains the company's portal, performing backups and ensuring user accessibility to the site. Monitors site traffic and helps scale site capacity to meet traffic demands for performance. Improves the company's efficiency and designs the look and feel for the site. Will often generate site statistic reports, troubleshoot hardware-related challenges, update security patches and software, and research and evaluate new Web hardware and software.

Qualifications

WEB DESIGNER (SITE DESIGNER)   Should be skilled in the areas of Web development, network administration, and PC technical knowledge. Required to have a working knowledge of HTML, JavaScript, and SQL. Solid knowledge of Web design and authorizing, as well as a strong background in Internet hardware technology, especially related to server hardware and security, as well as Intranet administration. Knowledge of Microsoft IIS 4.0 and Apache are essential as two of the most commonly used Web servers. May require a bachelor's degree in a related area and two to four years experience in the field or related area. Certifications and related experience can substitute for degree in the field.

Related Certifications

▶ Prosoft Master Certified Internet Webmaster (CIW) Network Administrator

▶ CompTIA A+ and Server+

Additionally, other certifications associated with Web design and programming may apply, such as:

▶ CompTIA i-Net+

▶ Prosoft Certified Internet Webmaster (CIW) Associate, Website Manager, Master Designer

Figure 12-29 is an example of a résumé for a webmaster.

Web Programmer (Web Developer)

Job Description

Various responsibilities depending on the specific needs of the company or client. Can include HTML authoring, programming Web applications, creating graphics and multimedia optimized for the Internet, or performing usability testing. May include integrating database solutions into the Web site. Depending on the size of the company or the complexity of the site, can be responsible for all aspects of the site or may work with team members who each play a role in the development of the site.

Qualifications

Most often responsible for coding content for Web sites in HTML and/or creating custom scripts with JavaScript and ASP. Additional required skills include proficiency in graphic design and page layout, and solid knowledge of image manipulation tools such as Photoshop. Additionally, some basic programming skills are beneficial, such as Java, Visual Basic, or C++, as well as knowledge of databases specific to the company, such as SQL. May require a bachelor's degree in a related area and at least two years experience in the field or related area. Certifications and related experience can substitute for degree in the field.

Related Certifications

▶ CompTIA i-Net+ Internet Technician

▶ Prosoft Certified Internet Webmaster (CIW) Associate, Website Manager, Master Designer, Master Administrator, Master Enterprise Designer

Figure 12-30 is an example of a résumé for a Web programmer.

Ross Leo

1965 Jerome Place #K204 ~ Shirley, CA 92663 ~ (555) 646-4193
rossleo@email.inc

KEY QUALIFICATIONS

- **Web Content Editor** with a solid background in writing for the Internet/New Media, as well as strong organizational and project management skills.
- Experience includes editing, copywriting, and promotional planning for an eLearning website for IT professionals.
- Exceptional technical skill set, including graphic and multimedia software, and HTML. Interpersonal skills with excellent problem solving skills, creativity, and ability to meet deadlines in a fast-paced environment.

EXPERIENCE

Web Copywriter, Online Learning Enterprises, Feb. 2001 – present

- Increased site activity by 40 percent through implementation of an innovative marketing strategy, including newsletters, email campaigns, and affiliate programs targeted at training and education decision makers for large corporations.
- Coordination, development, and project management of editorial schedule and site promotions, in addition to writing and editing articles, overseeing contractual writers, and keeping the site up to date and competitive in the industry.
- Track and document marketing efforts using Web Trends software to make suggestions for future campaigns and improve department performance.
- Development and coordination of an online community of more than 80,000 users to provide career guidance and résumé writing assistance, including certification and industry resources, and chats and support services from IT professionals.
- Designed the layout of the online community to provide easy navigation and comprehension for end-users, using HTML.
- Report on industry news and events, monitor newswires, write in-depth features, compile backgrounders, and attach encoded video and graphics to stories to keep users knowledgeable about items pertinent to their careers.
- Hosted online chats and monitored message boards to provide excellent customer service to clients and ensure accuracy of information.

TECHNICAL SKILLS

Proficient in Macintosh and PC applications, HTML, Dreamweaver, Adobe Photoshop and PageMaker, QuarkXpress, RealMedia, Microsoft Office and FrontPage, Windows 95/98/NT/2000, Mac OS 8/OS 9, FTP.

CERTIFICATION

Prosoft Certified Internet Webmaster (CIW) Site Designer in progress

ADDITIONAL WRITING EXPERIENCE

TU Wired Online Magazine, Staff Writer, 1998 – 1999

EDUCATION

B.S. in Mass Communication, University of California, Cum Laude, May 1999

AWARDS AND RECOGNITION

Eddie Ballard Award for Journalism, Online News Association Professional member, Vice Presidential Leadership Award, Golden Key National Honor Society

FIGURE 12-27   Sample résumé for a Web content editor

Erica Kate Harris, CIW

152 8th St. NW, Apt. 206 ~ Crookston, MN 58102 ~ (612) 555-1213
ekh@design.com

KEY QUALIFICATIONS

- Extensive **Web design** knowledge, hands-on experience and expertise demonstrated in instructing courses in design and programming at beginning-to-expert levels.
- Expert design and programming skills utilized in the creation of several corporate and educational websites, including e-commerce capabilities and complex flash animation.
- Skilled at building strong team environments and open communications; incredible creativity and ability to acclimate to new technology and situations with ease.

TECHNICAL SKILLS

Programming: HTML, DHTML, Cascading Style Sheets, Visual Basic 5, C/C++, Java, JavaScript, ASP

Graphics and Design: Adobe Photoshop, Macromedia Dreamweaver, Macromedia Flash, Macromedia Fireworks, Adobe Illustrator, Microsoft FrontPage

Networking: Windows 2000/NT, Linux, FTP

Applications: Microsoft Office 97/2000, Adobe Acrobat Writer, Corel WordPerfect, Photo-Draw and Photo-Paint

EXPERIENCE

Software Instructor, New Versions Computer Centers, 1/2000 – present
Instructing software and programming adult education courses in the following areas:

Adobe Photoshop 5.5	Macromedia Dreamweaver 3
HTML/DHTML/CSS	Macromedia Flash 4
FileMaker Pro 5	Corel Photo-Draw and Photo-Paint
Macromedia Fireworks 3	Microsoft FrontPage

Associate Web Designer

- Redesigned training portion of website to enable students to easily locate course details and access online training, increasing user satisfaction on the site.
- Gathered user requirements to produce project specifications and consulted with other project leaders on user interface related issues.
- Created Flash email campaigns to coincide with marketing strategies to increase enrollment and awareness of new courses and special offerings.

ADDITIONAL PROFESSIONAL EXPERIENCE

Exam Validator, Brainbench.com, 3/2000 – 4/2001

- Validated the appropriateness and content of the Core Web Designer exam.
- Provided recommendations to improve the quality of the exam content.

Websites Designed

- http://www.newversions.com/crookston/
- http://computerprogrammingclasses.net
- http://www.testyourITknowledge.edu

CERTIFICATION

CIW Site Designer Certification

FIGURE 12-28 Sample résumé for a Web designer

Caroline Homan, CIW

441 E. Hampton Lane ~ Las Vegas, NV 99201 ~ (555) 711-9090
caroline_homan@vegas.com

KEY QUALIFICATIONS

- Expertise in **Webmaster** skills such as HTML, XML, JavaScript, Dreamweaver, Photoshop, and Illustrator, as well as extensive experience in QA testing and research.
- 2+ years experience with website development, Internet and e-mail marketing, and strategies to increase website traffic.
- Strong technical writing background, interpersonal and project management skills, with ability to adapt to new technologies and applications proficiently.

TECHNICAL SKILLS

Programming: HTML, XML, JavaScript

Design Applications: Adobe Photoshop, Macromedia Dreamweaver, Macromedia Flash, Macromedia Fireworks, Adobe Illustrator, MS FrontPage, Corel Photo-Draw and Photo-Paint

Operating Systems: Windows 98/NT/2000, Mac OS 8 and OS 9

Applications: Microsoft Office 97/2000, Adobe Acrobat Writer, Corel WordPerfect, FTP

CERTIFICATIONS

CIW Master Site Designer

EXPERIENCE

Internet Marketing Manager, Nabiscox Corporation, May 1999 – Nov. 2001

- IT project management of the day-to-day maintenance and development of the corporate website, including content and Web page creation, page layout, and design.
- Contributed to a full site release for www.nabiscox.com from design concepts to launch, coordinating recommendations between marketing research firm and IS department.
- Constructed forms to enable support staff to efficiently answer questions and resolve problems related to the site and the development tools.
- Developed a standardized Web traffic report using Accrue HitList and MS Excel, generating reports on a weekly basis to measure site traffic and the success of e-mail marketing campaigns and partner launches.
- Quality assurance testing of all site development prior to launch to ensure proper functionality and consistency with graphical user interface.
- Organized and compiled a monthly email marketing campaign that enabled Nabiscox to effectively communicate with affiliates, and to promote the launch of new showcases.
- Spearheaded the promotion of www.nabiscox.com via search engine optimization strategies to increase company name recognition and site traffic.

EDUCATION

Bachelor of Science, Mass Communication, Marymount University, 1995

FIGURE 12-29   Sample résumé for a webmaster

Luladey Negatu

MCSE/CIW
1321 Prentis House Ct. ~ Columbus, OH 43235 ~ (614) 444-6720
lula@negatu.com

SUMMARY OF QUALIFICATIONS

Web Programmer with strong GUI design background and expert knowledge of HTML, XML, VBScript, JavaScript, ASP, ColdFusion, databases, SQL, and C/C++. Experience in building websites from conception to rollout, including e-commerce. Excellent project management and problem-solving skills with ability to work independently or in a team environment.

EXPERIENCE

Webmaster, BellSoft Corporation, May 2000 – present

- Designed and developed the full corporate website, creating the look and feel to emphasize the company's expertise in financial services and dedication to providing excellent customer service. Additionally, served as the team's interface designer, providing layout and graphics design for the e-commerce site.
- Integrated an HTML-based solution that evolved into an online corporate and retail store. Online software orders through this store now account for more than 75% of corporate annual sales revenue.
- Developed and implemented an installation and configuration procedure to ensure rapid deployment with predictable results for each new SHL RDIMS environment. Lead integration testing, troubleshooting the system, and developing procedures for introducing new, upgraded products.
- Lead installation and configuration engineer for the initial installation and acceptance trial of e-commerce security authorization system.
- Designed intranet for internal communication and support purposes, administering rights and functionality for more than 500 users.

TECHNICAL SKILLS

Programming: Java, JavaScript, HTML, DHTML, Cascading Style Sheets, ASP, ColdFusion, Perl, Visual Basic 5.0/6.0, C/C++, VBScript, XML, server-side programming (PHP, SQL).

Graphics and Multimedia: Photoshop, Illustrator, web animation such as ImageReady, Shockwave and Flash, streaming video and audio, plug-ins, web hosting (Linux, Apache, IIS, and other web servers), e-commerce development.

Additional: Project management, Visual InterDev 6.0, excellent Internet knowledge, Microsoft Office 97/2000.

CERTIFICATIONS

MCSD, Master CIW Enterprise Designer

EDUCATION

B.S., Electrical Engineering, Vanderbilt University, 1996

ASSOCIATIONS

IEEE Member since 1995, ACM member since 1999

FIGURE 12-30 Sample résumé for a Web programmer

Index

INTERNATIONAL CONTACT INFORMATION

AUSTRALIA
McGraw-Hill Book Company Australia Pty. Ltd.
TEL +61-2-9417-9899
FAX +61-2-9417-5687
http://www.mcgraw-hill.com.au
books-it_sydney@mcgraw-hill.com

CANADA
McGraw-Hill Ryerson Ltd.
TEL +905-430-5000
FAX +905-430-5020
http://www.mcgrawhill.ca

GREECE, MIDDLE EAST,
NORTHERN AFRICA
McGraw-Hill Hellas
TEL +30-1-656-0990-3-4
FAX +30-1-654-5525

MEXICO (Also serving Latin America)
McGraw-Hill Interamericana Editores S.A. de C.V.
TEL +525-117-1583
FAX +525-117-1589
http://www.mcgraw-hill.com.mx
fernando_castellanos@mcgraw-hill.com

SINGAPORE (Serving Asia)
McGraw-Hill Book Company
TEL +65-863-1580
FAX +65-862-3354
http://www.mcgraw-hill.com.sg
mghasia@mcgraw-hill.com

SOUTH AFRICA
McGraw-Hill South Africa
TEL +27-11-622-7512
FAX +27-11-622-9045
robyn_swanepoel@mcgraw-hill.com

UNITED KINGDOM & EUROPE
(Excluding Southern Europe)
McGraw-Hill Education Europe
TEL +44-1-628-502500
FAX +44-1-628-770224
http://www.mcgraw-hill.co.uk
computing_neurope@mcgraw-hill.com

ALL OTHER INQUIRIES Contact:
Osborne/McGraw-Hill
TEL +1-510-549-6600
FAX +1-510-883-7600
http://www.osborne.com
omg_international@mcgraw-hill.com